PAUSE.

moments to reflect

Managing Director: *Dale Tadlock*
Pause Editor: *Marnie Fisher-Ingram*
Production Assistant: *Amanda Short*
Copy Editors: *Becky England, Lynn Groom*
Art Direction: *Colleen Burroughs*
Designer: *Deanna Gardner*

3421 Sierra Drive
Birmingham, AL 35216
www.passportmedia.org

ISBN: 978-1-938810-07-7

fifty-two weeks of reflections
from the writers
of the devotional series
www.d365.org

PAUSE.

moments to reflect

One day at a time.

That's the way life's journey is taken. Some days are bright with promise; others are dark with foreboding.

For people who are trying to follow Jesus, the journey is one of companionship with Jesus and with others on the way. It's nice to remember that someone is alongside us – step by step.

We hope this collection of d365 devotions might also be a companion – a safe place to return to as you walk this journey of faith.

d365 *Nick Foster*
Editor, d365.org

d365.org *is produced by Passport, Inc., a national non-profit student ministry whose Christian mission is to empower students to embrace community and extend grace to the world.*

Passport produces d365.org in partnership with The Episcopal Church, Presbyterian Church (USA), and The Cooperative Baptist Fellowship.

"When I pray with the d365 community I feel as though I am a member of a cloud of witnesses around the globe: grounded in scripture and focused on God's word. I am eager to revisit, along with you, some of the devotions from across the years. I will treasure this collection, even though I know I will be giving it away to young friends and colleagues faster than I can finish reading. My hat is off to Passport for the amazing ministry partnership that we share."

Bronwyn Clark Skov
Officer, Youth Ministries
The Episcopal Church

"We all have longings deep within— for comfort, affirmation, inspiration and peace. Young people sit with these wishes and hope for connections to significant pieces of wisdom, great relationships, and solid friendships. The devotions of d365.org have been a simple, relevant mechanism that allow young people to connect their longings with God's heart. PAUSE is a timely resource that will give youth a tangible way to connect their hopes and their faith with God's word."

Gina Yeager-Buckley
Associate for Ministries with Youth
Presbyterian Church (USA)

"Daily devotions are an important part of spiritual formation and discipleship. You hold in your hands a powerful tool for helping your life be more formed in the spirit of Jesus. These devotions are timeless and deeply moving. Let God's Spirit guide you daily. Be changed and blessed in ways that are beyond your wildest imaginings!! Receive God's love and live on bravely!"

Bo Prosser
Coordinator for Missional Congregations
Cooperative Baptist Fellowship

Invitation to PAUSE

Breathe deeply. Rest. Be still . . .
PAUSE.

For years I have been a regular reader of d365 — as a great way to begin my day. d365.org is a 10-year-old daily online devotional site geared toward youth and young adults. Yet as an adult, I find the content very rich and meaningful.

This book is a collection of devotions from d365 by a group of all-star writers that cross denominational lines.

PAUSE is divided into 52 weeks. Every week begins with a centering word **(PAUSE),** and ends with a benediction **(GO)**. Printed only once, the "pause" and "go" statements bookend the daily devotions for that week. Reading them each day will deepen your devotional experience.

Each day then has a Scripture reference **(LISTEN)**, a devotion **(THINK)**, and a prayer **(PRAY)**. Have a Bible with you to thoughtfully read the day's scripture.

In the back, there's both a keyword and scripture index, to look up a topic or passage of interest, as well as a list of our writers.

Take the time to pause—to start or end your day with a moment of reflection and connection with God. It is my hope that these devotions will become a treasured part of your daily life, as they have become for me.

Peace and Grace,
Marnie Fisher-Ingram
Editor

Table of Contents

JANUARY

Praise to the Lord

Michelle Thomas-Bush

PAUSE.

God makes a covenant with us and we also covenant with God to bring forth our honest songs of praise.

If we are to be authentic and genuine in our praise, then let us accept the call to offer praise at all times: in times of thankfulness and celebration . . . with anger and in times of deep fear . . . and even in the dark of night.

May the act of offering honest praise to God guide you in your search to be more fully alive, even in these next moments.

LISTEN. JANUARY 1 **Psalm 40:1-5**

Praise, Faithfulness

THINK. We call them "God moments"—when we know deep in our souls that God is present. It happens in the spectacular, but also in just the ordinary movements of our lives.

After a tragedy, when we live out the commandment, "Love your neighbor," offering help to people we have never met. When a popular movie speaks boldly of redemption. When the light of your candle flickers at the candlelight service and you look around at the light spreading and know you are not alone. During a mission trip, when the people you are serving offer you so much that you know the mission is mutual. When you are offered a hand up, a place at the table, forgiveness and even something as simple as a smile.

Because of these God moments, we cannot keep silent. We are witnesses to God's grace that is so much more than amazing. We have seen the majesty and we cannot possibly keep silent. Praise be to God.

PRAY. God, thank you for your faithfulness that is much more faithful than mine. Open my eyes to see glimpses of your grace all around me, and give me the words offered back to you in praise. Amen.

LISTEN. JANUARY 2 **Psalm 40:6-11**

Stillness, Praise

THINK. I am a huge extrovert; I love Bible studies that offer good discussion and rich questions. When our teacher gave us 20 minutes to spend on our own, I was not all that excited. Solitude, quiet, and silence are three words that do not often find their way into my prayers. I walked, then sat. I folded my hands. I stood up. I glanced at my watch knowing that I was almost done. Six and ½ minutes, 13 and ½ minutes to go. I could not clear my mind. Plans were made for the weekend, a new playlist was created, my cuticles were even pushed back and then I began to hear music in my mind. It was one song that kept repeating. Finally, I stopped and listened to the words I had memorized in Sunday School as a child.

"Be Still and Know that I am God."

I sat listening as it played over and over. I looked around and watched an ant carry a large crumb across the bridge. I noticed the rays of sun coming through the canopy of trees and flowers just breaking through the soil. The trickle of water from the creek seemed to complement the song I began to sing..."Be Still and Know that I am God."

PRAY. Wondrous God, thank you for the voices of those who offer songs of praise for us. Thank you for those with whom we sing, whose recorded words become our praise to you. God, guide me as I seek to find my voice and give me courage to sing out loud. Amen.

LISTEN. JANUARY 3 **Isaiah 49:1-4**

Praise, Image of God

THINK. There are times when I doubt, times when I wrestle with my questions. There are times when I struggle with the existence of God. And then I look at my fingerprint, that can be lifted from anything I have touched, and speaks only of my identity. Out of the 6 billion people in the world, I am the only one with this particular fingerprint. Its curves and ridges are unique to me. How amazing is that?

When I was 7, I got a microscope for Christmas. I would make slides of my hair, dead skin, a fingernail...and just study them. My question was always, "How does this happen?" I knew how I came to be, but I still wondered (even if I didn't know it, I was addressing this question to God), "How can I be so complex?" And this was just the beginning. What about my thoughts, my feelings, my yearnings?

The only answer was God. God created every tiny, amazing, complex part of me. I am a child of God, created in the image of God. It is because of my fingerprint that I say, "Thanks be to God."

PRAY. God, you are so big and sometimes I cannot understand all the complexities of life. But I love our conversation. Continue to annoy, disturb, even provoke me in my questioning. Remind me of your promises. And most of all, remind me of your presence. Amen.

LISTEN. JANUARY 4 **Isaiah 49:5-7**

Hope, Fear

THINK. Isaiah was a prophet to a people who lived in fear. His words to the people were often disturbing, challenging, maybe even annoying. And yet they were words of hope. God has chosen you and will give you strength. We are a people who also live in fear—fear of failure, fear of rejection, fear of something incredibly bad happening to someone we love, and fear of the unknown. Out of the two basic emotions in life—fear and love—we choose to live in fear.

If you look around, the people who are the most happy choose to live in love. They still have fears, but they do not allow the fears to guide their lives. Instead, they love. They take a risk and they love themselves, they love those close to them, they love life, and they even love the people they have yet to meet.

We do not walk this path alone; we get the strength to love from God. God has chosen YOU and will give you strength. Thanks be to God.

PRAY. God, I am anxious about life, about love and even about what tomorrow will bring. Ease my anxiety and guide me to be more anxious to serve you and live in the love you offer that is without conditions. Amen.

LISTEN. JANUARY 5 **John 1:29-34**

Doubts, Questions

THINK. It seems like we have just celebrated Christmas. It was a celebration of the birth of a baby—Emmanuel, God with us. A baby that came with promise and offered us hope. The reality that I know often allows my doubts to surface, and I cannot see past a baby to One who can bring change. Today we are confronted by John the Baptist, who sees more than we can: "This is the son of God." If we open our eyes to this life of Christ through the scripture, we too will testify. We cannot ignore Jesus' wildly hopeful promises.

If we're too stressed to enjoy life, there is Jesus' relief-filled invitation: "Come to me all you that labor and are carrying heavy burdens, and I will give you rest." When we are confused about where to turn, Jesus boldly declares, "I am the way, the truth and the life."

Jesus brought forth a whole new way of living that calms our doubts, offers real hope, and fulfills the promises of our God of love. Praise to the Lord; this is the Son of God.

PRAY. God, let my questions and doubts bring me closer to you. Give me room to wonder, to seek and to know. Even when I do not have the answers, empower me to claim faith. Praise be to you, God. I pray this through your son, who loved the conversation and continues to offer me assurances. Amen.

LISTEN. **JANUARY 6** **John 1:35-42**

Following Christ, Faithfulness

THINK. Come and see. The star of Bethlehem was more than an arrow that pointed to the baby; it was an invitation to come and see. God knew that once we experienced Christ in our lives we could not help but follow. Come and see Jesus taking the ordinary and making it holy. Come and see Jesus reaching out to sinners and the outcast. Come and see Jesus telling stories so everyone might know. Come and see Jesus healing the sick, offering new life.

The invitation comes to us every day to follow in the footsteps of our Lord. Come and see as a youth group makes a difference, collecting a dollar from everyone who will watch the Super Bowl at their church and donating it to the local food pantry. Come and see as the church welcomes the homeless, someone in the midst of a divorce, the pregnant teenager, the person who has never been to church—living the ministry of hospitality Christ taught.

Come and see every day as people claim the new life and begin to follow in the footsteps of the one who is the Lamb of God.

PRAY. I have stopped from the chaos of my life, God. I have stopped so that I may hear your word. Take away the distractions, God - my responsibilities, the stress that I place on myself, and the pressures that threaten to overwhelm. Help me to focus on your word and, in listening, find what I need to grow in faith, hope and love. Amen.

LISTEN. JANUARY 7 **1 Corinthians 1:3-7**

Love, Faithfulness, Thankfulness

THINK. Throughout the scriptures we read wonderful accounts of God's people who are remembered for their faithfulness. Their story is part of God's story of redemption. I give thanks for the lives of Moses, Esther, Jeremiah, and Mary and Joseph and their child, Jesus.

I give thanks for the lives of Dietrich Bonhoffer, Martin Luther King, Jr., Mother Theresa and Bono. I give thanks to my God always for the people God placed in my life and the stories their lives tell. A little closer to home, I give thanks for my grandmother. She grew up in a home where her father was abusive, and her family lived in fear. In the darkest times, she found her strength in Jesus. It is her laughter and the relentless joy she finds in life that I celebrate. In celebrating those stories of faith, I realize that I, too, am called to play a role in God's ongoing drama of redeeming love. My story is an essential part of the story of God. Your story is part of God's story, too.

PRAY. I am here to worship you, Almighty God. Even though it is hard to admit, in this place it is not about me; it is not about what I need or want. It is about you and this family called the church. So come, then, hear my prayer I bring this day—not because I presume to have the right words but because you have promised to listen. Hear my prayers of thanksgiving for the teachers who have gone before me. Hear my prayers of celebration in my life. Hear my prayers to become the person you created me to be. Amen.

Go now, giving thanks that nothing can keep God from loving us.

"For I am sure that neither death, nor life, nor angels, nor principalities, nor things present, nor things to come, nor powers, nor height, nor depth, nor anything else in all creation, will be able to separate us from the love of God in Christ Jesus our Lord."

Romans 8:38-39

Growing Up In God

Caela Simmons Wood

PAUSE.

"What do you want to be when . . . ?"

You can fill in the rest. You've heard that question many times, usually from adults who were trying their best to start a conversation with a child.

Becoming a mature God-follower means giving our attention to the task of growing up every day. Give your attention now to who you are becoming under God's grace.

LISTEN. JANUARY 8 **Isaiah 44:6-8**

Trust

THINK. When I was a little kid, I was certain there was no other god but God. My Sunday School teachers told me this, and I believed them.

As I grew older, I started to have more questions. I found out about other religions and other ways of understanding my place in the world. I became friends with people who didn't believe in God at all. At some point in my early 20s, I kind of stopped caring about what other people thought. I stopped obsessively reading C.S. Lewis, trying to memorize his arguments for the existence of God.

I tuned into a feeling, a knowing, deep within me. I realized there were very few things I could say about God with 100 percent certainty, but I decided that there were at least three things I could hang on to as absolutely true: 1) God is always present, 2) God is always loving, and 3) God is a dreamer. This was enough for me.

I finally made it to the place where I can say, "There is no other rock; I know not one."

PRAY. God who is beyond labels and rational arguments, I celebrate you for whomever you are. I'm not 100 percent sure where you are or what you look like or how I should even talk to you, but I know you're there, and I know you are my rock. Thank you for just being you. Amen.

LISTEN. **JANUARY 9** **Romans 8:12-13**

Balance

THINK. Paul lived in a time when the world was divided into two realms: physical and spiritual. The early Christians bought into this Greek worldview because it was the dominant way of understanding things at the time. So when Paul described sin as coming through the physical, it made sense to his readers. It can make reading the Bible really confusing, though, because it's so different from the Hebrew Scriptures. In the Hebrew way of understanding the world, things of the body and the spirit were always bound together, no way to separate them.

There have been times in my life where I've been really into physical things, such as working out and eating good food, and times where I've been really into spiritual stuff, such as praying and reading Scripture. But the thing I've noticed over time is that the physical is usually better when I pay attention to the spiritual aspects, listening for God in my breath as I run. And the spiritual is often enhanced by paying attention to the physical, presenting my body as well as my words as a prayer. For me, it's not just one or the other. It's always body and spirit.

PRAY. God who is in both body and spirit, help me to stay in balance. Remind me to seek you in the physical as well as the spiritual. Deepen my spirituality by grounding it in my body. Thank you for the gifts of bodies and spirits. Amen.

LISTEN. JANUARY 10 **Romans 8:14-15a**

Security, Love

THINK. When I was a little girl, there was no place I felt safer than with my mom or dad. Knowing that I was their child, I felt secure that they would never let anything bad happen to me.

Growing older, I've come to understand there are things they cannot prevent, and I can't be protected from everything. But I also know that they would if they could.

Being someone's child means resting assured their love for you is so powerful, so intense, so pure, there is no greater love. Paul told the Romans in today's passage that we are all children of God. It's a phrase we throw around often, but rarely take the time to ponder. To be a child of God, beloved, held, cheered on. What a truly awesome gift.

PRAY. God our Mother and Father and beyond, what an incredible gift to be your child. I thank you, holy Parent, for your constant love. Just as I know I will never stop being my mother's daughter, I know I will never stop being your child. Amen and hallelujah!

LISTEN. JANUARY 11 **Romans 8:15b-17**

Following

THINK. Do you remember when you first realized being a Christian wasn't going to be totally easy? I do. I was in middle school and had gotten into a bad habit of talking about other people behind their backs. It was easy. It was fun. It was what everyone else was doing, and it was a great way to get some anger out.

But I also knew that God had other plans. I knew that, if I was supposed to try to be like Christ, I should try to do better. So I did my best to stop, cold turkey. It wasn't easy. I had to explain to my friends that I wasn't going to act that way anymore.

I'm sure I probably wasn't as much fun to be around. But I guess the goal of being a Christian isn't just to be fun, huh? I mean, sure, we can be fun, and we often are. But the goal of a Christian is to emulate Christ, to recognize that we are called to continue Christ's work in the world.

PRAY. God who calls us into suffering and glory, I stand amazed that you have called little ol' messed-up me to be the good news of Jesus Christ to the world. Help me to take my call seriously, God. Help me to do my best, each and every day, to let your light shine in the world. Amen.

LISTEN. JANUARY 12 **Romans 8:18-21**

Hope, Faith

THINK. There's always something to look forward to. Jesus shows us that, at the end of the day, God is always working for the betterment of creation. There are a lot of terrible things that happen in the world and some people get more than their fair share of misery. I don't think God heaps suffering on people. But even in the midst of great sufferings, I believe God is present, sometimes quietly lurking behind the scenes, sometimes loudly shouting to people to act!, sometimes weeping quietly and hoping for a better outcome. God is dreaming of a better future.

When I was a kid, I was a pessimist. I spent a lot of time worrying and noticing all the bad stuff happening in the world. For me, growing up has meant that I've become more deeply attuned to the reality that Christianity is a faith full of hope. Even when it seems silly and even when the odds are stacked against us . . . Christians hope. Even grown-ups. Maybe especially grown-ups.

PRAY. God who calls us into impossible optimism, I thank you for being a dreamer. When I am in the midst of trial, please help me to remember you are there with me, not causing the pain, but hoping for a better day. When things are going my way, help me to remember those who are not having a great day. Amen.

LISTEN. JANUARY 13 **Romans 8:22-23**

New Creation

THINK. Growing up ain't easy. Seems like we spend most of our childhoods wishing we could be adults, and then most of our adult years wishing we could be kids again. Something in us is always wishing to be and have what we can't. I guess that's part of the reason we're never really grown up, though, isn't it? We are always seeking to move, to change, to become something new.

And you know what? I think that makes God smile. God is a creative force. God loves things that are moving, changing, being made new. In fact, God is constantly moving in people, changing up the game, and making all things new. Sometimes it's not an easy process.

Sometimes it hurts pretty bad. But at the end of the day, we are constantly being remade into newer and more glorious creatures. It's never too late to move in a new direction or make major changes. And that's pretty great.

PRAY. God who moves and changes and makes new, I'll admit there have been times when I've wanted to stand still and stop changing. But I thank you for always pulling me along, calling me into new opportunities and helping me become the creature you made me to be. Amen.

LISTEN. JANUARY 14 **Romans 8:24-25**

Hopefulness, New Creation

THINK. Sometimes the anticipation of something great turns out to be even better than the thing we were waiting for. Do you remember being really excited about an awesome summer movie? Or trying to sleep the night before Christmas? There's nothing quite as pure as that feeling of excitement you get when you know something great is just around the corner. Sometimes it's even kind of sad when the great thing is over, because you don't have anything to look forward to anymore.

One of the amazing things about being in relationship with God is that there is always something to hope for. There's always something better coming just around the corner. There is always something new and amazing that God is working to make happen, and you're invited to be a part of it.

Tune in to those jumpy, happy feelings in your tummy that are telling you to be excited. Listen to the Holy as you hope for a new thing. Be a part of creating something new and wonderful with God.

PRAY. God who keeps us hoping, thank you for giving us a world that doesn't end. Thank you for teaching me there is always something new around the next corner that I can be a part of. When I doubt this, please gift me with people who can help me look forward to the future with a renewed sense of hope. Amen.

GO.

"In a word, what I'm saying is, Grow up. You're kingdom subjects. Now live like it. Live out your God—created identity. Live generously and graciously toward others, the way God lives toward you."

Matthew 5:48 (The Message)

The Salvation of the Lord

Brian Boyd

PAUSE.

In the midst of confusion, war, and pain . . . where is God? Though hard sometimes to believe, God is in the middle of it all. In these next moments, in the midst of whatever is happening in your life, open yourself to the saving grace of God present with you.

LISTEN. ## JANUARY 15 **Job 42:1-6**

Unconditional Love, Grace

THINK. These words of Job's are some of the most powerful in all of Scripture. As the story of this book begins, we find Job to be a man who has experienced all of the goodness life has to offer. Eventually Job lost everything, not just his property, but his entire family; his world was turned completely upside down.

During this great sadness, Job turned inward and examined himself. He looked inside to see what it was about him or his actions that would have brought these tragedies to him. As Job argued his case with God, God showed him that all people are in need of God. God showed Job that there are no arguments that can be made for salvation, but that salvation is freely given by a gracious God.

It is in this text that Job finally came to realize the fullness of God's love and grace. The language seems a little strong. Job even claimed to hate himself. However, the point of these verses is not to show us that we must hate ourselves, but rather that God's love is so beyond understanding that we fall to our knees and cry, "We're not worthy!" Take some time today to reflect on the absolute love that God shows us.

PRAY. Gracious God, I praise you today for the many ways in which you have shown me love. Your love is more complex and complete than the love offered by this world. You have loved me all my days. Today, I pray to see your great love in a unique and unexpected way. Amen.

LISTEN. JANUARY 16 **Job 42:10-17**

Mercy, Kindness

THINK. Today we see the fruits of Job's salvation. Yesterday we learned of Job's faith and his trust in his own arguments. We saw that Job was finally able to receive the fullness of God's grace. At the beginning of this text we are told something very interesting, that Job "had prayed for his friends." Job had been arguing with his friends about his tragedies. But immediately after experiencing unbelievable tragedy and then realizing the unlimited love and salvation of God, Job didn't rest. He prayed for others.

He prayed that his friends might experience the salvation that he had received. At this point, nothing had been restored to Job. He only had the knowledge of God's salvation.

The great Bible commentator Matthew Henry wrote of this passage, "His troubles began in Satan's malice, which God restrained; his restoration began in God's mercy, which Satan could not oppose." Mercy did not return when Job was disputing with his friends, but when he was praying for them. God is served and pleased with our warm devotions, not with our warm disputes. Take some time today to think about your friends and how you can put your disputes behind you.

PRAY. God of all, I pray that you help me to discern in my heart the places where I have been unkind and unforgiving as I relate to my friends and my family. Give me courage to offer mercy instead of anger and love instead of arguments. Amen.

LISTEN. JANUARY 17 **Psalm 34:1-8**

Salvation, Grace

THINK. Many of the psalms of David are prayers for comfort, songs offered up from a place of fear. David referred to himself as a "poor soul" who "was saved from every trouble." This doesn't seem like the strong king that we have come to know. This was a man who was seeking salvation.

But notice, as we have in the other devotions this week, that David did not seek salvation for himself alone. He asked his people to "magnify the Lord" with him. He spoke of his own experience of salvation, and then he invited others to share in the wealth of God's grace.

Once David's fears had been calmed, he didn't just go back to his daily routine. He sought out others to share in the saving grace of the Lord. We see that salvation is infectious. Once delivered, we want to share salvation with everyone. We want others to be whole. This is the beauty of God's gift to us. God's love knows no bounds. Today, take some time to reflect on how you can share the love that God has given you with others.

PRAY. God of love, give me the strength of character to love others as you have loved me. Give me courage to speak up for people in trouble and to offer comfort to my friends who are struggling. Let me be a beacon of hope in my relationship with others. Amen.

LISTEN. JANUARY 18 **Jeremiah 31:7-9**

Salvation, Community

THINK. This chapter of Jeremiah is about the restoration of Israel. When we think of restoring something, we think of bringing it back to its original state. Jeremiah spoke of God's salvation in terms of making us whole. He spoke of bringing together the parts that make us one.

When we experience the saving grace of God, we are brought back to God. We are brought back into the fullness and wholeness that God intended when we were created. Therefore, salvation affects our whole being. We become the beings that God created us to be. And as these "new people," we seek out others for community.

That community today is the church. Jeremiah prophesies the coming of Jesus and the church. It is our salvation that brings us to wholeness and to communion as the people of God. Today take some time to reflect on your role in the church and how you can contribute to the whole.

PRAY. Lord of all, I see the church struggling to be real to my friends. Help me to define my calling, my role in the life of God's people. Know my heart and my gifts and call upon me to use them effectively to share your unconditional love to a broken people. Amen.

LISTEN. JANUARY 19 **Psalm 126**

Salvation, Peace

THINK. The psalmist here shows two sides of salvation. First, we see the almost overwhelming joy felt by those who have been freed from captivity. However, as Israel experiences the joys of restoration to wholeness, they are quick to remember those who have yet to be freed from captivity. Then the psalmist lifts up his oppressed brothers and sisters in prayer to the gracious God who has freed Zion. And finally the psalmist claims the knowledge that salvation comes to those who are bound. He knows that God will allow God's people to share the joy that salvation brings.

Many times we find ourselves weighed down by the burdens of our busy lives. We have so little time to reflect on the places we have been. We tend to "live in the moment" and wait for a temporary fix to get us to the next moment. The psalmist calls us to remember where we have been. And with this remembrance, we are asked not just to thank God for God's saving grace, but to lift up those who now reside where we were.

Too often we look at salvation as a personal moment in time, but God calls us to participate in the salvation of all people. Take time today to pray for those who are struggling to find the peace that we have lived.

PRAY. Peace, begin with me. Peace, be still. God of peace, grant me peace this day as I go forward to bring peace to those who are struggling and afraid. Peace, begin with me. Peace, be still. Amen.

LISTEN. JANUARY 20 **Hebrews 7:23-28**

New Creation

THINK. In this chapter of Hebrews, the author is comparing human priesthood to the priesthood of Jesus. The difference is that as humans both we and our priests or pastors are imperfect. We need to perform sacrifices over and over again. We need to constantly second-guess ourselves. Out of fear, we seek out God's approval. But God doesn't ask for this.

God gave us the Son so that we could have everlasting life. The fact that we can live through the ultimate sacrifice Jesus made is a blessing beyond any that we have or will experience. Our self-doubt and lack of confidence melt away in the face of God's great gift of salvation in Jesus. Our old selves are made new as we are made whole by Jesus' love.

The knowledge that God demands no sacrifice from us, that God's eternal love is ours at no cost, instills in us the confidence of salvation. Take some time today to reflect on the areas of your life where you find doubt and those areas that affect your self-esteem. Recognize that through Jesus all of those doubts and questions are covered by Jesus, our high priest.

PRAY. Jesus, I struggle with self-doubt and fear that I am not what I am supposed to be. I sometimes feel less than others. Help me to live and breathe your love for me as I grow to love the creation of who I am in you. Amen.

LISTEN. JANUARY 21 **Mark 10:46-52**

Darkness, Light

THINK. Throughout this week we have learned many things about salvation. The story of Bartimaeus is a great story to end on. On its surface, it seems to be the story of a simple healing, but as Episcopal Presiding Bishop Frank Griswold said in his final Sunday sermon as Presiding Bishop: "While it is clearly an account of Jesus healing a blind man, it can also serve as an invitation to explore blindness as a spiritual condition in which we see but do not see."

One of the greatest metaphors used for salvation is going from the darkness into the light. When we are surrounded by the dark, we seek the light. Bartimaeus cried out just as David did for deliverance from darkness. And as with Job, it was his faith that allowed God to show him the light. Take some time today to reflect on all the ways that we see salvation, and especially the places where you have found the light of Jesus.

PRAY. Jesus, shine light into my darkness. Light the darkest corners of my soul so that I may fear nothing and be forgiven of even those things that I am afraid to admit are there. I pray that you heal me by allowing me to experience how much you love me. I know when you call my name you also call me your beloved. Amen.

GO.

Sing praise to God who reigns above, The God of all creation,
The God of pow'r, the God of love, The God of our salvation.
Johann J. Schutz (trans. Cox)[1]

Jesus the Prophet

Estelene Boratenski

PAUSE.

Only the passage of time reveals the vision of a prophet. At first, we dismiss as nonsense what time unfolds as astonishing perception. While the words of Jesus the human were rejected, the wisdom of Jesus the prophet transcends time and place.

Consider now how you can discover God's vision in your own world.

LISTEN. JANUARY 22 **Matthew 10:24-25**

Following Christ

THINK. What can we, who are less than prophets, learn from Jesus? The Spirit of God is revealed in the world through the spirit of the people who seek to follow the Teacher. We are charged with being the face of God to people in need, in time becoming teachers ourselves.

Jesus assures us that we will not always be welcomed. To be like him is to be different. And we don't have to look far to find evidence of how hard it is to be different. We can see it in the public's fascination with the singer Lady Gaga when she repeatedly tells her fans not to apologize for who they are, but just to declare, "I was born this way."

In such a society some people will offer thanks for us, but others may mock us for serving others in ways that will never make us rich. But we can shake the dust from our shoes—shake off our doubts—and know that we have heard the wisdom of the Teacher.

PRAY. Dear Teacher, thank you for those who have affirmed your Spirit in my life, and helped me to be the face of God in the world—a disciple, a teacher. Amen.

LISTEN. JANUARY 23 **Matthew 10:26-27**

Sharing Christ

THINK. "God is watching you, even when I'm not." Most of us have heard our parents use this or some variation of Jesus' words about secrets as a warning that we cannot hide our bad behavior. And there is truth in that. As Benjamin Franklin said, "Three may keep a secret, if two of them are dead."

In context, though, Jesus said these words not as a caution but as encouragement. Behind closed doors Jesus explained more fully to the disciples what he had sometimes spoken in public as parable and metaphor. He charged them to continue the work that his prophecies had begun, to share his message of grace and mercy with those whom he had not reached in his human lifetime.

We can feel confident to "walk in the light, as he is in the light." We need not fear of becoming God's presence in the world.

PRAY. Dear Teacher, thank you for your presence in the darkest moments of my life. Grant me the courage to share your encouraging light with someone in need. Amen.

LISTEN. JANUARY 24 **Matthew 10:28-31**

God With Us

THINK. Like human beings, sparrows come in a wide diversity of sizes, shapes, and colors. When Jesus asked, "Are not two sparrows sold for a penny?" it might be the equivalent of today's saying that something is "a dime a dozen." Sparrows are everywhere, yet Jesus told us that not one of them falls to the ground without God being near to them.

He used a second metaphor for added emphasis, that God knows at any given moment how many hairs we have on our heads. According to Encyclopedia Britannica, the average number of hairs on a person's head is between 100,000 and 150,000, and the average life of one hair is three to five years, so the number is constantly changing.

Think of that! It brings new meaning to "God with us." No matter what is going on in our lives, God is completely aware of every detail. God is in the muck with us.

PRAY. Dear God, thank you for the wisdom of Jesus the prophet in these verses. Help me to remember that you are always present with me, even when I may not think you are there. Amen.

LISTEN. JANUARY 25 **Matthew 10:32-33**

Ministering to Others

THINK. Jesus told us that God doesn't expect his message to stop with us. Yes, as the hymn says, "His eye is on the sparrow." And with that gift comes the expectation that we give what we have to others.

All of us know what it is to feel alone when life is difficult. When we feel that way, we may know that God is present, but we need something concrete that we can grab onto.

As Lily Hardy Hammond wrote in her 1916 book In the Garden of Delight, "You don't pay love back; you pay it forward . . . I've always said the most secure possession was the one carried in an open hand and free to fly at a breath."

Jesus told us that we are to be the breath and the face and the hands of God—the concrete, physical presence of God—by ministering to those who need help. In doing so, we keep a firm grasp on God's presence in our own lives.

PRAY. Dear God, thank you for Jesus' reminder of the gift of your love. Help me to find a way today to pay it forward. Amen.

LISTEN. JANUARY 26 **Matthew 10:34-39**

Unconditional Love

THINK. If we believe in a Prince of Peace and a God of grace, this is a confusing passage. How are we to read Jesus when he said he came with a sword to set family members against one another?

Perhaps this was a foretelling. He knew that his words would cause controversy thousands of years later, both within families and within humanity, who disagree about the nature of God.

And is it humanly possible to love God more than one's parent or one's child? As a mother, I would lay down my life for my child. How can I love an abstract spirit even more?

Jesus said, "No one has greater love than this, to lay down one's life for one's friends." Perhaps Jesus was telling us here that if we strive to have that same fierce love for God, we will find ourselves in the same way we do when the immense love we feel for other human beings brings out the best in us.

PRAY. Dear God, thank you for Jesus the prophet, even when I struggle to understand his message. Please help me remember that I can find myself by losing myself in you. Amen.

LISTEN. JANUARY 27 **Matthew 10:40-42**

Community, Grace

THINK. Jesus the prophet ends as he began, by talking with his disciples about community. While he began by warning them to expect rejection, here he focuses on how to be a part of a community. In a shrinking world where the Web has made it possible to be in fellowship with people in remote lands, the definition of community is changing. We can talk with people we have never met through social networks or in blogs that can turn ugly in an instant with one negative post. Or we can use this community to welcome and encourage "little ones" who are new to the family.

Jesus' disciples could not possibly have imagined a world like ours. But whether we are meeting with a small group as they did, or chatting with the vast online community, Jesus' command to pay it forward and welcome others is the same: The gift of kindness, "a cup of cold water" to someone who is thirsty, is a reward that returns to us in a world in need of God's peace.

PRAY. Heavenly Spirit, thank you for communities where I can find your peace, renewal, and encouragement. Help me to find a way today to pass on the peace of Christ. Amen.

LISTEN. JANUARY 28 **Psalm 86:1-7**

Helping Others, Unconditional Love

THINK. According to the New York Times, the United States owns a third of the world's wealth and Western Europe another third. While we may feel poor when we cannot afford the latest smart phone, few of us know what it means to be truly poor and needy in material goods. But all of us know what it is to be poor and needy when we face a "day of trouble."

Thornton Wilder says in his play Our Town, "We all know that something is eternal. And it ain't houses and it ain't names, and it ain't earth, and it ain't even the stars . . . everybody knows in their bones that something is eternal, and that something has to do with human beings. All the greatest people ever lived have been telling us that for 5,000 years, and yet you'd be surprised how people are always losing hold of it."

When we question God's steadfast love, we would do well to remember that, for thousands of years, writers have written about the certainty of God's Spirit.

PRAY. Gracious Spirit, thank you for your abounding, steadfast love. May I be mindful this day that you incline your ear to me and hear me when I am poor and needy. Amen.

GO.

Go now and seek to be God's breath and face and hands to a world in need of grace, knowing that when you lose yourself in the Spirit, you will find yourself indeed.

The Value of Knowing Christ

Nick Foster

PAUSE.

Day by day we make one choice after another, making decisions about how we spend our time, our money, and all our other resources. You have chosen today to spend these moments giving attention to the God who calls to you and leads you. Be attentive, then, to the marvelous treasure Christ offers you with this time.

LISTEN. JANUARY 29 **Psalm 19:1-10**

Guidance

THINK. "Now that is a sweet law! I love that law! Sweet!"

Imagine being pulled over in your car by a police officer who walks to your vehicle and, through your rolled-down window, explains that you have just broken a regulation that you did not even know existed. The above response is not something that, in the moment, you would likely say. Right?

Appreciation of any law comes in understanding its purpose. The psalmist, in today's text, understands that the laws of God are there not to put limits on our good times but to lead us to a deeper relationship with God. When we understand that, and live accordingly, we are revived in our spirits, we are made wiser, and we see things more clearly. Sweet!

PRAY. Dear Lord, help me to see and understand the direction you have for my life, yielding to your guidance. May I know you even better as a result. Amen.

LISTEN. JANUARY 30 **Philippians 3:4b-6**

Balance, Following Christ

THINK. You've seen one of those confrontations in the movies when two characters meet and it looks like there's going to be a fight. One guy finally says in a threatening way, "Do you know who you're messing with?" He can't believe that anyone would dare to take him on.

In today's text, Paul was saying a similar thing. If anyone had reason to be sure of himself, Paul wrote, it was him. He had all the background anyone would need to be deemed significant in Hebrew life. No one could question his credentials. He had done it all!

But it's not enough. Paul was setting himself up as an example. Even though he had and was everything needed to be considered worthy, there was one very important thing missing. Without a relationship with Christ, all that Paul was and all that he had done was nothing to him.

PRAY. Dear God, help me to keeps things in perspective. Especially help me to see that my relationship with Christ is important above everything else. Amen.

LISTEN. JANUARY 31 **Philippians 3:7-9**
Following Christ

THINK. As I write this, it is trash day in my neighborhood. Everyone has taken the stuff they don't need, don't want, and can't use out to the curb to be picked up by those wonderful folks who will throw it in a truck and dispose of it. And you know what?

It stinks! It smells really bad. It's no wonder we want to get rid of it.

Paul wrote in today's text of the stuff he saw from his past life, everything that came before knowing Christ, and said it was worthless to him. Worse, he described it all as being rubbish—trash, the stinky stuff.

That's quite the image, eh? Compared to anything else in the world, compared even to those things that many would consider to be of surpassing value, a relationship with Christ makes anything else like the stuff you take to the curb on trash day.

PRAY. As I move into my own future, O God, I pray that I will leave behind those things that are of no value. Instead, I want to give myself more fully to the greatest value—my relationship with Christ. Amen.

FEBRUARY

LISTEN **FEBRUARY 1** **Philippians 3:10-11**

Knowing Christ

THINK. Reading this part of Paul's writings, one gets the feeling that the apostle had been doing some serious soul searching. It's like he had been looking to discover that one thing that was of ultimate value to him, the one central part of his life.

He came down to this: What he wanted most in the world, above and beyond any other possibility, was simply to know Christ. More than being born into the right family, more than being a member of the right clubs and organizations, more than having graduated from the best schools, knowing Christ was of ultimate value.

And it was worthy of the ultimate cost, even losing his life. Paul realized that knowing Christ meant also knowing resurrection. That one thing that many fear most, death, is made of no concern when one is in relationship with the One who has overcome the ultimate enemy.

PRAY. Help me today not to be afraid, Lord. Help me instead to search my soul and find my center in you. Amen.

LISTEN. FEBRUARY 2 **Philippians 3:12-14**

Following Christ, Faithfulness

THINK. Have you ever run a marathon or some other long-distance race? For those who compete in these events for the first time, the experience can be intimidating. Weeks and months of training are required, and the commitment cannot waver. But if you choose to be a part of such a contest, you have to expect all of that.

In the long-distance event called "life," though, it's a different story. No training is provided; no preparation is available. We are in it from the beginning for the long haul. We learn all along the best way to run.

A marathon has an end point, the finish line. Life is different here, too. To be sure, there is an end, but we can never be sure where it will be. In the meantime, as we live our lives, we are called to press on and know Christ better and better along the way.

PRAY. Lord, I want to be a committed follower of Jesus. Help me today to run the race of faith with faithfulness and determination. Amen.

LISTEN. **FEBRUARY 3** **Matthew 21:42-44**

Example of Christ

THINK. Before quoting the Psalms here, Jesus told a parable of tenant farmers who killed the son of the man in whose vineyard they worked. They thought that by eliminating him they would be able to take the vineyard for themselves.

It's as if they didn't know who they were dealing with. So Jesus used a psalm to remind his listeners that you can never be certain who you encounter in even the most casual relationship. Any person we meet on any particular day might turn out to be more important than we think.

In fact, in another place Jesus told us that we really should treat every person as though that person were Jesus himself. If we value our relationship with Christ, we will value everyone who enters our lives. To reject anyone is to risk missing out on the promised kingdom of God.

PRAY. As I walk through this day, O God, show me the value of every single person I meet. Make me an accepting person and friend, following the example of Jesus himself. Amen.

LISTEN. **FEBRUARY 4** **Exodus 20:1-6**

Putting God First

THINK. Have you ever come to the end of a cafeteria line and been faced with that spectacular display that requires your final and perhaps most difficult decision? Dessert.

What will it be, coconut cream pie or chocolate cake? Lemon bars or fruit parfait or chocolate chip cookies? It all looks so good, but you've been instructed, and you know it's best, that you can choose only one.

How do you pick the one that you want most, that will provide the greatest sweetness experience?

God tells us that, when it comes to the sweetest deity experience, our choice is clear. There are many "gods" out there that call to us from behind the "god display," but only one stands out as the obvious selection of greatest value: the one who made us, sustains us, and loves us through every day.

PRAY. You are the center of my life, O God. I give myself to you again as my first choice, the one and only God in my life. Amen.

GO.

Go into this day with the sure knowledge that you are known and loved by the Christ who walks alongside you. May your knowledge of Christ grow as you turn your mind and heart continually to your Lord.

A Hands-on God

Bo Prosser

PAUSE.

The presence of God, the very hand of God on our shoulders as we walk through a troubled world—this is what we want. We need to know that God is not distant, unconcerned, and uninvolved. Consider today how you see God's hand at work in your close-by world and the whole world 'round.

LISTEN. **FEBRUARY 5** **Jeremiah 1:4-10**

Child of God

THINK. Just as the Word came to Jeremiah, the Word comes to you today! And God is affirming you today in the same way, too. God loves you and has loved you from the beginning of time. How awesome is that?

So, today, be confident in the life you are living. Don't let fear keep you from sharing God's love in the world. Don't let insecurities keep you from sharing God's love in the world.

You may sometimes feel like a "little boy" or "little girl," but you are growing up in God today. You may sometimes be treated like a helpless child. You may feel that you have nothing to offer the world. But God knows better.

You are a child of God filled with confidence and security. God has touched you and appointed you. Feel God's touch upon you today. Feel God's Spirit strengthening your spirit. The world is waiting and hoping for you.

PRAY. God help me to be more childlike and less childish. Help me to feel your touch upon my life and your Spirit upon me. Help me to live with confidence and strength today and every day. Amen.

LISTEN. **FEBRUARY 6** **Luke 13:10-17**

Confidence in God, Healing

THINK. Jesus has always been about bringing freedom to the world. His healing touch has always healed hurts and provided freedom.

Today, you may be feeling "bent over" like the woman in the passage. You may be burdened by some overwhelming ailment that keeps you bound up and bent over. Let Jesus touch you today. Let Jesus free you from your pain.

Not everyone will celebrate your freedom. The religious leaders were not happy with Jesus; he didn't follow the rules. Some won't be happy with your healing either. Big deal! When Jesus heals you, you're freed up.

The crowd had a party! One of their friends was free from 18 years of pain. Your friends will celebrate your healing today. Receive the healing touch from Jesus. Seems like a good day for a party!

PRAY. God, touch me today that I might stand up straight. God, touch me today that I might be free of my burdens. God, take away my hurt and pain and let me celebrate your love in my life. Amen.

LISTEN. FEBRUARY 7 **Hebrews 12:12-13**

Ministering to Others, Child of God

THINK. Look at your hands, really look at them. See the specialness of your fingerprints. Examine your fingers, and see how they bend and how they lay straight. Look at your hands and know that God is working through them.

Look at your knees, really look at them. Think about how your knees support you as you run and jump and walk and kneel. Think about how God strengthens your knees to give you purpose.

Look at your feet, really look at them. Think about how your feet are special as they help you move from place to place. Think about how your feet direct your footsteps as you follow God's leading. Think about where God is leading you and how your feet will carry you.

God continues to tell you how special you are. As you play today, or work with your hands today, or send text messages to your friends, remember that you are being healed in God's love.

PRAY. Thank you, God, for my hands and knees and feet. Help me not to waste the energy that is flowing through them. Help me to serve you through my work and play, my rest and my activity. Amen.

LISTEN. FEBRUARY 8 **Hebrews 12:14-17**

Example of Christ, Grace

THINK. Esau was selfish and greedy. He sold everything precious to him, both present and future, for a single meal. He thought only of himself, wanting things "right now!" Know anyone like that in your circle of friends?

Be an example to them today. Show them the goodness of God so they will see beyond their selfishness. Show them the joy of sharing and of giving.

Be an instrument of peace to them today. Refuse to be trapped by their arguments so they will see what true friendship looks like. Help them to understand the grace and love of God.

Be a good friend to them today. Good friends share grace with those who might not deserve it. Just as others have been good friends to you, today is your turn to be a good friend.

Show your friends the holiness and love of God. They'll be glad you did!

PRAY. God help me to be patient with my friends today. Help me to be an instrument of grace to those around me who are slow or angry or mean. Help me in the face of selfish friends to be your example. Amen.

LISTEN. FEBRUARY 9 **Hebrews 12:18-24**

Unconditional Love, Grace

THINK. Some people are afraid of God. Some people let negative images of God separate them from God. Even Moses related to God at times with trembling fear. What negative images try to invade your thoughts and keep you distant from God?

Today, imagine God in extreme beauty and joy. Imagine God as your best friend. Imagine God as your favorite place. Imagine God as the best party you've ever attended. Just know today that God is good.

Don't be afraid of God; instead, rejoice that God loves you! There are no greater feelings in life than loving and being loved. That is what heaven will be like. Take a moment to glimpse yourself in the midst of the heavenly party right now.

PRAY. God, forgive me for the negative thoughts that keep me distant from you. Forgive me for the times I've disobeyed and not trusted. Help me today to live in the goodness and beauty of your love and your grace and your peace. Amen.

LISTEN. FEBRUARY 10 **Hebrews 12:25-29**

Security

THINK. Have you ever seen those snow globes? You know, the glass ball that has the glitter and stuff in the water, and you shake it up. The scene looks like it's snowing inside the ball.

Have you ever felt as if you were living inside a snow globe? Perhaps you felt that someone was shaking your world upside down and swirling it. Perhaps you have friends who are feeling that way now. Being shaken up constantly is certainly no fun.

God promises that the kingdom of heaven will not be shaken. There is stability in God's love. The challenge is to pay attention to those who struggle in their own "snow globe world." Help them understand what we already know. God's kingdom is eternally stable for those of us who follow. No more shaking!

PRAY. God, thank you for the stability that you bring to my life. Thank you for the times, when I was being shaken, you brought security. Help me to pay attention to my friends today and share with them the good news that I already know. You are strong, stable, and to be trusted. Amen.

LISTEN. **FEBRUARY 11** **Psalm 71:1-6**

Comfort, God With Us

THINK. God is always near us and involved with us. God is present for us in times of trouble, in times of our friends betraying us, in times of our critics being hurtful to us. God is "hands-on" and involved in the daily activities of our world.

God also desires our friendship. Just as the psalm writer was talking to God, God also wants to hear from us. God has been with us from the beginning of the world, from the beginning of our lives, to whatever happens next. You can trust that God knows and that God cares.

So live fully in the moment without fear. God is our refuge! In our bad days, we can go to the refuge for comfort and security. In the good days, we can go to the refuge for praise and celebration.

PRAY. Thank you, God, for being a refuge of strength in my life. You are there for me in good times and bad. You are there for me when critics hurt me and when friends desert me. Thank you for the love and security you give me. Amen.

GO.

All through the hours of a good day, God is at work.
In every hour of a bad day, God is at work.
Through the highs and lows of all the rhythms of life . . .
God's hand is upon you.

What God Does

Richard Vinson

PAUSE.

We know that God is at work in the world. It's just not easy to always know how that work is taking place or how we can recognize it.

Take time now to think about what God is doing in your life. Be open to the ways God may be at work even now.

LISTEN. FEBRUARY 12 **Romans 8:11-17**

Child of God

THINK. Know anyone who was adopted? Were you? In our culture, adoption is complicated, time-consuming, and expensive. Everyone wants to make sure that the new family will treat the child well.

In Paul's time, adoption was pretty easy. If parents had a baby they didn't want, they could just leave it somewhere public, and anybody could take it home. Many abandoned children were raised to be slaves for the household, but occasionally a family would adopt an abandoned child and raise it as their own.

In our culture, there are adoption papers, legal documents that the new parents sign saying that the child is now their child. In Paul's time, the only official document was the new will naming the child as an heir. Once the will was filed, the child could claim the family's ancestors and inherit the family property.

God has adopted us, Paul said, making us God's daughters and sons instead of slaves. We have no written documents; instead we have God's Spirit inside us, helping us to learn to speak to God as "Parent."

PRAY. Our Father who art in heaven, hallowed be thy name . . .

LISTEN. **FEBRUARY 13** **John 14:8-10**

Example of Christ

"Just show us God. That's all we're asking! One little peek, and we'll be satisfied."

THINK. I suppose Philip wanted something zippy-zappy: Jesus would wave his arms, there would be a big cloud of smoke, and God would be standing there in front of them. What would God look like? Would God be holding a lightning bolt?

Maybe Jesus considered whacking Philip upside the head, because he had missed the point of what Jesus had been saying over and over in this Gospel. "What? How can you ask me that? Whoever has seen me has seen God. My words are God's words. All those miracles—God did those through me."

Boil down the Gospel of John to one sentence: If you want to know God, get to know Jesus. Sure, you can know God in other ways—by caring for God's creation, by treating other people with God's compassion, by listening for God's voice inside you. But always check your conclusions about God by comparing them to Jesus. God hasn't left us in the dark; anytime we want, we can check out the example of Jesus in the good old B-I-B-L-E.

PRAY. Lord, thank you for showing God to me, and for answering all my questions. Help me to pay close attention when you speak. Amen.

LISTEN. FEBRUARY 14 **John 14:11-14**

Prayer

THINK. Lord, please help me pass this algebra test.

Lord, please let my mom live.

Lord, please . . . well, you get the idea. People pray all sorts of things. Jesus' promise was so big—ask anything in Jesus' name, and he'll do it. Sometimes it works just that way. Yet sometimes we pray really hard, and what we ask for doesn't happen.

Jesus promised to do what we ask in order to glorify God, and some things we ask for wouldn't honor God. He also said that we need to believe in him—be committed to him, in other words, so that we want what he wants. Those limits on the promise may explain why some things we pray for happen, but not everything.

Prayer isn't like putting money in a candy machine. It's conversations with somebody who knows you inside and out, somebody whom you get to know better the more you open up. So ask for what you will, but then ask what God thinks, and trust that God will help you understand.

PRAY. Help me to want what you want for me. And help me to pay close attention when you speak. Amen.

LISTEN. **FEBRUARY 15** **John 14:15-17**
Holy Spirit

THINK. Search for the Tallis Scholars' version of Thomas Tallis' "If ye love me, keep my commandments." It's so beautiful that it always makes me a little sad when it's over.

Jesus spoke these words the night before he died. He had already predicted that one would betray him and another deny him, and that none was ready to face what he was about to go through. But ready or not, his hour had come.

So he made them a promise: I will ask the Father to send you another Advocate, another "Comforter," as the King James has it. A "comforter" sounds, well, comforting, something warm to snuggle under or your favorite foods when you're sick.

But this comforter does more than make you feel better; the Spirit represents you in your struggles. If you pay attention, the Advocate can remind you of Jesus' commandment to love each other and can teach you how to respond when the world is a hostile place.

Life isn't always as lovely as that song. But God is merciful, and gives us a strong Advocate to coach us through the tough parts.

PRAY. Thank you, Lord, for your Spirit within me. Amen.

LISTEN. FEBRUARY 16 **John 14:25-27**

Peace, Eternity

THINK. Caesar Augustus was proud of having brought peace to the Empire. But the Roman Peace, the Pax Romana, came at a high cost: nations conquered, peoples enslaved, armies slaughtered. A defeated chieftain is supposed to have said, "They rob, butcher, plunder, and call it 'empire'; they make a desolation, and call it 'peace.'"

Jesus' people knew all about that, having been "pacified" by the Romans twice before Jesus was born. Judea paid Rome money every year for the privilege of having Roman soldiers stationed in their country to keep them under control.

That's what Jesus meant when he said that his peace was not like the world's peace. It doesn't cost you money, and it isn't enforced by spear and sword.

We know Jesus' peace when we realize that we have God's Spirit in us, and that we can never be apart from God. You always have God's ear, and God always has your back. Rest easy, then. Empires come and go, but God is eternal. Empires will use you up, but God wants to build you up. This is a peace that can do you good.

PRAY. Help me to know your real peace. And help me know the difference between what the world offers and what you give. Amen.

LISTEN. **FEBRUARY 17** **Acts 2:1-4**

Spirit, Power of God

THINK. Sometimes there's a moment in sports when one team or individual just gets hot. Somebody makes a steal and takes it down for a thunderous dunk, and then everybody else plays a little harder, looking for the chance to break the game open. It's that extra bit of confidence or surge of emotion. You can't predict it, but as an athlete you wait for it and when it comes, you ride it, and it's amazing.

Pentecost was the day when Jesus' followers caught fire. In today's text, Jesus' followers amounted to 120 men and women meeting quietly to pray, to remember Jesus' teachings, and to share meals with each other. But after Pentecost, they piled out into the streets, telling people who had even heard of Jesus about how salvation could be theirs.

"Filled with the Spirit," Luke calls it. Jesus taught that the Spirit lives in us all the time, but this must have been one of those special moments when God's presence and the Spirit's power felt . . . well, amazing. That's what they had been waiting for, and when it happened, it changed them, and then they changed the world.

PRAY. Lord, fill me with your Spirit. Change the world through me. Amen.

LISTEN. **FEBRUARY 18** **Acts 2:14-21**

Will of God

THINK. This passage is amazing. It says that God's Spirit makes prophets of all of us—men and women, young and old, slave and free. All who belong to Christ are filled with God's power to preach ("prophesy"), to know God's will ("see visions"), and to imagine plans for the future ("dream"). Everybody is gifted, everybody is empowered, and everybody is responsible. Two questions: Is that how things work in your church? Is that how you think of yourself?

If you answered no, then you are not alone. Maybe you feel like your church doesn't listen enough to the youth. Pray for God's guidance, and talk to a church leader you trust; think of a way to raise the issues respectfully.

Think about this: God wants your voice, your perspective, your energy. Yeah, you. God poured the Spirit into you, and you've got something God is calling you to do. How about it?

PRAY. Lord, empower me with your Spirit. Then help me to act with confidence to do your will. Amen.

Go into this day now with the assurance that God is at work in your life. Open your spirit to make way for what God can and will do.

Impartial Love

David Woody

PAUSE.

It's easy to love when we feel loving toward another. It's much more difficult when the other seems unlovable to us.

Jesus provided another model, a way of offering love to whomever he encountered, regardless of their status or "loveliness."

Think about how you might follow that example.

LISTEN. FEBRUARY 19 **Mark 7:24-30**

Life in Christ

THINK. One of the nice things about a job is that it has a beginning time and an ending time. When we're off the clock, we don't have to worry about any job-related responsibilities; we get to do what we want to do. In today's reading, Jesus wanted some time alone and tried to hide from all the people. He was tired and wanted some time to rest.

While he was resting, a woman found him and begged him to help her daughter. Jesus could have easily told her to leave him alone, that he wasn't working right now. But Jesus didn't. With patience, love, and grace he listened to her, had conversation with her, and healed her daughter.

Jesus always has time for us. He is never too busy. We can go to him with our concerns, our questions, our fears, and our celebrations. Jesus wants to spend time with us. He loves us so much that he is never off the clock.

PRAY. God, thank you that you have all the time in the world for me. Help me to come to you and share all of my life with you. Amen.

LISTEN. **FEBRUARY 20** **Mark 7:31-37**

New Life, Unconditional Love

THINK. Have you ever thought how great a basketball player you would be if you were six inches taller? Or how great a musician you would be if you could read music? Or how great a whatever you would if you only had . . . ? How many times have you thought about all the obstacles in your way of becoming something different than what you are?

Jesus faced this question all the time. Folks came to him with all sorts of problems. Their problems, though, weren't about becoming the next great athlete, musician, or whatever. They wanted to be whole. They all had something that kept them from being complete.

Through his love and compassion, Jesus made them whole. He loved them, all of them, so much that he radically changed their lives so that they would live in a new way. Jesus' intense love is not just reserved for the lame, the blind, and the deaf. His love is for you and for me. What is it that is keeping you from being whole and complete? Take it to Jesus. He loves you and wants to take care of you.

PRAY. God, let me tell you about the things that keep me from growing into the person you call me to be. Make me whole and complete. Make me new in you. Amen.

LISTEN. FEBRUARY 21 **James 2:1-4**
Unconditional Love

THINK. Every morning we face a vital decision for the day—what clothes to wear. The clothes we wear are important and are the visible witness of who we are. Deciding what to wear every day can be stressful when so much of our love and acceptance from others seems to hang from the curtain rod. We want to wear the right colors or style or labels so that we will fit in and be accepted and loved.

We all judge others by the way they look and the clothes they wear. We might not say anything out loud, but deep inside of us, we have a running commentary on the way others look. Fortunately, God doesn't do that. God isn't concerned about our shirts, pants, or jewelry; our clothes are temporary and disposable. We are not. God loves us and accepts us just the way we are. We don't have to wear the "right" clothes to fit in with God. Thanks be to God!

PRAY. God, thank you for loving me the way I am. Thank you for seeing who I am and not for who I pretend to be. Help me to see others through your eyes. Amen.

LISTEN. **FEBRUARY 22** **James 2:5-7**

Loving Others

THINK. Have you ever thought about why you love certain people? I'm not talking about romantic love. I'm referring to the kind of love or attraction that makes you want to hang out with someone, be their friend, and spend time with them. A lot of times we love people who are a lot like us: they may come from the same part of town, go to the same school, have similar interests, or look like us. The other people, those from the other side of town, those in different groups, and those who look nothing like us, barely get a passing glance from us. If they do get noticed, it's only because they are so different than we are.

Loving people like us is easy. We know who they are, because they are like us! Loving those who are different from us is difficult. We don't know what they think or what they will do or what they like and don't like. When we start putting people in categories, cool or uncool, like me or unlike me, rich or poor, and stylish or style-challenged, we limit ourselves and the love that we share with others.

PRAY. God, help me to see all people for who they are. Knock down the categories and stereotypes I use and open my heart so that I might love others the way you love me. Amen.

LISTEN. FEBRUARY 23 **James 2:8-10**

Loving Others

THINK. One of the first Bible passages I memorized was "You shall love your neighbor as yourself." I remember that verse being very easy to live out because I didn't know my neighbors. In my childish mind, my neighbors lived on my street in my neighborhood. If I didn't know them, I didn't have to love them. That worked for me then. It doesn't work now.

With ever-changing technology, my neighborhood stretches around the world. I can just as easily have a conversation with my friend in Indonesia as I can with my neighbor who lives next door. As my neighborhood has grown, my understanding of the idea of neighbor has grown, too. Jesus calls us to love our neighbors—all of them! His words aren't merely a suggestion or an option; they are the way it is supposed to be. Can you imagine a world where love was the dominant emotion instead of fear or hatred or jealousy? When we love our neighbors, we start to spread God's love around the world.

PRAY. God, move me to be more loving, and help me to do what I need to do to show that love to others. May all of my neighbors know that I love them. Amen.

LISTEN. ## FEBRUARY 24 **James 2:14-17**

Loving Others

THINK. How do you show someone that you love them? With candy, flowers, or a card? What if you don't have romantic love for someone? How do you show love then? Flowers and candy aren't really the best gifts for that kind of love. Love is a gift, a free gift, with no strings attached. We love because something within us wells up and we want to do something for or say something to the other person.

God's love for us is that "something within us." When we are filled with God's love, our own love just comes out. If we are serious about loving others, then our love will be exhibited through our words and our actions. We have daily opportunities to love others. Whenever we interact with someone else, we have the opportunity to say a kind word, meet a need, provide something they lack, and serve them in the name of Christ. We can love our best friend that way, and we can love a stranger that way. Let our love flow to all that we meet.

PRAY. God, let me feel your love, and let me be filled with your love so that when I see others your love comes flowing out of me. Help me to meet needs, have conversations, and use the right words of love with everyone. Amen.

LISTEN. FEBRUARY 25 **Prov. 22:1-9, 22-23**

Loving Others, Actions

THINK. Have you ever thought about how people talk about you? "Sarah is a great student, but doesn't talk much." "Rashaad is a little mean, but he can play a great saxophone." "Mollie is so sweet." "Kyle is a bully." We all have our opinions about others, and others have their opinions about us. The way we act and treat other people is the way people remember us and treat us. If we are mean, people will be mean back. If we are quiet and reserved, people tend to leave us alone. If we are kind and loving, people will come to us and want to be around us. Other people like being around nice, loving people.

We have the choice of how we want people to remember us. If we follow the example of Jesus, people will remember us because of our love. It's the kind of love that is blind to fashion, cliques, stereotypes, money, and power. It's the kind of love that accepts everyone for where they are and for who they are. It's the kind of love that says, "I love you, and I want to do something special for you." It's the kind of love that people remember for a long, long time.

PRAY. God, let me sow love in my life so that others might see your love from me. Give me the courage to love the unloved, the patience to love the difficult, and the openness to love the different. Basically, God, help me to love like you. Amen.

GO.

In Christ there is no east or west,
In him no pride of birth,
The chosen family God has blessed
Now spans the whole wide earth.

In Christ there is no east or west,
He breaks all barriers down;
By Christ redeemed, by Christ possessed,
In Christ we live as one.

Michael Perry (from a line by John Oxenham)[2]

The Way, The Truth, and The Life

Luke Fodor

PAUSE.

Waymaker, Truthgiver, source of abundant life, on this Journey to the Cross help me to live in the wideness of your love. Jesus, you came to this earth to become my path to God. When I follow the lead of your life, I always find my way home.

LISTEN. FEBRUARY 26 **Philippians 1:9**

Doubt, Fear, Trust

THINK. If you have ever been lost, not just sort of lost, but truly lost, like being lost on a hike in a forest, you know what a jarring, disorienting, and frustrating experience it is. Your surroundings become totally unfamiliar, and you are unable to make any progress in finding your way.

If you have ever been lost in the woods, you know what a relief it is when you finally spot the trail marker. But, sometimes you still wonder. What if that isn't really the marker and I made a mistake? Now it's getting dark. Ultimately, you have to believe that the trail marker points the way and follow it.

Jesus is like the trail marker, providing a path for us to find our way back to God. We may have doubts, but if we believe that Christ is the way, the truth, and the life, we'll find our way.

PRAY. God, Waymaker of my life, so often I am confused and lost. My life spins out of control and I lose my way. Jesus, you have provided a way for me, a way back to God. Calm my troubled heart and teach me to follow your path. Amen.

LISTEN. **FEBRUARY 27** **John 14:8-14**

Image of God

THINK. Have you ever seen one of those old Matreshka dolls? You know, the painted, wooden, bowling-pin-shaped dolls that have progressively smaller dolls nesting inside of each larger one? Although they appear to be just one figure, when you unpack all the smaller dolls there are three, four, or perhaps five smaller, almost identical dolls standing side by side.

In today's reading, Jesus tells us that our relationship to God is like the Matreshka dolls. Christ is in God, and we are in Christ, and through Christ the Holy Spirit is also in us. Now that Christ has ascended to heaven, like removing the one layer of the dolls, we Christians are the remaining visible image of God. Because God has chosen to be close, like the smallest Matreshka doll, we are surrounded by God, by Jesus, by the Spirit.

If the people in our world are to see God, they have to see God in our lives. Do your friends and family see Christ in you?

PRAY. God, you promised to reveal yourself to us. Reveal yourself in a new way to me today, so I can reveal you to the world. Keep me close to you, so close that I become a reflection of the good gifts you long to give. Amen.

LISTEN. FEBRUARY 28 **John 14:15-17**

Spirit of God, Following Christ

THINK. Sometimes we receive a gift we just cannot seem to appreciate. Have you ever received a book or a sweater for your birthday instead of the latest gadget you wanted so badly? It is difficult to not be dismissive of certain gifts we might not want, even when they are given with love. We receive these gifts, but we are unable to see their value.

God has given us a gift that is precious. God gives us the Holy Spirit—a helper, counselor, and advocate—who dwells in us, enabling and encouraging us to love God and keep God's commandments.

Much like that unread book on the shelf or the sweater buried in your closet, we sometimes forget about God's gift of the Holy Spirit. The Spirit is our helper, who encourages us to walk in faith and follow the example of Jesus. And yet, we often live our lives as if the Spirit had never come. Have you forgotten God's gift?

PRAY. Come, sweet Spirit, make me aware of your indwelling. Tune my ears to hear you. Focus my eyes to see you. Warm my heart to feel your presence. Help me to acknowledge you, God's gift to my life. Amen.

LISTEN. **FEBRUARY 29** **John 14:18-24**
Presence of God

THINK. Through the internet we are connected to a web of relationships. Email, instant messaging, blogs, and social media create places to encounter other people. Those of us who communicate in these ways often have friends from around the country and around the world, most of whom we have never spoken to, let alone met.

In today's Scripture, Jesus told his disciples that he was going away, and though the world would not see him, they would continue to see him. "How is it that you will reveal yourself to us, and not to the world?" asked one disciple. This question is important for us today, as well.

The living Christ is seen best by those who dare to follow. Jesus is alive and active in the life of the church, in the fellowship of God's people, in the celebration of the holy communion, in the reading of Scripture, and in the practice of prayer. Have you encountered Christ recently?

PRAY. Be present, Christ Jesus, be present. Teach me to see your life in the people who surround me. Make me aware of your presence and help me to keep your words. Amen.

MARCH

LISTEN. **MARCH 1** **John 14:25-31**
Comfort, Peace

THINK. Have you ever studied really hard for a test and felt prepared to answer any question the teacher might throw at you, only to forget the answer as soon as the test was in front of you? It is a frustrating experience that we have all faced. We sit in our chairs, racking our brains, straining to remember the answer.

In today's Gospel, Jesus promises us that we will not encounter a similar experience in the classroom of faith. The Holy Spirit will always be with us to teach us and remind us what Christ said. When our faith is tested, we don't need to be troubled or anxious about remembering the right answer. If we are attentive to the indwelling Spirit, each test becomes an open book exam. Jesus tells us that we have been given this peace, so why should we worry about the tests of faith we tackle? Don't be caught worrying. "Rise, let us be on our way."

PRAY. Peacegiver, Waymaker, still my anxious heart. Remind me that your spirit indwells me. You are with me as much in the difficult times as in the easy times. Don't let me forget your gift of peace. Amen.

LISTEN. MARCH 2 **John 12:24-25**

Example of Christ, Following Christ

THINK. When I was in the fourth grade, my class celebrated Earth Day by planting trees. My teacher brought in a pinecone packed with seeds. Each student got a seed that we germinated in the back of the room. When my seed sprouted, I took it home and planted it in my yard. That pine tree is still in my parents' yard today, towering over 20 feet tall.

Jesus gave us a simple picture that accurately portrays the season of Lent, when we prepare for the passion and mystery of Easter. Using the life cycle of a grain of wheat, Jesus was able to explain his own death in a way that makes sense to us. Jesus' death was the start of the church. When he died, he planted a seed that has produced fruit for two thousand years. Through baptism we have entered into Christ's death, and we must remember that our life doesn't belong to us but to God. As lovers of life we must learn to follow Jesus' example; we must learn to give our lives away.

PRAY. Christ, remind me continually of your gift of life. In the season of Lent, help me not cling to my life, but rather lose it for your sake; for I know this is the only way to find eternal life. Amen.

LISTEN. **MARCH 3** **John 13:33-38**

Love, Kingdom of God

THINK. Do you remember being a young child and your parents leaving you with a babysitter because they were going to a party? In a fit of tears you asked them, "Can I come with you?" And of course, they said, "No you can't."

That's just how Jesus' disciples must have felt, like little children! Jesus was leaving them, and they couldn't come with him. Just like the disciples, we are little children left by ourselves. Jesus has gone before us to a party, a party in God's house, which we will one day attend.

In the meantime, we have the opportunity to throw a pre-party here on earth while we wait. But to gain access to that party, we need to follow Jesus' commandment and love one another as Christ has loved us. God's kingdom starts here on earth if we are willing to truly love each other.

Do people know that you are a Christian because of your love?

PRAY. Jesus, even though you are away I know that you love me. Help me to love those around me as much as you love me. Teach me to celebrate the kingdom of God here on earth. Amen.

GO.

And this is my prayer, that your love may overflow more and more with knowledge and full insight to help you to determine what is best, so that in the day of Christ you may be pure and blameless, having produced the harvest of righteousness that comes through Jesus Christ for the glory and praise of God.

Philippians 1:9-11

Blessing in Hunger and Thirst

Heidi Hagstrom

PAUSE.

Through the season of Lent, we take a look at ourselves; we examine our lives to find those things in us that need to be changed. Search your heart; become deeply aware of your longings, and of your desire for the compassion and love of God to fill you.

LISTEN. MARCH 4 **Psalm 42:1-6, 8**

Child of God, Childlike Faith

THINK. A simple walk down the street in my Chicago neighborhood would make one wonder if our whole society suffers from insatiable thirst. It seems everyone carries a water bottle. Because I can turn on the tap and drink the water in my home, and because I have the resources to buy bottled water, I have not known thirst. But I have known the kind of thirst that the psalmist talked about. This kind of thirst is more like a deep longing for, or thirsting after, God.

The gift of Lent for me is the awareness of my sinfulness, and I long to be drawn closer to the heart of God. I become aware of the patterns of thinking and being that distract me from God's purpose, and that pull me away from my true self—God's beloved.

Listen to the longing in your own heart this week, and take initiative to turn it homeward. Acknowledge the obstacles and distractions, and ask for what is yours as a child of God. Ask for the same intimacy with God that a suckling child enjoys with its mother. Ask for faith to persevere, even when asked, "Where is your God?" Seek the treasure of your heart. Seek God.

PRAY. All-loving Savior, I yearn to be one with you. Like a comforting mother, draw me close to your heart and give me the courage not to run away. Bless my desire to be an instrument of your love, offering refreshment to those who, like me, are thirsting for your love. Amen.

LISTEN. MARCH 5 **John 4:7-15**

Prayer, Stillness

THINK. I once spent a few days with this text on retreat. I used my imagination in prayer. I was the woman sitting next to Jesus. In my prayer I was naked, a metaphor for the shame I felt in the presence of the Holy One. I couldn't look at Jesus, let alone talk to him. So when he asked me for a drink of water, I dropped my head in my hands and started to sob. How could he possibly want anything from me? I was keenly aware of my unworthiness. Then Jesus did something amazing. He took my head in his hands, drew his face close to mine and said, "Beloved, lift your eyes." I looked into Jesus' soft eyes and followed his invitation to stand. There I was, naked, literally and figuratively, before my God with no place to hide.

The miracle of that moment for me came in Jesus' next action. He took his ample cloak and wrapped it around me. It was like being bathed in purifying love, so powerful and unfamiliar I wanted to flee, yet the Spirit gave me the grace to remain still. Ever since that day, I can pray "Search me O God, and know my heart; test me and know my thoughts. See if there is any wicked way in me, and lead me in the way everlasting," knowing that in the praying I am entering nothing more than the scrutiny of love.

PRAY. Gracious God, I beg for the grace to pray today, "Search me, O God, and know my heart." I know that you are all love. Help me to remain still in your presence because I know that you judge me only with the scrutiny of your love. Amen.

LISTEN. MARCH 6 **John 6:47-51**

Knowing Christ

THINK. I am a food addict, carbohydrates in particular. I especially lose all control around bread products. A friend who is a recovering alcoholic has taught me much about addictions. We often talk about the addiction to alcohol being different than the addiction to food. You can live without alcohol; you can't live without food. She can avoid alcohol; I can't avoid food. I can moderate my behavior toward food but that is more easily said than done.

Because of my unhealthy relationship with bread, the image of God as the Bread of Life has not been helpful. The kind of bread I buy at the bakery is not life-giving. I am never satisfied, and trying to satisfy the hunger only causes shame and insecurity, drawing me deeper into the chaos of addiction.

Then it dawned on me when receiving holy communion. It was the chaos that Jesus redeemed. When I leave the Lord's Table, fed with the Bread of Life, my head is satisfied with the truth of Christ; my heart is content with Jesus as the object of my affection. My hope is nourished and my desire satiated, for what can I wish for more than to know Christ—hungry no more.

PRAY. God, grant me the serenity to accept the things I cannot change, courage to change the things I can, and wisdom to know the difference. Amen.

Serenity Prayer by Reinhold Niebuhr[3]

LISTEN. MARCH 7 **Isaiah 55:1-2, 6-9**
Food that Satisfies

THINK. I invest too much energy feeding my soul with "food" that doesn't satisfy. Most times I'm left empty, and sometimes I'm consumed by the things I pursue. In today's Scripture we are asked, "Why do you spend money for what is not bread, and your wages for what does not satisfy?" Our heart's deepest longing, it says, can be satisfied in God alone. There is satisfaction in feeding on mercy rather than revenge, truth rather than cheating, peace rather than conflict. So we choose Christ, again and again.

As a child I was fascinated when my Roman Catholic cousins crossed themselves. We didn't do that in my Lutheran church. As an adult I am learning the beauty of the practice. Morning and evening I make the sign of the cross, saying, "In the name of the Creator, the Son, and the Holy Spirit. Amen."

This is a sign of discipleship, a reminder that I am claimed by Jesus and marked with the cross of Christ. The Greek word is the same for the mark a shepherd put on a sheep and a general put on a soldier. For me, making the sign of the cross is a declaration that I belong to Christ. Always a good investment.

PRAY. Gracious God, you know my many hungers for approval, security, justice, healing, peace, freedom, (add your own). Do not delay in feeding my hunger with what is good. Grant me the grace to choose wisely. In this moment, I choose you. Come into my heart, Lord Jesus. Amen.

LISTEN. **MARCH 8** **Jeremiah 23:5-6**

Peace, Example of Christ

THINK. The prophets, including Jeremiah, always talk about endings and beginnings, dying and new life, suffering and hope. Their radical language disrupts the community. The Israelites can't believe that what they are hearing could even be possible. Now there is a new leader who will "deal wisely" with the people, and "execute justice and righteousness" in the land. The Israelites are told they will "live in safety." Could it be?

Fast forward. In the Bible we are told that Jesus will establish a kingdom of peace and righteousness, and that the world will be a safe place. Could it be? Don't we sometimes stand with the Israelites in disbelief that the promise could come true?

I get glimpses of God's promise occasionally, mostly when I am focused on others. One of the great gifts of the Lenten disciplines is the opportunity to participate in bringing about the reign of peace and righteousness by following Jesus' lead: accompany the poor in spirit and those who mourn, practice meekness, seek righteousness, be merciful, remain pure of heart, make peace, stand firm for the sake of righteousness (Matt. 5:3-10).

PRAY. God of Promise, let there be peace on earth and let it begin with me. Let there be peace on earth, the peace that was meant to be. With God as our Father, brothers [and sisters] all are we. Let me walk with my brother[s and sisters] in perfect harmony. Amen.

Lyrics by Jill Jackson Miller and Sy Miller[4]

LISTEN. MARCH 9 **Matthew 3:13-17**

Kingdom of God, Image of God

THINK. Eddy was just tall enough to see into the baptismal font. This doe-eyed, round-faced child of Russian immigrants, elbows on the baptismal font, chin in his hands, stared deeply into the inviting water. Eddy was not alone around the font. His sister stood next to Matthew's wheelchair; Caleb was there; sweet Miguel was timidly holding his position; and the pastor's lanky son stood next to another child with fair skin.

The pastor compared the promise of the good life often attributed to money to the promise of everlasting life through Jesus. Eddy's five-year-old brain wasn't engaged by the analogy, but that water was beckoning. One arm dropped, his chubby fingers touching the plane of the water. He cast those big eyes coyly up to the pastor, waiting for a response. "Go ahead and touch it." To my delight, Eddy put his hand in the water, and immediately made the sign of the cross on his forehead. He'd seen it done before. "Can I do it again?" Then all of the kids did it, and a splashing, grace-filled gala ensued.

I glimpsed the kingdom of God that morning, a diverse group of young humans gathered living water. And a word came from heaven: "You are my beloved. I am well pleased with you."

PRAY. Jesus, help me to grow into the person you want me to be. I want to live like your beloved. Remind me today that I don't need to live by bread (things) alone, and fill me with your Word, the source of real life. Amen.

LISTEN. MARCH 10 **Matthew 5:10-12**

Following Christ

THINK. Jesus moves quickly from peacemaking to persecution in the Beatitudes. I think his movement reveals a truth. However hard we try to live peacefully, some will refuse to live at peace with us. Certainly today we are aware of politicians and political systems that each oppose, despise, and criticize the other. But how often do we think of the opposition as persecution?

Someone defined persecution as a clash between two opposing value systems. Even in my small world, I have experienced the tension of opposing value systems. My niece experiences it at school when she refuses to participate in a scheme to cheat or be drawn into a mean girl's cruel assault on another.

God has chosen us to represent Jesus' way by patiently enduring and even overcoming persecution as part of our Christian witness. We are to face persecution remembering "that the sufferings of this present time are not worth comparing with the glory about to be revealed to us" (Rom. 8:18).

During Lent we become aware of the times when we are persecuted for the sake of Christ. Persecution brings us into communion with the sufferings of our Savior, a blessed and necessary step on the journey with Jesus to the cross.

PRAY. Stir me, O Lord, to care; for a world that is lost and dying, for values that are rejected and scorned for enemies that hate and malign me. Amen.

Prayers From the Heart by Richard J. Foster[5]

GO.

Go now, beloved child of God; go in the knowledge that you are blessed. Be aware that the God whom you desire to know and to love is reaching out also to you, to be known by you, to fill you with righteousness.

Signs

Bruce Reyes-Chow

PAUSE.

How can you tell?

That's a fair question whenever someone makes a prediction of what is going to happen, or even when they give an explanation for what is happening now.

There are signs for those who will see them. Take time now to watch for the signs God has for you.

LISTEN. MARCH 11 **Psalm 25:1-5**

Example of Christ

THINK. It seems that every time I turn on the TV or read some article online, there is a politician, religious leader, or commentator making some disparaging remark about a person with whom they disagree. Too often the words are mean, violent, and deny the very humanity of the other. There have been times when words like that have been turned my way. From stupid fights in high school to arguing about church with adults, hurtful words have been flung my way and I usually want so very much to strike back.

Then I remember that, like today's psalm says, the ways we act during conflict may not be God's ways. While striking back against an enemy might feel good, I suspect God's way would be a path that shows our enemies that we live differently, a way that shows God's presence in the world, a sign of love, lived through us. It's not an easy task, but living in the path of God never is.

PRAY. God, when I am feeling overwhelmed in a world of chaos and struggle, show me, teach me, guide me, and make yourself known so that I may follow your way. Amen.

LISTEN. MARCH 12 **Genesis 9:8-11**

Promise

THINK. "I promise" is one of those things we say all the time when we make an agreement. If it is really serious, we might even "pinky promise," shaking with our pinkies as a way to seal the deal and add a little oomph to the promise made.

More times than not, we probably break those promises. Life gets busy, we get distracted, and we forget promises that we have made, even the pinky ones.

God does no such thing. God's promises are never broken.

We are promised that no matter what, God will be with us. God promises to give life to all that is around us now and forever, and so we take comfort in the fact that even in our most difficult times, God has promised to be there.

PRAY. God, thank you for life. Thank you for the life around me. And thank you for your promise to always be present. Amen.

LISTEN. MARCH 13 **Genesis 9:12-17**
Journey with God

THINK. Every Christmas as my family hangs ornaments on the tree, we take a walk down memory lane. The baby's-first-Christmas ornaments, the baked clay person from kindergarten, and the starfish bought during a vacation in Hawaii. One by one, ornament by ornament, we are reminded of our journey together as a family. We are reminded of the love that has bound us, one to another.

God often leaves these reminders for us as well. God spread a rainbow to remind Noah of the promise made, but for you it may be something else. Maybe God reminds you of the promise made through the picture of a loved one that you walk by each morning, maybe a friend who always remembers your birthday, or maybe it's an afternoon rainstorm that cools the earth.

Whatever it may be for you, when those reminders pop up, take a moment to remember and thank God for the love and life that has been promised to you.

PRAY. God, may you show me a sign of your love in unexpected ways and let me remember, and live as if it matters. Amen.

LISTEN. **MARCH 14** **Mark 1:9-11**

Journey with God, Child of God

THINK. There are few phrases that a parent can say to his or her child that are any more important than the words, "I am proud of you." Being proud of a child is not always about winning a game, getting a good grade or completing a task, but it's about who that child is becoming. When I say that I am proud of one of my children, it's because they are making choices that I clearly see as showing them growing into the person God intends them to be.

When Jesus was baptized and came out of the water, it's not just that he was baptized, but that he began to know who he was—a child of God. This realization was holy, and God, as a parent, was proud. As you live your life, know that God's hope for you is not about success, but about making choices that bring you closer to being the person God intends for you to be.

Whether it is baptism, treating others with kindness, or sacrificing your own time in order to serve others, know that as you do so, God is well pleased.

PRAY. Loving God, help me live in a way that allows me to become the person you intend for me to be. Amen.

LISTEN. **MARCH 15** **Mark 1:12-13**

Struggle, Presence of God

THINK. I wish life were easy. Wouldn't it be easier if there were no struggle, no conflict, and no stress in the world? Sure does seem like an ideal situation, but without some struggle in life, we don't grow, we don't learn about ourselves, and we don't learn how to make choices in life that are of God and not of the world.

I don't think Jesus was sent into the wilderness to suffer. I think he was sent there to learn how to be faithful. It was not about punishment or testing, but about the need for some tension in order to become disciplined and intentional about one's faith.

You too are sent into the world, not to be tested, not to suffer, but to live. In that living, you may find times when it will be difficult and choices will be hard to make. But always know that God, even in the struggle, is there.

PRAY. God, for your presence in the times of struggle, I am thankful. Help me to sense today that you are near. Amen.

LISTEN. **MARCH 16** **Mark 1:14-15**

Following Christ

THINK. I am a procrastinator. I like to tell myself that I do better under pressure. The truth is, I like to put things off until the last minute when a deadline is staring me down and I have to get it done. The pressure of a due date is enough to get me moving to finish the project.

Faith is sometimes like that. Sometimes things happen that jolt us into the realization that to follow Christ is to live differently—not tomorrow, not next week, but today.

Unlike writing a paper, though, it's not about the adrenaline rush and performance under pressure, but the reality that God calls us every day to be different and better than we were the day before. And that is not something we can put off until tomorrow.

PRAY. God, thank you for the ability and challenge to live faithfully, today, tomorrow, and always. Help me to take on that challenge gratefully. Amen.

LISTEN. MARCH 17 **Psalm 25:6-10**

Forgiveness

THINK. I still remember once getting caught in a lie by my mother. I told her I was in one place when I was in another, and I got busted . . . big time. As a parent now, I can imagine how she felt—worry, mixed with anger, topped with disappointment. I'm not sure how she ever forgave me, let alone let me out of the house again. But she did, and while I had to serve my time being grounded, in the end I was forgiven. Once she felt that I was truly sorry and some time had passed, it was as if it never happened.

Now I am sure that she never truly forgot, and was always keeping a little closer eye on me as I grew up, but she never held it against me. God, too, is like that.

When we mess up, God may get worried, angry, or disappointed, but God's love overrides it all; our faltering is not held against us. When you mess up or when you make choices that are not the best, God forgives and allows you to keep trying. So when you do find yourself in those kinds of struggles, be humble in seeking forgiveness, and be bold in living as God intends.

PRAY. God, for the times that I have faltered, forgive me and give me the courage to keep trying. Help me to remember that you are still on my side. Amen.

GO.

Go now with open eyes.
Go now with listening ears.
Make your way with the assurance
That God is leading you.
God is providing the signs you need
To see, To hear,
To find your way.

The Resurrection and the Life

Susan Hay

PAUSE.

With palms waving in the air, I remember the journey you took to the cross. This week, teach me to walk the road with you, to remember the life you lived. Like Lazarus, Mary, and Martha, I long to know you—my resurrection and my life.

LISTEN. **MARCH 18** **John 11:1-6**

Waiting

THINK. Lazarus must have been sick, really sick, or the sisters would not have sent for their friend Jesus. It's a message to a dear and trusted friend: "He whom you love is ill." Beneath the words I hear, "We need you. You bring us comfort. We can get through this with you here."

Aren't there friends you desire to be with in your times of great need? There are those people you know that love you, and you love them, and you know just by their presence everything will be all right. And you wait, but they can't get there when you need them most. Can you remember how you felt? What happened?

As with the sisters, we put expectations on Jesus, especially in times of great need, or grief, or suffering. This passage of Scripture calls us to reflect upon what kinds of expectations we put on Jesus and to look closely at how we react to God's timing in relation to our need.

PRAY. Whenever I feel pain or crisis, I want you there immediately. I am not good at waiting for you when I am afraid or insecure. Help me to know you are there even when I don't sense your presence. Help me to claim for myself that I too am one whom you love, and you never, never leave me. Amen.

LISTEN. MARCH 19 **John 11:7-16**

Struggle, Darkness, Light

THINK. Jesus was talking much deeper than actual day and night here. He sneaked it in when he said, "because the light is not in them." It's not about darkness as nighttime; it's about darkness inside.

I don't know about you, but nighttime for me is more often than not the time when I feel my insecurities the most. It's when my doubts and fears can become manifested, and then the night goes on forever, and I wonder if daylight will ever come so I can see.

Struggling in the night does not reveal lack of faith or even weakness; it provides opportunities for a holy encounter where we can grow in compassion and knowledge of God. It is where we can face our fears and doubts and in return be blessed. It is where we learn that God is always here, not only at dawn, but through the darkness of the night as well.

PRAY. As more of your light gets in me, I wrestle less in the night. As more of your light gets in me, I stumble less in the night. As more of your light gets in me, I discover with wonderful delight you have been there all along, that I have never been alone in the night! As more of your light gets in me, I realize you are the light of the world, and you are the light of me. Amen.

LISTEN. MARCH 20 **John 11:17-27**

Believe, Faith, Trust

THINK. Martha went out to meet Jesus and immediately hit him with "Lord, if you had been here, my brother would not have died." Her encounter with Jesus was part rebuke, part desperation, part regret, part grief, and part faith: "I know that God will give you whatever you ask of him." Martha believed Jesus was more than friend; he was also a righteous man whom God listened to in prayer.

Martha's faith in Jesus came through knowing and trusting him. Isn't that what faith is all about, knowing and trusting the other? When Jesus said to her, "I am the resurrection and the life . . . Do you believe this?" her reply was not a response to any sign of a miracle. It was her expression of faith, and believing Jesus' words, "I am the resurrection and the life." She responded, "Yes, Lord, I believe."

Whom do you know and trust no matter what? When did you first come to trust them, to believe in them? Do you believe Jesus to be the Messiah, the Son of God, as Martha proclaimed . . . no matter what?

PRAY. O most merciful redeemer, friend, and comforter, may I know you more clearly, love you more dearly, and follow you more nearly, day by day. Amen.

LISTEN. **MARCH 21** **John 11:28-37**

Sadness

THINK. Jesus wept over the death of Lazarus, a beloved friend. Was he weeping partly because of the chiding words of both Martha and Mary? "Lord, if you had been here . . ."

Did he weep at the hardness of heart of some of those present, those who always looked for something to complain about no matter what he did? "Could not he who opened the eyes of the blind man have kept this man from dying?"

Did he weep at the thought of his own death at the hands of "godly" people—people so sure of God, yet so disrespectful of life? Jesus wept at the death of his friend Lazarus.

When have you seen Jesus weep? Are those the same things that cause emotions to well up in you?

PRAY. Jesus, teach me to weep with you when I see injustice in my world. Guide my journey and teach me compassion. Let me draw from the deep love that respects and values life. Amen.

LISTEN. **MARCH 22** **John 11:38-44**

New Life, Wholeness

THINK. What were you thinking, Lazarus, as you were being called forth from the grave? Did you want to come back? Were you, too, thinking, "Four days in the tomb, it is finished. I am gone, my spirit has departed"? After all, wasn't it Jewish belief that the spirit lingered around the body for three days hoping for life to reenter, and then on the fourth day departed forever?

After four days, Lazarus, death was all you knew. When you heard your name, did you want to be called out from that tomb, back from something that now felt so normal? What did you fear the most, Lazarus: exposing the rot or responding to God calling you back to life and wholeness?

I wonder how long I have been in my tomb? Four days? And what do I fear the most: exposing the rot of my life, or the possibility of God calling me to life and wholeness?

PRAY. Gracious and loving God, as I sit here you are present, breathing life into me and into everything that is around me. Give me the strength and the desire to trust myself totally to you and to your love. Bring me to life; I desire to be made whole. Amen.

LISTEN. MARCH 23 **John 11:44**

Freedom in Christ

THINK. You've got to be kidding. Unbind him? Lord, he stinks; rot has set in! You want me to touch that? No way. Surely there must be another way to do this without it being so messy, without getting my hands dirty. You called him out of the tomb, surely you can strip away the cloth yourself. Why me? Why did you turn and motion for me to unbind him? Why not you? Why not someone else? Why not the priest and ministers? I'm just a disciple.

Unbinding and freeing people is always messy business. It requires getting our hands dirty, sometimes even coming away smelly from the stench that was beneath the bindings. Are there those you've been invited to set free but you are afraid of getting your reputation tarnished through the association? Is there someone today in need of unbinding? Can you be the one to do it?

PRAY. Today, God, as I sit quietly, allow me to see the names or faces of people who through just a word of kindness from you today could be given some freedom from their binding. Today, God, as I go, give me the courage to get my hands dirty. Amen.

LISTEN. MARCH 24 **John 11:49-50**

Putting God First, Loving Others

THINK. Caiaphas was right. I mean, this made perfect sense. Isn't it always better to get rid of the thorns in our sides than get to know them? Isn't it better to go to war rather than seek a peaceful solution? Isn't it better to say to people who are different from us, "Get out of the way, you don't matter," than to offer friendship? Isn't it just better to say, "Get out of my way, your life has no significance"?

When did we come to the belief that human beings are expendable? Or more specifically, that some human beings are expendable? When did we get caught up in the belief that human life is unimportant, that life is not significant—more specifically, that all life is not significant?
Jesus was expendable. Caiaphas said so.

And now, Jesus is dead, in the tomb.

PRAY. Oh God of resurrection and life, forgive me when I see people as objects to do my will or to just get out of my way. May I come to hold everyone as having significance, eternal significance. You are the source of all that is significant. Help me to live and proclaim a life centered in you, where no one is expendable. Amen.

GO.

Go now, knowing that light lives beyond the darkness. Go now, believing that life can come in death. Go now, and find life in remembering the journey of Jesus to the cross.

Withdraw

Andy Watts & Amy Dodson-Watts

PAUSE.

Wilderness is a symbol for places and experiences in our lives that bring us silence, fear, uncertainty, and loneliness. It can cause us to withdraw from our relationships with our friends, our family, and from God.

Can it mean something else? Should we ask, "What can the wilderness do for me?"

LISTEN. MARCH 25 **Matthew 4:1-2**

Temptation, Wilderness

THINK. People who own horses often provide salt licks for them. Horses tend to drink less water in winter because of the cold, and dehydrate more quickly in summer because of the heat. Salt helps the body retain water, but it also replenishes minerals caused by dehydration. Salt not only nourishes bodies but also teaches them to seek what they need.

Jesus was led into the wilderness, isolated from the clamor of life's demands. He was led, possibly without knowing why, by the Spirit that intercedes when we need it. In the wilderness he was confronted with more than hunger; he was tempted to forsake his calling. Often we don't know why we enter into wildernesses that come our way.

Often our wilderness is emotional, like anger. Or it is physical, like sickness. Other times, it is spiritual, like guilt and shame. Like Jesus, sometimes we feel depleted when we act on the Spirit's urging, but the wilderness is a place where we might learn the most about ourselves.

PRAY. Beautiful and loving God, I hunger for healing. I thirst for you. Lead me to you, like the deer to water. Amen.

LISTEN. MARCH 26 **Psalm 32:3-4**

Unconditional Love

THINK. A great Christian philosopher once asked a question in story form. What if a mighty emperor thinks to send for a day laborer, a poor man who never dreamed that the emperor knew he existed? What if the emperor told him he wanted him for a son-in-law, to join the royal family? What would the poor man think? Would the laborer be embarrassed, self-conscious, and puzzled? What would the neighbors think? Would they say the emperor was making a fool of him? How could he guarantee that this was not an absurd joke? What if he had to believe it on faith? Would the laborer have the courage to dare to believe it true? Or would he humanly and honestly confess, "Such a thing is too high for me; I cannot grasp it?"

Often we withhold our most intimate confessions from God in silent embarrassment. Is it because we can't see that God's unlimited love is the hand that lies heavy on us, holding us close?

PRAY. Creator God, it seems so absurd that you would love me with all my secrets and all my faults. Teach me to have the courage to trust you. Amen.

LISTEN. MARCH 27 **Exodus 16:1-3**

Assurance of God, Journey with God

THINK. Thick burger. Super-size. One-pound burger. These are the meals of our world, not the Israelites'. If he could, Moses probably would have super-sized any edible thing set in front of them. Instead, God's people complained about going from stuffing their faces under Pharaoh to starving under Moses. The wilderness became their resentment.

If we're not careful, we could resent God's presence with us much as the Israelites did. Most of us are used to stuffing ourselves with the biggest, the most, the best, and the latest. In the land of plenty, most of us are not used to the food deserts, entertainment deserts, clothes deserts, and pleasure deserts symbolized by the wilderness. Even our churches stuff and super-size our faith experiences like the food court at the mall.

Yet God beckons us away from our overstuffed lives. We are called to places of interconnectedness to God and this "whole assembly" we call community. We can resent the experience or we can find it both healing and nourishing.

PRAY. Loving God, the places you ask me to go are sometimes scary. I fear I'll be alone, or that my needs won't be met. Assure me with your love, merciful God. Amen.

LISTEN. **MARCH 28** **Psalm 32:5-7**

Wilderness, Forgiveness

THINK. Sometimes we do things that aren't consistent with our character. Sometimes we injure and disappoint ourselves. Other times, we injure and disappoint others. This is called brokenness. It is something God knows very well; God understands sin. The Bible is full of stories where people break and injure themselves and others and their relationship with God.

We feel guilty about our wrongdoing, but we don't know what to do with our feelings. We don't understand that responsibility for our wrongdoing can only be absolved by someone else. We punish ourselves. This affects our self-esteem and destroys our joy. Racked with guilt, our souls are diminished. We hide from the very people who could help us live forgiven. We hide from God. We turn a wilderness moment into a lifeless desert.

This is the psalmist's point. Sometimes a punishment handed down by another is not as bad as a punishment we inflict on ourselves. In the wilderness, we might discover that God forgives our guilt—judges our culpability—with a punishment of forgiveness and grace.

PRAY. Lord, when my understanding fails me, deliver me from my guilt and secure me with hope. Amen.

LISTEN. MARCH 29 **Matthew 4:3-4**

Presence of God

THINK. Former country music duo Brooks and Dunn sing, "You can take the girl out of the honky tonk, but you can't take the honky tonk out of the girl."

After fasting for 40 days, Jesus faced three temptations that tested his character and self-understanding. The first concerned turning stones into bread. Bread might seem like a big temptation after you've been fasting for this long, but the body gets used to not eating. In this light, the temptation seems to be about more than material things. The adversary wanted to take Jesus out of this sacred place in a quick and unnatural way, such as turning stones to bread. He wanted Jesus to "get on" with being God immediately. Jesus, however, recognized the trap. His fast from food was ending, but his feast on God's provision continued.

Once we find ourselves alone with God, our hearts sing, "You can take the beloved out of the wilderness, but you can't take the wilderness out of the beloved."

PRAY. Dear God, so many things compete for my attention. Keep me in your presence. Nourish me with your love. Amen.

LISTEN. **MARCH 30** **Matthew 4:5-7**

Journey with God, Security

THINK. As Jesus stood at the top of the pinnacle of Jewish faith, he probably had feelings of exhilaration. Even after fasting for 40 days, he probably felt an invincibility of spirit. The tempter recognized this and urged him to prematurely force God's intervention for his life. But Jesus saw through this ploy. In the wilderness he learned that God's presence is as strong in suffering as in strength. He turned and scolded the adversary for speeding up the seasons of God's provision and care.

Just as a mirage in the desert gives a false sense of confidence that all will be well, our emotions often give us an exaggerated confidence in our faith. They work most powerfully in times of spiritual struggles. They jump in to quickly fix our pain. Exhilaration feels much better than uncertainty and confusion.

Yet when we withdraw into God's care, we are sustained at a deep level. We are loved even when we can't muster confidence or excitement.

PRAY. Lord Jesus Christ, settle my soul when it seeks to run too quickly from the depths of your love. Amen.

LISTEN. MARCH 31 **Matthew 4:8-10**

Community, Presence of God

THINK. Jesus' experience in the third wilderness temptation is like a superhero movie. The sinister villain attempts to dominate the world, and the superhero defeats him in battle. The third encounter between Jesus and the devil couldn't be more different, however. The devil offered Jesus power over all the kingdoms of the world. He enticed Jesus to worship him with a dominating power—a controlling, competing power. Jesus, knew about that kind of power, and he rejected it.

Archbishop Desmond Tutu, a church hero who helped bring down Apartheid in South Africa in the 1990s, teaches ubuntu. Ubuntu is a Bantu word that means people are dependent upon one another for individuality and community. It means that each person's being is caught up with the being of others, including God's being. That is the power of creative love.

In the wilderness, we meet God's power as ubuntu. It neither competes with us nor seeks to dominate us. It loves us, shares itself with us, and sustains us.

PRAY. Dear God, forgive me for the times I have withdrawn from you. I did not understand you wanted me to share in your overflowing being. Thank you for your empowering peace. Amen.

GO.

We have been told in the letter to the Hebrews that Jesus journeyed to this unfamiliar place before us as a forerunner on our behalf. Wherever you are, Jesus waits for you as the sure and steadfast anchor of your soul. Trust him.

APRIL

Love Comes to This

Peter Hanson

PAUSE.

Love has its reasons, they say.

Love has its purposes, too. It's not out there "just because," only to make us feel good, or even, as it does sometimes, to drive us crazy.

Love intends a result; love has an end in mind. When we say "God is love," we need to remember that.

LISTEN. APRIL 1 **Psalm 107:1-3**

Praise, Assurance of God

THINK. Several years ago, in the movie *Broadcast News,* one very lucky character says to another (who has not been quite so fortunate), "What do you do when your real life exceeds your wildest dreams?" "Keep it to yourself," responds the other.

This is not the way it is with the people of God. God's people, who are set free from big and small things, are called to share this good news. God's people, when they have been comforted in times of trouble, don't keep it to themselves. They tell others about God's love and mercy, how God's forgiving presence lasts forever. God is good all the time. Let God's people say so!

PRAY. Good and gracious God, thank you for your love, which lasts forever. Help me to rely on you in times of trouble, and help me to tell others when you've helped me out.

LISTEN. **APRIL 2** **John 3:14-15**

New Life

THINK. After 10 years overseas, one of the new buzzwords I've discovered in US slang is "repurposed." It is somehow stronger than any of the usual "re-" words: reduce, reuse, or recycle, for example. It suggests a more profound change—a change of meaning, of direction, of intention.

Both of the symbols alluded to in today's passage have been repurposed. Snakes were a symbol of plague and sudden death in the desert until Moses lifted one up on a stick. The cross was a symbol of capital punishment and humiliation throughout the Roman Empire until Jesus was lifted up on Golgotha. In both cases, the symbols have been repurposed, becoming signs of healing, wholeness, victory, and new life.

In what ways might God be calling you to repurpose your life? How is God offering you healing, wholeness, and new life?

PRAY. Jesus, Son of God, Son of Man, I look to you for new life. Give my life a calling, a direction, a purpose. Be lifted up in all I do. Amen.

LISTEN. APRIL 3 **John 3:16**

Unconditional Love

THINK. The Fulani people of west and central Africa have two different words for "we." One is called the exclusive "we," and the other the inclusive "we." A football captain uses the exclusive version when speaking to the other captain after a coin toss: "We will receive the kick-off." A mother speaking to her children uses the inclusive version: "We are having meatloaf for dinner."

Within the Fulani church, believers are intentional about their use of the inclusive "we," claiming God's love not only for themselves but for all of God's people.

Here is the gospel in a nutshell: God loves us. All of us. The whole world. No exceptions. God doesn't just love the church, the insiders, the "good people," the saved. God's love is inclusive. It is for all of us.

This is good news.

PRAY. God, you love the world so much. Thanks for including me in that love, for including me in your "we." Expand my thinking to include others—all people, the whole world—in your gracious love. Amen.

LISTEN. **APRIL 4** **John 3:17**

Unconditional Love, Salvation

THINK. For many years, there was someone at NFL games holding up a sign that said "John 3:16." Usually it was a guy wearing a rainbow wig or some other outrageous outfit in order to draw attention to himself and, of course, his message. A professor of mine once said he felt this weird need to stand next to this guy holding up a sign that said "and 3:17!" just to show how much these two thoughts go together.

God loved the world enough to send Jesus. But this Jesus was not sent here to tell us how bad we are, to condemn us, to point the accusing finger at us. Jesus came to show us how much God loves us—loves us all. Jesus came here to help us, to make things right in this world that God created. Jesus came to save us.

PRAY. Jesus, show me again how much God loves us all. Tell me again and again that you have come not as a judge and jury, but as a brother and a friend. Help me to be that kind of friend to others, too. Amen.

LISTEN. APRIL 5 **John 3:19-21**

Darkness, Light

THINK. There are certain things that are better done during daylight hours. I became much more aware of this living closer to the equator, where the days don't get much longer during the summer, and where nights stay more or less the same in the winter. As soon as the light comes—as soon the day dawns—people tend to get up and get on with their day to get as much done as possible while it is light outside.

In Jesus, God's light has come into the world. That light scatters the darkness of sin and evil, but also guides the way for us to do the good we are called to do. We know that there will still be times of darkness in our lives, times of questions, of confusion, of uncertainty.

But when the light comes—as soon as Christ's new day dawns for us—we can get on with the good God is calling us to do.

PRAY. Christ Jesus, you are my light and my life. Scatter the darkness in my life, and help me to live in the sunshine of your love. Amen.

LISTEN. APRIL 6 **Ephesians 2:1-7**

New Life

THINK. For some reason, our culture has seen a craze of zombies in movies, television shows, comic books, and video games. Something about the walking dead appeals to a lot of people. Maybe that's how many of us feel from time to time, that we're stumbling around, not quite alive, but not fully dead. Going through life, but not quite living it.

Even if we find ourselves in a state of not quite living life, God still loves us. We could feel dead because of what we've done, or as a result of another's actions. God still loves us. Through Jesus, God brings us out of our zombie-like existence, whether "dead through trespasses" or simply undead in a haze of questions and confusion.

Whatever our condition, no matter how "dead" we are, Jesus raises us to new life. And not just to stumble through life, but to really, truly live it.

PRAY. God, you love me even when I don't know what I'm doing. Even when it seems like I'm walking around in a haze. Even when I feel dead. Thanks for making me alive, for giving me new life through Jesus. Amen.

LISTEN. **APRIL 7** **Ephesians 2:8-10**

Service, Grace

THINK. As much as I love to improvise with certain tools, at some point I have to give up and concede that they don't always work for things they weren't designed to do. I've determined that a potato peeler does a better job peeling potatoes than a kitchen knife does. A Phillips head screw really does need a Phillips screwdriver. Duct tape just dosn't repair evertyhing.

We were designed to do good works, created to perform acts of kindness in our neighborhoods and to do justice in our world. Yes, we are saved by God's grace through faith in Jesus Christ, so it's tempting to think that we don't have to do anything at all. But that's what we were designed to do. We're hardwired to do good things for others, not to be saved, but rather because we are saved. It's just the way God made us.

PRAY. God, you created me to want to do good things for others. Help me to be humble in my service, and to remember that it is your free gift of grace that allows me to do anything I do. Thank you for that gift. Amen.

GO.

Jesus loves you;
This you know,
For the Bible tells you so.
Little ones—like you—
To God belong.
You are weak;
But God's love is strong.

Changed

Cindy Gaskins

PAUSE.

Sometimes, depending on the situation, we resist change; other times, we can't wait for change to happen.

But our lives and the lives of others are always changing. How is God at work in and around you as one day gives way to another, and things do not stay the same?

LISTEN. **APRIL 8** **Psalm 146**

Hope, New Beginnings

THINK. It's a Declaration of Dependence! The psalmist is bold in proclaiming: Lifelong honor and praise to God! Hope and unfailing help in God! Champions remembered by God! This songwriter starts with praise and reminders of what works and doesn't work when it comes to trust. God is the way-maker for every person. To be sure we don't miss who can get help from God, the psalmist tells us it's not the strong who get God's attention and care—it's people who are oppressed, hungry, vulnerable, helpless, captive, and alone. We are in a place for God's grace to change us even though we may be weighed down, held captive, vulnerable, blind, hungry, weak, or alone. We can trust God, who is faithful.

God delights in us when we ask for help. We are blessed, strengthened, renewed, and changed by God's work in and for us. There is a long line through generations that can speak God's praise when hope from God was all they had. Through stories from slaves past and present, the Holocaust, school shootings, apartheid, war, famine, tsunamis, epidemics, earthquakes, and persecution, declarations of dependence have been made. Champions remember and give their praise. Make a declaration today!

PRAY. Maker of heaven and earth, thank you for the hope of change, new beginnings, and courage for when life is hard. Believing you will be my help, I ask you to be the way-maker for this day. With thanks, I pray in Jesus' name. Amen.

LISTEN. **APRIL 9** **Luke 7:11-17**

Changed, New Beginnings

THINK. A dictionary.com definition of change is "to make the form, nature, content, future course of something different from what it is or from what it would be if left alone."

The widow who was watching her son's body being carried had no hope that the lifeless form would change back to her breathing, laughing, living son. But what she didn't know was that the very nature of God had walked into the scene. Jesus' tender compassion and comfort called out, and a gift was given. Jesus didn't leave the mother's world of death and grief as it was. It was changed. The lifeless form was breathing, living, maybe even laughing within minutes. Everything had changed: a dead body being taken away became a life being given back to his mother; a sad crowd was filled with awe and praise for God. A change had taken place and recognition was made: "God has come to help us."

Where has God been a help to you recently? Where do you need God to come help you? Through Jesus, God came to change . . . everything! God doesn't want to leave alone what is broken, hurt, hungry, trapped, and forgotten.

PRAY. Dear God, you know what is dead in me. You know what needs to be awakened and resurrected. Thank you that you have come to help. May today be a day filled with awe and praise because you are near. Amen.

LISTEN. **APRIL 10** **Galatians 1:11-12**

Journey with God

THINK. "I want you to know." That's the way my daddy used to start and end his letters. He and mom were living a missional life in Southern Africa. My sisters were in boarding school 1,500 miles away, and I was in college in America. In that age of letter writing, dad would write "I just wanted you to know I was thinking about you this morning . . ." or "I want you to know . . ." There was a comfort and confidence passed on to me in consistent, personal words.

In today's passage, Paul was doing the same thing for Christ-followers in Galatia. He wanted them to know the truth about his words. He wanted them to know he hadn't created a system he wanted others to live by. The words he shared weren't his invention. The truth of Jesus Christ had changed him. And he wanted them to know that without a doubt.

Who is writing or speaking truth to you? Who creates comfort and confidence in the words they give you? God wants you to know the life that is given to you freely through Christ Jesus and empowered by the Spirit. God wants you to experience truth. God wants you to know.

PRAY. God, thank you for providing truth to me. Help me to not miss what you want me to know today. Amen.

LISTEN. APRIL 11 **Galatians 1:13-17**

Brokenness, Changed

THINK. I love home makeover TV shows. The "before" scenes capture the broken down, falling apart, and messed up houses that people are living in. For a variety of reasons, people have come into hard times, and they are chosen because someone thinks they deserve better. The "after" scenes are amazing, a work of tearing down the old and watching transformation take place. The change happens right before our eyes.

That is the power of the Good News. All of us are broken, falling apart, and messed up. For a variety of reasons we are where we are today. The life-changing words are "but when God." But when God is welcomed into our messes, when God breaks into the hurt, confusion, and disappointment of our lives, the old can become new. Change can take place.

Paul often told his before and after story of the change Jesus had begun and the way it continued to shape him.

Consider the broken places in your life that have been transformed. Remember the "but when God" moments when you knew divine change was happening. Give thanks that God is always able to renovate. Pray for a willing partnership in the renovation work!

PRAY. Dear God, thank you that I am your workmanship, created, redeemed, and gifted in Christ Jesus to do good works that you planned before time began. Renew and redo the places in me that need your restoration. I trust your continuing work in me. Amen.

LISTEN. APRIL 12 **Galatians 1:18-24**

Changed, New Life

THINK. A college friend and I reconnected after more than 25 years. He said to me, "I remember you being fatter in college!" Not that it matters, but I guess this friend has had a certain image of me for all these years because of that one sophomore year when I carried some extra weight around.

Don't we do that with others? A certain event, reaction, or circumstance shapes our thoughts about someone, and that is what we carry in our heads (and sometimes hearts). We don't give people the chance to grow up, or change, or head in a new direction.

The apostle Paul had plenty of scary stuff in his past that lots of people knew about. But in the early years of Paul's changed life, people began to see the difference that his nature, his form had taken on. He let his life speak. What he once tried to destroy, he now cherished. What he ripped apart through persecution now became his passion to build up and protect. And those who saw this change worshiped and praised God.

Has anyone noticed change in you? Has anyone worshiped God because of the change they see in you?

PRAY. You, O God, are never surprised by the paths I take. Thank you for the grace and mercy you give when I don't deserve it. Today may your conversation to me and through me bless and build someone up. May I worship you with a song in my head even if my lips don't get it out. Amen.

LISTEN. **APRIL 13** **Psalm 30:1-5**

New Life, Changed

THINK. Missionary friends wrote about a man described as a pit dweller. He stood for everything against the gospel of Jesus. There was no goodness, joy, or kindness for those around him. He made life hard for others. One day this man died, and cultural preparations were made for his funeral. The body was wrapped for burial and kept in a village house for the night. The next day, strange sounds began to be heard. Following the sounds, his wife went to the house and discovered the body that was pronounced dead was moving and making noise!

Removing the burial clothes, the man was able to tell how a man who said he was Jesus visited him and told him he had a second chance to choose to follow Jesus. With joy and surprise the man began to declare his love and thanksgiving for the second chance of life. He was changed for life!

Today, remember no matter what pit you may be in, no matter what sadness has draped itself over you, there is a God who loves you and can lift you up, dress you in dancing clothes, and remind you that you are precious.

PRAY. God of miracles, thank you for the pits that teach me there is no place where you are not there. Thank you for second chances. Continue to change my heart so that my life invites others to dance. With hope, I thank you. Amen.

LISTEN. APRIL 14 **Psalm 30:6-12**

Praise

THINK. My son plays basketball for a school where Caucasians are in the minority. He stands out, being the whitest and one of the tallest on the team, and so does his mom, who cheers loudly in the stands for him and the team. Most of the parents know to sit away from me if they want to be in a quieter part of the crowd. But a funny thing happened this season. I missed one game, and parents let me know they didn't like the silence of the stands! They gradually joined in the cheering, even standing for our team at every turn!

The psalmist knows he has to cheer before God. There is gratitude and joy because God changed his life. The psalmist calls on the saints to join in the celebration. It is not just one voice that cheers; it is the crowd cheering together.

To be changed is to be different from what you were or from what you would have been if left alone. Our God changes us, and others get to see that mysterious, transforming work. What fun when they embrace God's offer of change and choose to dance in celebration with us!

PRAY. Dear God, how is it that you want us to be like you? Today I want my voice to be one among many who cheer, celebrate, and dance for your honor. May your kingdon on earth be a happier place because I have worshiped you. Amen.

GO.

I appeal to you therefore, brothers and sisters, by the mercies of God, to present your bodies as a living sacrifice, holy and acceptable to God, which is your spiritual worship. Do not be conformed to this world, but be transformed by the renewing of your minds, so that you may discern what is the will of God—what is good and acceptable and perfect.

Romans 12:1-2

True Love

Julie Ball

PAUSE.

What good is love, really, unless it is true? Actually, love requires trust, and none is more trustworthy than our Creator.

Trust God now to show you trustworthy love, and to grow it more deeply within you.

LISTEN. APRIL 15 **1 John 4:7-8**

Loving Others

THINK. When I first created my social media page, easily filling in my name, email address, and hometown, I was suddenly stopped short by the blank labeled "Religious Views." How could I sum up my religious views in that little space? After a few moments' reflection, I typed, "God is Love. The rest follows from there."

I think the apostle John would say something similar if he were around today. Legend has it that the aging apostle was asked at every worship gathering to offer a word to the congregation. No doubt those around him wanted to hear exciting stories from his days with Jesus, but each time John simply said, "Love one another." The people, confused and frustrated, finally asked him why that was all he ever said. John answered, "It is the Lord's command, and if this alone be done, it is enough."

PRAY. O God of love, thank you for being exactly who you are. Your love, which creates, sustains, and saves the entire world, is more than enough for me. Amen.

LISTEN. APRIL 16 **1 John 4:9-12**

Love

THINK. It's hard to show love from a distance, isn't it? Phone calls, texts, emails, and cards are all well and good, but they just can't compete with a genuine hug.

God had shown love to the world from the beginning, through nature, covenants, leaders, prophets, miracles, and the Hebrew Scriptures. Those were just not the same, though, as reaching out and physically touching the people God created and loved.

So God sent Jesus into the world in order to give love in the most direct and personal way. Jesus then sent his followers out to continue the work. Because God lives in us, we are the presence of God on earth. When we love one another, God's love reaches through our hands and arms to hug the world.

PRAY. Loving God, thank you for all the ways you show love. Thank you for showing love to me and through me. Open my eyes every day to the people to whom I can give your loving touch. Amen.

LISTEN. APRIL 17 **1 John 4:13-16a**

Holy Spirit, Love

THINK. In Acts 8:26-40, Philip met a man from Ethiopia who was reading the book of Isaiah. Philip asked him, "Do you understand what you are reading?" And the man replied, "How can I, unless someone guides me?" So Philip sat down and taught him the words' full meaning.

The Holy Spirit is our guide, much like Philip guided the Ethiopian. With the Holy Spirit in us, we experience the love that God showed the world in the person of Jesus. With the Holy Spirit shining forth from us, we are the evidence that the very same love is still alive today.

In the story from Acts, it was the Spirit who guided Philip to the Ethiopian in the first place. The Holy Spirit may also guide us to unexpected people and places. Wherever we may find ourselves, we can be sure it will be for the purpose of sharing God's love.

PRAY. Holy Spirit, be my guide today. Teach me the full meaning of God's love. Show me what to do and tell me what to say in the place where I am. Amen.

LISTEN. APRIL 18 **1 John 4:16b-18**
Love, Loving Others

THINK. Think about the rules your parents gave you when you were little. They probably told you things like "stay in the yard" and "don't hit your sister." You probably obeyed those rules most of the time. But did you obey them because you really understood that they were for the best, or did you obey because you were afraid of getting in trouble?

The words "perfected," "perfect," and "perfection" in today's Scripture passage are all from the same Greek root word and could also be translated matured, mature, and maturity. Mature might be easier to understand than perfect. Mature people do what is right because it is right, not because they are afraid of getting caught and being punished for doing something wrong.

God's love matures us. It makes us grow up. When God's love makes its home in us, we love others because that's what is best, not because we're afraid God will punish us if we don't love.

PRAY. Dear God, thank you for your maturing love, which is constantly at work in me. Make me a more loving person each day, and remove any fear that tries to get in the way. Amen.

LISTEN. APRIL 19 **1 John 4:19-21**

Love

THINK. Throughout history, people have done drastic things to try to please the God or gods they believed in. They have sacrificed animals and even people. They have waged crusades. They have hunted witches. They have burned heretics.

Those events probably sound archaic and foreign to us, but how about these? We end friendships. We divide families. We point fingers. We close doors. We call names, all in the name of the God we are trying to serve.

Jesus never instructed or gave us the authority to judge and condemn. Rather, "the commandment we have from him is this: those who love God must love their brothers and sisters also."

Maybe it's human nature to want to do drastic things to please God. There is nothing more drastic than loving everyone, regardless of whether we agree with them, understand them, or even know them. That's a huge thing to do, so huge it requires a God-sized love. The good news is that's exactly what God gives us.

PRAY. Amazing God, I want so desperately to please you. Help me remember that you haven't asked me to win battles or even arguments for you. Thank you for giving me only the task of love, and for equipping me to do it. Amen.

LISTEN. **APRIL 20** **John 15:1-6**

Balance

THINK. These words Jesus spoke used to frighten me a bit. Did you notice that every branch is subjected to the pruning shears, even the good ones? Yikes! I didn't like the sound of that.

What relieved my fear was the realization that pruning is a natural part of everyday life. We trim our hair and nails so they don't become nuisances. Our skin is constantly shedding dead cells to make room for new ones. When we get too busy, we cut back our schedules. When our rooms become too cluttered, we get rid of the stuff we don't use anymore.

An apple tree with lots of skinny branches will produce fewer apples than one with a few large, sturdy branches. Our lives are like that, too. Jesus wants to trim away the things that crowd our lives, so that we have more room to grow and bloom in him. We need not be afraid. Instead, we can be thankful.

PRAY. Dear Jesus, my life gets so busy and crowded sometimes. Help me let go of excess stress, worry, want, and activity so that I can be free to stretch my arms out to you. Thank you! Amen.

LISTEN. APRIL 21 **John 15:7-8**

Unconditional Love, Journey with God

THINK. My all-time favorite movie is *The Princess Bride*. From the very beginning, Westley shows his love for Buttercup by responding to her every request with "As you wish." The boy to whom this story is being told whines and asks his grandfather to skip over the mushy parts. But at the end, when the boy asks to hear the story again tomorrow, his grandfather answers, "As you wish."

Just as Westley feels for Buttercup, and as the grandfather feels for his grandson, God loves us and delights in doing good things for us. Like the boy, as we grow and mature in God's love, we learn to ask for more mature things. I have prayed for a lot of childish things that I've never received. But when I ask God to stay close by me, to help me love others, and to prepare a path for me, I feel sure I can hear God say, "As you wish."

PRAY. O God, thank you for your generous love. Help me to grow and mature in your love each day. Enable me to say to the people crying out for love all around me, "As you wish." Amen.

GO.

Hear the voice of God so tender, gathering us in righteousness.
Giving, as our sure defender, Steadfast love and faithfulness.
Bless God's holy name together, as the Spirit brings new life.
Giving, as our sure defender, Steadfast love and faithfulness.

Lavon Bayler[6]

God and Suffering

Daniel Ingram

PAUSE.

Someone once wrote, "There is nothing so tragic as wasted suffering." In every struggle, in every difficult passage of life, we are given the opportunity for personal growth. Is such a gift offered to you today?

LISTEN. APRIL 22 **Job 38:1-7**

Patience, Questions

THINK. We live in an age of accessibility. Everything is within reach. If you don't know it, you can look it up on the web. If it's on a map, you can get there. If you want it, you can buy it. If you can't afford it, someone will lend you the money. If you are in a hurry, you can drive-through. If you missed it, you can watch it on your DVR.

I must admit, this convenience has made me really impatient. It frustrates me when I pick up the phone and can't reach someone on the other end, or when I have to wait an entire day for a response to an email. Where did I get this sense of entitlement that I should be able to have, achieve, and know everything that I want when I want it?

God reminded Job there are things in this world far beyond Job's understanding and ability. It's interesting that God responded to Job "out of the whirlwind." Out of what whirlwinds do you need to see God?

PRAY. God, I don't understand why the world is the way it is, and it scares me when I don't understand how you are the way you are. Comfort me when I am impatient. Amen.

LISTEN. **APRIL 23** **Job 38:34-41**

Doubts, Journey with God

THINK. Several years ago, there was a sausage commercial where a dad dressed as the sun was making breakfast for himself and his daughter. He explained to the young girl that he often didn't have time for breakfast.

She asks, "But why?"

He responds, "I have to be at work early . . . to light and heat the earth."

God invited Job to step for a moment into God's shoes. The Lord offered a glimpse at the complexity and balance of design in creation. To fully comprehend a piece of it is to take on all of it. It is important to note that God did not portray creation as a set of dominoes carefully set up to fall in a certain order. Rather, God communicated God's relationship to creation as provider and friend.

We are all scientists, in the purest sense of the word. We are always searching, and we make decisions based on observations and experiences, either our own or those that are handed on to us. This search, too, is a gift from God, and though we will never comprehend it all, we may find holiness along the way.

PRAY. Loving Creator, forgive me when I doubt you. I don't often understand why things happen as they do, but I'm thankful that you are with me on the journey. Amen.

LISTEN. APRIL 24 **Psalm 104:1-9, 24**

Creator

THINK. In southwest Virginia, there is a trail in the midst of the Appalachians called Dragon's Tooth. It's a fairly rugged hike, requiring nimble hands and feet to ascend. But the hard work is most definitely rewarded at the summit.

At the top of the mountain is a 30-foot rock structure, which again requires quite a bit of effort to climb. From the top of Dragon's Tooth, though, you can see for miles in any direction, and with little indication of civilization. And in the fall, when the leaves are every color under the sun, there are few places that I would rather be on any given day.

Sometimes I need creation calibration, something that reminds me of just how large, complex, and beautiful God's creation is. My worldview is so quickly altered by watching the evening news that I need to be reminded of God's loving, artistic, and creative energy.

PRAY. God of all creation, thank you for so generously and carefully sculpting the natural world. Help me care for it the way you need. Help me today to see the world in all its glory—again. Amen.

LISTEN. APRIL 25 **Isaiah 53:4-9**

Suffering, Hurting

THINK. Between television, movies, and the Internet, we are not in short supply of images of suffering. We rarely need to walk far from our doorsteps to be among those who are in anguish. Maybe we don't even need to leave our homes to be near suffering. Suffering takes on many forms, and it is difficult to gauge its severity; few can say, "My pain is worse than yours."

Isaiah offered a unique image of suffering, a servant who has taken on the pain of us all. And how should this image make us feel? Maybe we should feel ashamed that our sin, either individually or collectively, is so immense. Perhaps we should feel pity for the one who has been given this great burden. Should we be disturbed or even angry that God has laid this on one person, and not just let us cope with our own share?

Perhaps it's some combination of the three. And then, when you are ready, there is even room to move toward thanksgiving.

PRAY. I confess, Lord, that I don't know what to make of the great suffering in the world. Forgive me for my part in it. Thank you for loving me through it. Amen.

LISTEN. **APRIL 26** **Psalm 91:9-16**

Questions, Doubts, Hope

THINK. We yearn for security, to know that we are going to be OK. When we are young, we want to fit in, to have friends that will support and affirm us. Being singled out is a dangerous thing; blending in is our best defense.

As we get older, we look for new securities, primarily money. Money can secure a livable future and sustain a family. Money buys safer cars, protected houses, and superior healthcare.

Who wouldn't want security? And this is the temptation of our religious beliefs, that we will be guaranteed some amount of personal safety because of what we do, say, and believe. In fact, even Jesus was tempted by this very passage while fasting in the wilderness.

The truth is there is a lot more insecurity than safety in this world. We may be able to mask it, but the veil is thin, and there are many lovers of God who are in great suffering.

I wish I could offer you a clear explanation for why God allows this to happen, but I don't know. There is, however, goodness in this world that cannot be explained apart from we what we experience as God's love.

PRAY. God of love, give me words of hope for a world of insecurity. Amen.

LISTEN. APRIL 27 **Hebrews 5:1-10**
Example of Christ

THINK. What words would you use to describe Jesus? I can list some: friend, savior, Messiah, love, companion, teacher . . . and the list goes on. You can probably exhaust your vocabulary on this exercise.

The author of Hebrews uses a word we don't often associate with Jesus—priest. Really? Priest? The same Jesus that toppled tables at the temple and confronted religious leaders everywhere he went? Jesus was called many things, but I don't think anyone, either for Jesus or against him would have called him priest.

But maybe it's not so far off base. In Jesus we get the clearest image of who God is. It is through Jesus that we experience best God's love and God's power. We experience God in a very real and vibrant way. If we take seriously the way that Jesus lived out his relationship with God and with his neighbors, then we will experience most clearly God's will for the world.

PRAY. God of many names, thank you for sending your son Jesus and sharing even more of your love with us. Let me be a part of your healing, redeeming work in this world that you made most evident through Jesus. Amen.

LISTEN. APRIL 28 **Mark 10:35-45**

Service, Example of Christ

THINK. You probably know some people like James and John. They may be called teacher's pets or corporate go-getters. These two, nicknamed Sons of Thunder, craved power. They'd seen Jesus exercise power like they had never seen it before, and they wanted to be a part of it. And this is understandable. Following a powerful leader can be thrilling!

Jesus cleverly played along, promising that they would share in his ministry; they would share in his baptism and in the cup. Then, Jesus redefined the idea of power.

We are given power, for sure, power enough to lay down our lives and to concede, power enough to come in last and to be a servant to all. It's a countercultural understanding of power. With this power we find worth in our relationships—with God, with each other, and with the work that we are called to do.

PRAY. God, it is scary to think about what it means to become a "slave of all." As I study your gospel, show me through Jesus how I can better serve you by serving others. Amen.

GO.

We do not have a high priest who is unable to sympathize with our weaknesses. We have one who in every respect has been tested as we are, yet without sin. Let us therefore approach the throne of grace with boldness, so that we may receive mercy and find grace to help in time of need. Hebrews 4:15

Witness to God's Justice

Michael Sciretti

PAUSE.

To see God at work in the world, we often have to be very intentional about watching for the evidence of the Lord's hand. Upon seeing that work, we are moved to act in partnership with God in what we see being done. Watch for the hand of God to be revealed today in the written word of God. Then feel deeply to discover how you might respond.

LISTEN. APRIL 29 **Jeremiah 23:23-29**

Transformation, New Life

THINK. Listen to your heart. This message comes to us in many ways, especially in songs, TV shows, and movies. But from a Christian perspective, we must be careful when it comes to the heart. Jesus told us that the "pure in heart" are blessed. And in today's passage we are told about prophets who preach "the deceit of their own heart." Since our hearts can become impure and deceived, what are we to do?

Listen to the Word. That's what the prophets were not doing. They were only listening to their own desires. They ignored the Spirit of truth, which uncritically holds a mirror to us and shows us what we're like right now, warts and all! The people of Israel needed to change their ways, but they only listened to the voices telling them, "You're OK. No need to change!" That message doesn't give life; it only makes a person lazy and stops growth. God tells us to be transformed by the renewing of our hearts and minds. And as we submit to this purifying process, we become God's faithful prophets, able to hear, speak, and do God's justice and love.

PRAY. Create in me a clean heart, O God, and put a new and right spirit within me. Do not cast me away from your presence, and do not take your holy spirit from me. Restore to me the joy of your salvation, and sustain in me a willing spirit.

Psalm 51:10-12

LISTEN. APRIL 30 **Luke 12:49-53**

Putting God First

THINK. Prince of Peace. Isn't that what some call Jesus? So what does it mean that Jesus did not come to bring peace to the earth? This might really challenge your image of Jesus! How do you picture him? Is he kind or confrontational, ? Can you imagine Jesus as the one who brings division?

Division. What was Jesus saying we must separate from—parents, friends? On the surface it might seem like it, but I don't think it's what he really intended. Jesus said to seek first God's kingdom. Stronger loyalty to family, country, or even religion is not permitted, at least not if you want to be free.

Freedom. Jesus is calling you to separate from what is not as important so that you can experience inner freedom. Let go of your obsession to make a certain person like you. Stop anxiously trying to earn a particular person's respect. Let go of your "need" to have new clothes or to check your cell phone all the time. This is the kind of division Jesus calls us to. It's the beginning of justice, the end of which is real love.

PRAY. Close your eyes and place your hands palms down on your knees. This symbolizes your desire to let go of the things of your day that might prevent you from seeking God's kingdom first. Tell God what you need to let go of.

Now turn your hands over with your palms up. This symbolizes your openness to receive God's peace and strength for the day. Sit for a few moments in God's presence.

MAY

LISTEN. **MAY 1** **Luke 12:54-56**

Kingdom of God

THINK. Hypocrite. Ouch! That one had to hurt. Jesus, seemingly out of nowhere, started calling the people hypocrites. That word was a favorite of his, a name he mostly used on Pharisees. But Jesus wasn't simply calling people names. Hypocrisy is a serious offense, but not just to God. It might be a greater offense to the one committing it; it is a sin against yourself!

To be a hypocrite is to be an actor, someone who chooses not to be one's self. When you're being a hypocrite, you're not being real, which means you're not really living. Wake up to life.

Jesus was not afraid to tell it like it is. Sometimes we need someone to confront us with the truth about ourselves. We need the shock in order to wake up to what is real. For the people in today's text, their hypocrisy prevented them from experiencing God's kingdom. The kingdom was present in Jesus. They knew how to see the change in the weather, but they couldn't tell the change in the season, the God-season they could experience in and through Jesus. What prevents you from experiencing God's kingdom right now?

PRAY. Ever-present God, wake me up today . . . to the miracle of my body . . . to the good in others . . . to the needs of my friends . . . to your Spirit within me. Amen.

LISTEN. MAY 2 **Hebrews 11:29-31**

Faith, Courage

THINK. Faith. This is a little word used a lot in the Bible, and especially in this passage. But what does it mean? For example, is faith simply believing that Jesus died and was resurrected? I don't think so. Faith does not equal belief. You can believe Jesus died and rose from the dead but not trust him enough to let him transform you. So faith is not mere belief; it demands action and courage.

Courage. It took courage to leave Egypt and go to the Promised Land. It took courage to trust God to work a miracle. It took courage for an outsider, a prostitute, to peacefully welcome enemies into her home. There is no faith without courage. But this courage isn't something that comes from you. It comes to you as you open yourself to God.

Reflect on one of these questions today: What's your personal Egypt, the negative thing, person, or event you can't let go of? Are you trying too hard to make something happen your way? What is one way you could welcome and love your enemy?

PRAY. Today, Lord, with your help, I will let nothing disturb me, I will let nothing frighten me. All things pass away, But you never change. Through patient endurance All things are

LISTEN. MAY 3 **Hebrews 11:32-38**

Journey with God, Faith

THINK. Promises. There are many of them in the Bible. Genesis says God promised never to flood the earth again. Exodus tells of God's promises to Israel to guide and protect them. The prophets (such as Isaiah and Amos) recount God's promises to hold God's people accountable for their wrongdoings. And all throughout the psalms people are remembering God's promises. They even try to remind God of the promises!

Even though there are many promises in the Bible, it means nothing to you until you personally experience them. Knowing in your mind that God loves you and will guide you is good. But you don't really understand these truths until you open your heart, receive them, and live your daily life in light of them.

Receive. This is the first step. Take the promises for yourself. This is what your ancestors in the faith did. Through faith they took the promises for themselves. This means you have to work at it; you have to make some effort. Start small. For example, today live in light of Jesus' promise, "And remember, I am with you always" (Matt. 28:20). Today, try to remember that the spirit of Jesus is with you.

PRAY. Faithful God, I am now open and receptive to your living Spirit—within me and around me. How blessed I am to simply remember you. Amen.

LISTEN. **MAY 4** **Hebrews 11:39-12:2**

Child of God, Hope

THINK. Life. It can be so confusing and messy. We never know what life will bring us—a new friendship, a death in the family, or a change in scenery. Yet, no matter what happens, life is what you make it. The writer of Hebrews tells us to see life as a race; the goal is to be like Jesus. So life is a means of becoming who God wants you to be. But it takes effort. It's a race, not a stroll in the park!

Get ready. As a Christian, let go of the things that hinder you from becoming like Jesus. If you were in an athletic contest, you would dress appropriately. It's the same here. Take off "clothes" that hold you back. Let go of negative thoughts and emotions that trip you up and cause you to lose your focus on Jesus. Today, try to pay attention to a negative emotion, such as jealousy. When you catch yourself feeling this way, let go. Picture yourself taking it off of you like a jacket. And remember your goal—to become like Jesus.

PRAY. Savior, teacher, Lord, and friend, give me courage to see myself for who I am. Give me faith to trust your Spirit within me. Give me hope to see myself as I can be. Give me love, and I'll have everything I need. Amen.

LISTEN. MAY 5 **Psalm 80:1-2, 8-19**

Transformation, Faith

THINK. A parable: There was a young man trapped on the ledge of a cliff. He couldn't go back the way he came. He was scared and anxious. There was nothing with him that could help him survive, no food or water. He felt helpless. All he could do was scream for help. Then he saw it. A rope was seemingly connected to the sky right above him, its end dangling just a foot from his reach. The only way to grab hold of it was to jump straight up. It looked safe enough, but he couldn't see where it led. What was it attached to? It disappeared into the clouds. He had to make a decision. He jumped.

A reflection: Usually, in order to receive God's help, we need to change our thinking. All too often we only see and dwell on our problems and obstacles. The solution is to start thinking from a higher plane. Instead of asking God to save you from a particular circumstance, ask God to transform you through the circumstance. God always answers this prayer. The way of transformation is always there if we will only take the jump.

PRAY. Be pleased, O God, to deliver me. O Lord, make haste to help me!

Psalm 70:1

GO.

Rejoice in the Lord, O you righteous. . . . For the word of the Lord is upright, and all his work is done in faithfulness. He loves righteousness and justice; the earth is full of the steadfast love of the Lord. Psalm 33:1a, 4-5

The Creative Spirit

Brian Foreman

PAUSE.

What does it take to bring something into being, something that simply did not exist before? Can you imagine a time "before time?"

The God we worship is not concerned about such constraints; God works totally outside our perceptions of time and space.

This is the God who awaits you now in quietness. Seek the freedom to be in touch with your Creator.

LISTEN. **MAY 6** **Genesis 1:1-2**

Creative, Image of God

THINK. Do you remember when you could be given a container or two of modeling clay and be entertained? Do you remember the way it felt when you squeezed it between your fingers or rolled it out like a snake? As we got older, our fascinations with toy clay might have transferred over to sand at the beach. I once watched a boy and his mother let wet sand run out of their fingers to create beautiful, unique towers of sand. Perhaps you have done similar things.

When God created the heavens and the earth, all was formless. God essentially had a giant lump of clay and from it, creation happened. God is the original creative spirit. You are made in the image of God. Your creative spirit comes from God. For some, this spirit is utilized to make clay into beautiful pottery, or plain words into amazing poetry. For others, the creative spirit finds expression in the way problems are solved. In it all, God made you to be creative. How are you expressing this gift?

PRAY. Creator God, I praise you for the gift of creativity and how it allows me to connect to you. Continue to shape me into exactly what you want me to be, and remind me that I am beautiful in your sight. Amen.

LISTEN. MAY 7 **Genesis 1:3-5**

Darkness, Light, Actions

THINK. Imagine that first moment light came to be. All I can equate it to is going to the restroom in the middle of the night and clicking the light on, only to be blinded momentarily.

God did this from nothingness. God spoke light into being from the darkness. Does light still require creativity? Sure, Thomas Alva Edison had to be creative to create the light bulb, but let's think for a minute about creating light from darkness. Light and darkness take many forms, especially using them to describe situations. Human trafficking is darkness. Disease due to unclean drinking water is darkness. War orphans live in darkness.

Creativity is a light in several ways. God gives you passion, gifts, and talents to share light in the world. One way to use creativity is to shed light in places where darkness reigns. Another is to be creative in finding solutions. Creativity gives you unlimited ways to be Christ's presence in the world.

PRAY. God of Light, thank you for creating me to think, act, and create. My prayer is that you continue to direct me in ways that use my gifts and passions to share your light with the world. Amen.

LISTEN. MAY 8 **Mark 1:4-5**

Call of God

THINK. Have you ever known someone to whom you were just immediately drawn? It's hard to explain why they interested you; they simply did. I can't explain why people were going out to the Jordan River to hear the man whose message called them to confess their sins; they were just drawn to him.

Notice that John is described as appearing in the wilderness, and that people from the whole countryside were going to him. I don't know about you, but I knew the pastor that baptized me for some time, and I was still skittish about him holding me under water.

Yet there is something about John and his message. I think he must have been a creative spirit. People were drawn to him, including Jesus, to be baptized; but John also knew that one greater than him was coming (John 1:22-23). He thought in ways that were not necessarily those of the religious authorities. John was open to the call of God on his life.

PRAY. God, while I may struggle in my search for what you want for my life, I pray that I am always open to the creative leading of your spirit, so that I may join you in whatever wilderness into which I am called. Amen.

LISTEN. MAY 9 **Mark 1:6-8**

Courage

THINK. Fashionista is probably not a word used to describe John, although today fur is a popular trim on many coats. While John could have been a fashion trendsetter, his dietary habits have not taken hold. John was peculiar enough in his dress that Mark noted it in his Gospel.

Often it takes someone willing to stand out from the crowd to be noticed and heard. John shared a vision that was far different than that of many prophets of his time, or those claiming to be so today. John claimed that someone much greater was coming. John was open to a new way of thinking and a new way of doing.

John talked about one who would baptize with Spirit, not just water. In our culture, much is made of those who are rational, with well-thought concepts and well-drawn schematics. God can use those types, but in the case of announcing Jesus to the world, God used someone who our culture might very well cast aside.

PRAY. God of the unique, when I judge, forgive me. When I rationalize myself away from serving you, have mercy on me. When I find the courage to take a bold creative stand, thank you for your faithfulness to me. Amen.

LISTEN. MAY 10 **Mark 1:9-11**

Peace, Sharing Christ

THINK. Some things are far more peaceful than others: a football player versus a figure skater, a firecracker versus a waving flag, a thunderstorm versus a crackling fire, a falcon versus a dove. The Spirit of God descended upon Jesus like a dove. When you close your eyes and picture that scene, what does it look like to you?

He would die a violent death for preaching good news, but Jesus' ministry was begun by God with a peaceful gesture of the Spirit. God then spoke to Jesus, expressing God's pleasure. In Genesis, God was also pleased with creation.

In Jesus, God was creating a new covenant with humanity, a new way that we would relate to and know God. The peace of God is offered to you in the midst of the busyness of a new year. Much as Jesus must have been affirmed and assured at the moment of the descending dove, so you too can know that God is pleased with you when you are sharing God's love with others.

PRAY. God of peace, please help me to experience the peace that only you can give when I am searching for wisdom and direction. Please help those who are tormented and without peace to find it deep within the comfort of your Spirit. Amen.

LISTEN. **MAY 11** **Acts 19:1-7**

Call of God, Sharing Christ

THINK. To fully understand what it means to be a Green Bay Packers fan, you must live in Green Bay and attend football games in subfreezing weather while wearing a plastic foam cheese wedge on your head. This is the way to be baptized into Packer fanhood.

Being baptized into a sports culture is quite different than the baptism of the Spirit to which our text today is referring, but there is a similarity. Whereas John baptized based on knowledge of one who was coming, Paul baptized into the spirit of the one who had come. Once they went from knowledge of Jesus to being in baptized in his name, they received the Spirit of God.

From this baptism, new disciples began to share the good news of Christ. Once again, God creatively sent out another twelve to share the gospel in ways they were previously unable to do. God is constantly calling new people to share that gospel with the world in new ways. How will God use you?

PRAY. Spirit God, I pray that I know you intimately rather than in "fair weather" ways. I pray that others will see you in me, and in doing so they see the difference between one who knows of you and one who knows you. Amen.

LISTEN. MAY 12 **Psalm 29:1-4, 10-11**

Praise, Creator God

THINK. Expressions of the creative spirit come through song, through fine art, through poetry and drama. We find expressions of God's creative spirit in sunsets, mountain ranges, rushing rivers, and the pattern on the back of a turtle's shell.

Take a moment to experience and appreciate the creative spirit of God, who weaves together colors, sounds, tastes, and smells with laughter, voices, prototypes, and music. While God created from the void, we create from what God has made and what God has given us the ability to imagine.

The psalmist expressed appreciation through the praise of God. The psalmist credited God with strength, glory, and graciousness. All things are given by God to the people of God. Read the words of the psalm aloud and imagine the sounds and sights used to describe the power, majesty, and awe known to be God. Ultimately, David's prayer of blessing is that God give God's people strength and peace for the journey that is life.

PRAY. God of glory, I pray for the peace that you give. I pray for the strength that is yours and worship you in the splendor of the created order around me. For in you all things were, are, and ever will be. Amen.

GO.

Creator God we sing, a hymn of joy we're making;
Our grateful love we bring, as the new day's light is breaking.
God made the sea and land; the sun and stars came rolling
From God's own loving hand, their Creator's love extolling.
Alleluia, alleluia!

Creator God we sing: Alleluia!
From "Cantemos al Creador" by Carlos Rosas[7]

Loss & Redemption

Kerri Peterson-Davis

PAUSE.

You win some, you lose some. To be sure, we all know what it means to have good days and bad days. Sometimes it all seems out of our hands. We do have responsibility to live as best we can, and then we can leave the rest to God. God's purpose over all is to redeem our days, both good and bad. Prepare yourself now to receive that redemptive work of our Maker.

LISTEN. MAY 13 **Psalm 65:1-8**

Forgiveness, New Beginnings

THINK. Have you ever just completely messed up? Maybe it was texting a friend and having them share it with the person who had made you mad in the first place. Maybe you were complaining about your parents and found out that they heard every word you said. Or maybe it was something worse. It's called "losing face." It feels awful. You wish you could take everything back and start over, but you can't.

The psalmist can relate: "When deeds of iniquity overwhelm us . . ." In other words, when we've done so many things wrong we can't see a way out, it is as if we are drowning and there is no one there to hear our cries for help.

But there is. The psalmist reminds us that our transgressions, our sins, are forgiven. Filled with images of hope, we are reminded that God will silence the roar of the ocean and calm the noise that we've created through our actions. God does hear our cries for help! God is stronger than any mess we create and the promise of hope is true—no matter what.

PRAY. Thank you, God, for giving me a fresh start and a new beginning today. Instead of being overwhelmed by my sins, I am overwhelmed by your graciousness. It is hard for me to believe that you will redeem me and make me whole. Give me the courage to believe in your love for me. Amen.

LISTEN. **MAY 14** **Joel 2:23-29**

Joy, Example of Christ

THINK. When was the last time you played in the rain? I spent one summer in a beautiful mountain setting where most afternoons a storm would descend upon us without warning. One day I was walking with my daughter and her friends when the downpour began. There we were—no jackets, no umbrellas. I was so frustrated. My daughter and her friends were thrilled; they found every puddle to splash in while laughing, singing, and squealing with joy. All the while I was trying to push them along so we could get to lunch without getting too wet. What was I thinking? I finally gave up, and what fun I had!

We need the vision and perspective of others to remind us that life doesn't have to be so serious. The prophet Joel reminds us that it is our sons and daughters who will see life in a new way. We can't help but be overwhelmed by all that is going on in the world, but we have been given the promise of God's presence in the midst of it. Thanks be to God for sons and daughters who aren't afraid to live life to the fullest!

PRAY. God of new eyes, give us courage to live a life filled with joy and laughter! Open us to your Spirit that pours out on us like rain, soaking us through and through. Allow us to be agents of hope in your world, offering a glimpse of your reign to others. Amen.

LISTEN. MAY 15 **Joel 2:30-32**

Darkness, Child of God

THINK. It was a deep, dark pit, and she could not get out. She could tell that the world was going on around her, but all she could see was the darkness closing in. She could smell the dank wetness surrounding her. Her voice was a faint whisper, not strong enough to cry out. She was stuck, and it felt as if life would not, or could not, go on. Hope no longer existed in her world.

Depression is a horrible feeling. It consumes not just your mind and spirit, but your body, too. Feeling hopeless is awful, and it is hard not to feel as if you are the only one who has ever felt so bad. This short passage from the prophet Joel reminds us that feelings like these are not unique to us, nor are we the only ones who have ever been without hope. Even in the midst of such pain, the promises of God are true. God does hold us near even when we don't feel God's presence. If you don't have a voice to cry out, then find a friend you trust to cry out for you. You are not alone. You are God's child.

PRAY. Hold me up, O God. Give me strength to cry out to you. Be there for me when life is too hard. Surround me with people who will cry out for me. Give me a glimmer of hope so that I can make it through any difficult day. Amen.

LISTEN. **MAY 16** **Luke 18:9-14**

Child of God, Loving Self

THINK. The Who sings a song called "Who are you?" (You may have heard this while watching the TV show *CSI*). It reminds us that the world does indeed want to know who we are. We are expected to sell ourselves pretty much everywhere: introducing ourselves to our friends, filling out college applications, describing ourselves on social media, the list is never-ending.

Jesus told a story about a Pharisee who sold himself, even to God. With great detail, this religious leader told God just how good he was. Don't you think God already knew all that the Pharisee had done? Was it really worth the breath it took to speak those words? Apparently not. Jesus reminds us in this story that humility, being true to ourselves and not hiding our mistakes, is enough. We don't have to sell ourselves to God. God already knows who we are and loves us anyway. What an amazing gift!

PRAY. Thank you for not expecting me to sell myself to you, gracious God. It is humbling to know that I can come to you as I am without fear, and that you will respond with love and grace. Give me the courage today to just be myself. Amen.

LISTEN. MAY 17 **Ephesians 1:17-23**

Presence of God, Relationship with God

THINK. Where did you see God at work today? It is a great question, but it isn't necessarily easy to answer. How about asking it this way: What was a struggle for you today? Or, what gave you great joy today? The technical word for these sorts of questions is examen. In other words, you examine your life and pay attention to the Holy Spirit.

Knowing God takes work, just like getting to know a new friend requires time and energy. Relationships don't just happen. You have to invest lots of time and hard work. Just as Paul prayed for his friends in the town of Ephesus, there are many praying that you, too, may come to know Christ more fully and experience the power of God's Spirit. But you have to put some energy into this relationship.

The more we ponder where we see God at work, the more likely we are to have the eyes of our hearts enlightened, opened up to the amazing work of God in our lives and the lives of those around us. Are you up to the challenge?

PRAY. Keep open my eyes, O God. Keep open my ears, O God. Keep open my heart, O God. Amen.

LISTEN. MAY 18 **2 Timothy 4:6-8**

Love, Faithfulness

THINK. One step after another . . . that is all it takes to finish the race. At least that's what I tell myself when I'm running a half marathon. It's a mind game, really. I am still running 13.1 miles, but if I think of it in one step increments, it seems easier.

Keeping faith is a tough job. There are pressures and demands that make living as Christ intends for us just plain hard. Paul knew that; he had faced more challenges than most of us can even imagine. But today's text is cause for celebration. Paul had made it to the finish line, and the party was ready!

How about you? Can you sit back for a moment and give thanks that you have made it? Can you rest in the truth that the promises of God are true for you, too? Take a deep breath and drink in God's Spirit.

PRAY. Your faithfulness and grace give me courage to keep moving toward you, loving Creator. I need your encouragement to keep the faith. Fill me up with your overflowing love so that my spirit will not run dry. Amen.

LISTEN. MAY 19 **2 Timothy 4:16-18**

Faith, Journey with God

THINK. All alone. It doesn't matter how many people might be around you, there are times we feel all alone. I still remember the day I returned to school after getting in a huge fight with my friends. My stomach was in knots as I walked to my first class, and peering out from underneath my bangs, I would look up just long enough to make sure I didn't run into anyone or anything. I was sure that everyone knew what had happened, and that I was the talk of the school. It was an awful day that I can easily recall many years later. Like the writer of this passage, I felt deserted.

Somehow I made it past that day.

There will be days when all we have are the promises of God to stand upon and to give us strength. It takes trust to live on promises, and that is no easy task. But then, no one said the life of faith was easy!

PRAY. Hold me up, God, when there is nowhere else to turn. Give me your strength to face those days when no one will stand with me. Redeem the painful parts of my life, and give me new life. Amen.

GO.

O give thanks to the LORD, for he is good; for his steadfast love endures forever. Let the redeemed of the LORD say so, those God redeemed from trouble.

Psalm 107:1-2

In the Midst of the Storm

Cory Goode

PAUSE.

Wouldn't it be nice if life were always calm and serene? We know that difficulties often arise for us, and sometimes in ways that leave us wondering.

But God is always consistent, always with us, always true to God's promises, seeking what is best for us.

In the midst of your life's calm or storm, reach out with your very soul to the God of serenity—and turmoil.

LISTEN. MAY 20 **Job 38:1-11**

Questions

THINK. Do you ever have days when you like to think you've got it all figured out? There are times when I like to assume that I possess enough intellect and experience to know what's best for me, in addition to what's best for everyone else in the world. If only they would listen to me, all the world's problems could be solved!

The truth is that I don't have all the answers. In fact, the older I get, the more I realize that I tend to have more questions than answers. But it's the questions that keep my pride in check. It's the questions that cause me to search for wisdom. It's the questions that keep my feet on the path toward God. I believe in a God that created all things, knows all things, and reveals all things. It's the same God that Job and his friends encountered in the whirlwind. And I believe that if we could all admit that God knows more than we do, the answers to our questions might not seem so hard to find.

PRAY. Lord of all creation, you have promised to grant wisdom to those who seek it. Today I open my heart and mind to you that I may receive all that you offer me. Amen.

LISTEN. MAY 21 **Mark 4:35-41**

Peace, Storms of Life

THINK. Storms are a common occurrence where I live during the spring months. Some are capable of causing serious damage to the things that lie in their paths. When one of these storms approaches my home, my family and I take shelter inside a small bedroom closet and wait for the storm to pass, hoping that everything will turn out fine. It's during those storms that I can best relate to the fear and anxiety the disciples expressed in this passage the wind and the waves tossed their boat about.

I imagine that we've all sensed those same emotions. Whether we've had to endure actual tornadoes, hurricanes, and thunderstorms, or we've experienced the storms of broken relationships, stress, or loss, we've likely sought safety in the calming presence of God. If Jesus had the power to calm the wind and waves by simply speaking to them, surely he has the power to speak peace into the storms in our lives.

PRAY. Grant me peace, Lord, in the moments when I feel overwhelmed by the storms of life. Help me not to be afraid, because you are with me. Amen.

LISTEN. MAY 22 **2 Corinthians 6:1-2**

Holy Spirit, Presence of God

THINK. There is no shortage of movies based on comic book superheroes. We love to see the impossible become "reality" as they save the day. When I leave the theater, however, I'm a little disappointed that such heroes aren't around when I need help. It's true I've never found myself stuck on a speeding train racing toward a collapsed bridge or been held captive by a criminal mastermind, but there are times when I could use some supernatural intervention. Who am I supposed to turn to?

When the disciples realized that Jesus wasn't going to be with them much longer, they wondered the same thing. Who would save the day? Jesus told them that he would send the Holy Spirit to guide them in the ways and truth of God so that they might continue their ministry even after he was gone.

God has not left us to live on our own. We can work together with God to change the world through the power and presence of the Holy Spirit, knowing that we are not alone. God is here. God is helping. God is saving the day.

PRAY. I place my confidence in your power, God. Grant me strength and courage to do your work in the world today. Amen.

LISTEN. MAY 23 **2 Corinthians 6:3-8a**

Example of Christ

THINK. With very few exceptions, no one knows who you are better than you. No one else knows what's going on inside your mind from one moment to the next. No one else knows what you say and do when you're all alone. There are things about you that only you know, and when you compile those private thoughts, words, and actions, the result is your character.

The Scriptures indicate that character is important to the life and witness of those who follow Christ. Proverbs 27:19 states, "Just as water reflects the face, so one human heart reflects another." You can pretend to be something you're not for a time, but who you are on the inside will ultimately determine who you are on the outside.

So take a moment to consider this. Are you the same person in bad times that you are in good times? Are the things you say you believe reflected in the things you do? With God's help, seek to live a life that is consistent and without blame so that others "may see your good works and give glory to your Father in heaven" (Matt. 5:16).

PRAY. Help me live today in such a way that the faith I claim is the faith I live. God, be glorified in me. Amen.

LISTEN. MAY 24 **2 Corinthians 6:8b-10**

Journey with God, Life with Christ

THINK. No one ever said it would be easy (being a Christian, that is). From the beginning, Christians have been stereotyped, misunderstood, underestimated, taken for granted, and even persecuted because of their faith in Jesus Christ. Paul experienced that firsthand. But Paul had also experienced the grace of God firsthand, and he knew that the life of faith offered rewards that far outweighed the hardships he endured.

God never promised us an easy life. We will all face hardships and obstacles at some time. In spite of this, we can take comfort in knowing that God has given us everything we need to endure and even overcome such adversity through our faith in Christ. Even in the midst of our hardships, we find hope in the promise that there is absolutely nothing that can "separate us from the love God in Christ Jesus our Lord" (Rom. 8:39). Paul's words remind us that a life dedicated to God is not an easy life, but it is the best life.

PRAY. The life you have given me is a gift, dear God. Through every challenge and every triumph, I am thankful to live this life with you. Amen.

LISTEN. MAY 25 **2 Corinthians 6:11-13**

Loving Others

THINK. It's a common practice during the weekly youth gatherings at my church to reflect on all that's taken place in our lives over the past week. One of the questions that we ask one another is: "How have you both given and received love over the past week?" There are a few obvious answers that pop up on a regular basis, but the challenge is to dig deeper and really think about how we have shared and experienced love in meaningful ways.

Paul made no bones about his feelings for the people of Corinth. The heart-wide-open kind of love that he expressed was modeled after the love he received from God. God's love knows no constraints or boundaries, and it is given freely. As recipients of that love, the challenge for the people of Corinth was to love in a similar fashion. "Open wide your hearts also," said Paul.

What might our world look like if we were willing to give and receive love with our hearts wide open? Could we even begin to imagine the difference it might make for others to encounter God's love in us in such a way? Try living with your heart wide open today, and see what happens.

PRAY. Open wide my heart today, God, that I may receive your love for me and that I might show it to others. Amen.

LISTEN. MAY 26 **Psalm 9:9-14**

Storms of Life, Assurance of God

THINK. The Scriptures never let us forget about God's faithfulness toward God's people. From beginning to end, we read countless tales of God delivering people from the direst situations and restoring to them their health, their dignity, and even their very lives. No matter what storms these people faced, all could speak of God's presence with them in their moment of need. Each account credits God's saving power as the means by which God's people and the world in which they lived were redeemed and made new. If I were to ask you to recount the times you've experienced God's saving power firsthand, how would you respond?

The ways in which we have experienced God's deliverance are as unique as the situations from which we have been delivered. Sometimes things turn out the way we want. Other times the end result is much different than what we had hoped. No matter the outcome, we can find comfort in knowing that God is ever present to those in need. No matter what storms you face, you can look to God as "a stronghold in times of trouble."

PRAY. In the midst of life's storms, I turn to you, dear God, for deliverance. I place my trust in your power and abiding presence today. Amen.

The LORD bless you and keep you; the LORD make his face to shine upon you, and be gracious to you; the LORD lift up his countenance upon you, and give you peace.

Numbers 6:24-26

God's Search

Courtney Jones Willis

PAUSE.

The Bible tells us that God is very active, always reaching out to renew the relationship between God and the human beings God has made.

How might God be searching for you today? Will you allow yourself to be found?

LISTEN. MAY 27 **Psalm 51:1-2, 10**

Forgiveness, New Life

THINK. Have you ever wanted a chance to start over, or wished for a clean slate? Maybe you did poorly in a class at school, broke your parents' trust, or did something that really hurt someone else. Wouldn't it be nice to take those things back and start fresh?

In the psalm today, not only is the writer asking God for another chance, but the writer, David, is asking God to help him start over completely, making changes from the inside out. Most often, our actions are a direct reflection of our hearts. When our hearts are pure and clean, we make good life choices. When our hearts are not in tune with God, we tend to make choices that don't reflect God's love for us and others.

The good news is that God wipes our slates clean if we simply ask. God will forgive us when we mess up, and God will even clean out our hearts so that we can make better choices in the future. We simply have to ask God to do it.

PRAY. God, please forgive me for the times that my actions have not reflected your love. I want to live a life that shows love and respect to your world. Please let me start fresh with a pure heart and good intentions that come from knowing you better. Amen.

LISTEN. MAY 28 **Luke 15:1-2**

Loving Others

THINK. In today's passage, Jesus was about to speak, and the "least wanted" people were making their way closer and closer to hear. Pharisees and scribes were close by. Since they believed that following laws was the key to being a believer in God, they didn't want anything to do with the folks who were crowding around Jesus. In fact, they didn't think Jesus should want to be around those people either. The Pharisees and scribes starting mumbling and grumbling among themselves, criticizing Jesus for letting the sinners be close and even eat meals with him!

What Jesus understood is that we are all sinners. All of us are guilty of messing up; Jesus came to tell us that God loves us anyway! Jesus had a reputation for hanging out with the people no one else wanted to be with. Jesus was setting an example for us to follow. God wanted to teach us that we are all equal in God's eyes. Nothing you do can make you any better or worse in God's eyes. We shouldn't judge others, but we should be open and willing to share God's love with everyone.

PRAY. Dear God, help me to see who I am treating unfairly. I know that you love all of us equally, and I want to try to do the same. Amen.

LISTEN. MAY 29 **Luke 15:3-7**

Grace, Journey with God

THINK. Can you think of a time when you felt like you weren't very close to God? Everyone goes through different phases of faith, and sometimes we feel as if we are far from God's reach. Jesus' parable reminds us just how important each of us is to God. In those times of feeling far from God, you are like the one sheep who is lost. Not only does God care that you are lost, but God actively looks for you. God reaches out to you to bring you back to the comfort of God's love and grace.

Once you come to a place of closeness with God, God rejoices! God celebrates your return with joy, because ultimately it is your choice. God will reach out to you, but you have to decide to take God's hand and let God lead you. Each time you make that choice, God is thrilled. You are not just another number to God. You are special, and you are worth searching for, even when you are feeling far away.

PRAY. Dear God, thank you for looking for me even when I feel far away from you. Thank you for rejoicing when I come back to your presence. Help me to always remember the love and grace that is only found in being close to you. Amen.

LISTEN. **MAY 30** **Luke 15:8-10**

Following, Child of God

THINK. Do you realize how important you are to God? You are an incredible person to whom God has given a special purpose. Perhaps you don't know what you're going to do with your life yet, but you do have a clear purpose. Your purpose is to love God, accept God's grace, and to share that with others you meet. You don't have to wait to go to college, or get a job, or become an adult to accept that purpose and the responsibility that goes with it.

To God, you are like the lost coin in today's parable. Before you accept your purpose, God reaches out to you and longs for you to receive God's grace. When you decide to accept your purpose as a child of God, God and the heavens rejoice! It is important that you commit your life to God, and that you fulfill the purpose God has intended for you. No one else can fill the exact role that you are called to fill. No one else has the exact life that God has planned for you. When you choose to follow God, you are giving God reason to celebrate.

PRAY. Dear God, thank you for reminding me that I am special. Help me to fulfill my purpose in this world, and to see the ways in which you are guiding me. I want to honor you and give you reason to celebrate. Amen.

LISTEN. MAY 31 **1 Timothy 1:12-14**

Following, Sharing Christ

THINK. When we are faithful to God, we can expect God to ask us to reflect God's love and grace through our lives. This looks different for each of us, but it's an expectation of every one who follows Christ. It doesn't matter how you've acted in the past. It doesn't matter who you might have hurt, or put down. God gives each of us a fresh start, to begin loving God's people immediately.

One of the great things about God is that God never calls you to do something that God does not also equip you to do. When you rely completely on God, it becomes easier to see exactly how you should live. With God's love pouring into your life, you can't help but share that love with others. How can you share God's love with someone today?

PRAY. Dear God, thank you for loving me just as I am, warts and all. Thank you for using me to love others, even though I don't always follow you the best way I should. Help me to be faithful to you and help me love people better. Amen.

JUNE

LISTEN. JUNE 1 **1 Timothy 1:15-17**
Sharing Christ

THINK. When you decide to commit your life to God, you can be sure God is going to be excited, and God is going to start using you. That's right; God wants to use you to show others how great it can be to follow Christ. The scripture today reminds us that Christ came to the world to save sinners—that's all of us.

So, no matter what you've done in your past, when you accept Christ you are also accepting the responsibility of helping others come to know Christ as well. This is not just a job for folks who are especially "holy." It's not just the job of ministers in churches. It's not just the job of the adults you know. It is your job. God is so proud of who you are and wants your help in leading others to know God. You never know when a kind word you say or a helping hand you offer might give someone a glimpse of who God is.

PRAY. Dear God, it's a little bit overwhelming to know that you're giving me such a big task—helping others know you. But I am honored and humbled that you would use me, a regular person with faults and struggles, to share your love. Help me to show you to those around me through everyday ways. Amen.

LISTEN. JUNE 2 **Psalm 14:1-2**

Faithful, Love

THINK. There are a lot of people in the world who doubt God. They doubt God's existence. They doubt God's presence in the world. They doubt God's goodness and love. God knows this and is not threatened by it. God is bigger than those who don't believe.

God wants believers to be diligent in their faithfulness, to make good choices and be positive influences in the world. Despite all the negative in the world, God believes in us. God believes there are followers who lead healthy, honest, wholesome lives. God seeks out believers, those who are struggling to believe, and even those who do not believe at all.

God hopes you will choose to be one of the believers instead of someone who fills life with negativity and unhappiness. God is searching for you and wants you to make wise choices that reflect God's love.

PRAY. Dear God, I want to be wise, and someone you search for. Help me to make good choices and to be faithful.Thank you for loving me and for accepting my love for you. Amen.

GO.

For thus says the Lord GOD: I myself will search for my sheep, and will seek them out. As shepherds seek out their flocks when they are among their scattered sheep, so I will seek out my sheep. I will rescue them from all the places to which they have been scattered on a day of clouds and thick darkness.

Ezekiel 34:11-12

Deliverance

Tracy Hartman

PAUSE.

Deliverance is the way of escape, Lord, a good way out of a bad situation. Teach me today of how you have delivered others and show me how deliverance can be part of my life as well.

LISTEN. JUNE 3 **Esther 7:1-6**

Boldness, Deliverance

THINK. Deliverance is the theme for this week's devotions. At first glance, the book of Esther is a classic deliverance fairy tale: the beautiful orphan girl from the 'hood suddenly finds herself queen and is called upon to save her people from destruction. As the story unfolds, the evil villain Haman is exposed and vanquished, good triumphs over evil, and the Jewish nation is saved.

There is more to this story, however, than meets the eye. In this short book, the author deals with themes of racism and genocide as well as responsible and accountable authority.

In today's passage (as in the entire book of Esther) we see God at work not through miracles or some other divine intervention, but through Esther who is willing to risk everything and step up to the plate when the situation calls for her to do so. Sometimes deliverance comes by taking a stand against an oppressive system, but in this case, Esther follows the system and works from her already established role in it.

PRAY. God, today help me to be aware of ways that I can be your agent of deliverance right where I am. Help me to know how to utilize the resources already available to me to help bring about your will and work in the world. Amen.

LISTEN. JUNE 4 **Esther 9:20-22**

Deliverance, Sharing Christ

THINK. It's time to party! Mordecai is declaring a national holiday, an annual two-day celebration for the specific purpose of remembering the deliverance of the Jewish people from total genocide. It is important for every people's communal identity to remember their history, to lament the low points, and to celebrate the high points. After a difficult period in Israel's history that included military defeat and forced relocation to foreign countries, this was indeed a high point worth celebrating. These were to be days of feasting and celebrating, days of sharing food with one another and of giving gifts to the poor. At low points, these days would serve as reminders of God's provision.

We have similar holidays in our culture. On July 4th we celebrate independence (or deliverance) from the oppression of English rule. Every January, near the birthday of Martin Luther King, Jr., we honor his work and celebrate the ongoing progress of ending segregation and racism in our society. Each year at Easter we celebrate the deliverance that Christ offers us personally and collectively. As we party, may we remember to pass on the stories that gave birth to our "feast days."

PRAY. God, thank you for days of celebration that remind me of your deliverance of your people. As I read of your works in Scripture and celebrate deliverance holidays in my community, help me to remember your work in my life and help me to be faithful in sharing your story with others. Amen.

LISTEN. JUNE 5 **Psalm 124**

Unconditional Love

THINK. In this psalm, the writer states that if God had not been on the side of the Israelites, their enemies would have destroyed them. As we read this psalm today, we must ask the question, "Whose side is God on today?"

Here in the United States, it is easy to assume that God is for us. We often pull up behind drivers sporting bumper stickers saying "God bless America" and "Support our troops!" But we must remember that God's blessings are not just for our nation. In the Gospel of John, we read, "For God so loved the [whole] world." God is for all of us.

Verse eight of our psalm reminds us, "Our help is in the name of the LORD, who made heaven and earth." This verse reminds us that as much as we may try to help ourselves, and each other, our true help comes ultimately from God. May God deliver us all from ourselves and from our assumptions that God is only for some of us!

PRAY. God, I thank you that you are for me as you are for all your children. Help me to live as one who acknowledges that you create each person and that you love us all. Amen.

LISTEN. JUNE 6 **Numbers 11:4-6, 10-14**

Trust

THINK. What do you complain about? What do you crave? Often we focus on what we think we are missing (and deserve) instead of focusing on what God has provided for us. In today's text some Israelites were complaining and craving the meat and produce they ate in slavery in Egypt. But they were not the only ones who were complaining. Moses was complaining about the burden of leading dissatisfied people. "It's too heavy," he said. "I can't do this anymore."

God responded differently than we might imagine. For Moses, there was help. God instructed Moses to gather 70 trusted leaders together. God came and met with them, and empowered them to help Moses shoulder the leadership responsibility. Those who were craving food were not so fortunate. The next day they found an abundance of quail outside of camp, but when they ate the meat, they were struck dead from a plague.

Why the different responses? Today's text reminds us that it is not our complaining or laments that anger God; Scripture is full of such laments. God is much more troubled when we crave or seek earthly things (such as meat) more than we crave the spiritual food of God's presence.

PRAY. God, today remind how you have delivered me in the past and of the ways that you continue to provide for my real needs. Forgive me when I crave things more than I crave you, and remind me to be careful what I complain about. Amen.

LISTEN. JUNE 7 **Isaiah 46:8-13**

Putting God First

THINK. "Listen to me," says God, "you stubborn of heart, you who are far from deliverance." How does one get far from deliverance? In this case, the people of Babylon were crafting and worshiping idols. In verses 1-2 of chapter 46, these idols are described as heavy burdens that propel the carriers into captivity. In the Scripture for today, we are reminded that there is one God, and that God is the one who will bring deliverance.

During this time, the Babylonians held some of the Israelites captive. Away from their homeland, their temple, and all that they knew, I imagine they, too, felt far from deliverance. In today's text, God declares that a man from the east (Cyrus of Persia) will be the agent of deliverance for the Jews. "I bring near my deliverance," God said, "it is not far off."

What puts you in a position to be far from deliverance? What idols do you carry that are weighing you down? Who (or what) might be the agent of deliverance for you?

PRAY. God, reveal to me this day what idols I am carrying, and help me to put them down. Remind that you are my God and my deliverer. Help me to worship you in spirit and in truth. Amen.

LISTEN. JUNE 8 **James 5:13-20**

Community, Deliverance

THINK. "No one is an island." "It takes a village to raise a child." These sayings are not scriptural, but I think the author of James would agree with them. In this letter he addressed issues related to community. Early in the book, he warned readers that our words and deeds (or lack of them) can harm community. In our passage today, he reminds us that sometimes deliverance comes from God through the positive words and deeds of the community.

Society often models for us the survival of the fittest. The sick are ignored or marginalized because we are afraid, or because they slow down the rest of us. Those who make mistakes (commit sin as James described it) are often cast out of our families and sometimes even our churches.

James' words solidly refute this thinking and challenge us to model a better way. The sick are to call the elders who will come to pray and minister. We are all to confess our sins to one another, so that we may all be forgiven and healed. Think about how different the world might be if we were all such agents of deliverance.

PRAY. God, thank you for your reminder today that I am not alone, and that deliverance often comes through those with whom I share community. Help me today to be both a giver and receiver of deliverance in my community, whether it be home, school, work, or church. Amen.

LISTEN. JUNE 9 **Mark 9:38-48**

Ministering to Others

THINK. Aren't you glad we're not supposed to take all of Scripture literally? If we took today's Scripture that way, we'd all be physically disabled in some way, for we all stumble at one time or another! In these verses, Jesus was using a metaphor that would have been familiar to his listeners. It would be better to lose a body part, Jesus was reminding them, than to cause someone else to fall into sin. We are to be about the work of deliverance, not causing others bondage.

The Gospel today speaks to our theme of deliverance as well. Here, John perhaps thought he would be praised for trying to stop someone who was an outsider from delivering those who were demon-possessed. But Jesus was not happy. "Don't stop him," Jesus said, "for whoever is not against us is for us." Unfortunately, sometimes we tend to be like John, thinking that we, or our churches or programs, have the corner on ministry—on healing and deliverance. But the world is large and the needs are great. And we serve a God who can minister through whomever God chooses.

PRAY. God, forgive me for times when I have caused others to stumble, or times when I have failed to see you at work through those I call "other." Help me to always be an agent of your grace and help me to affirm the work of deliverance that comes through others, whomever they may be. Amen.

May the God of deliverance go before you, showing the way of liberation in your life and in the lives of your sisters and brothers around the world. Join God in the joy of rescue and relief.

Godliness and Wealth

Tim Tate

PAUSE.

Money can't bring happiness, we say. Then we work like mad to get money, thinking that maybe we were wrong. What is the best we can do in relationship to financial resources? What does God want us to do with whatever money we have?

LISTEN. JUNE 10 **Luke 16:25-31**

Caring for Others

THINK. Lazarus meant little to nothing to the rich man when they were alive, but on the other side of death, Lazarus was the one who could potentially bring relief. On this side of death, Lazarus meant nothing, but on the other side, he meant everything. On this side of death, the rich man had wealth, but on the other side, none of his wealth could relieve his pain; only Lazarus, the forgotten one, could help.

I wonder if the story would have turned out differently if the rich man had shared his wealth with Lazarus. I wonder what his eternity would look like if he had seen his wealth as a gift to be shared, rather than something to be hoarded.

The rich man was far away from Abraham, Lazarus, and relief because in his life he did not reveal the kingdom of God, rather he created his own kingdom. Great was his reward in this life, but great was Lazarus' reward in heaven. What kingdom are you living in? What might be your reward if you were to die today?

PRAY. God who bestows upon us gifts to share, soften our hearts and open our hands so that we might be privileged to feed and care for the Lazaruses of the world. Amen.

LISTEN. **JUNE 11** **Luke 16:25-31**

Listening, Following

THINK. "If they do not listen to Moses and the prophets, neither will they be convinced even if someone rises from the dead." Recognizing his own fate, the rich man thought about his family who was still alive. He wanted them to be warned not to live the same way that he did, relying on himself rather than God. He wanted Lazarus to be sent to give that warning, convinced that if they received the message of repentance from someone who was dead, then they would surely listen. But Abraham essentially said, "They have all they need to hear the message, and they will not be changed, even if someone rises from the dead."

Jesus has given the world the message of repentance and truth, and Jesus rose from the dead bringing back with him that same message, so that the world would be saved. Does the world listen? Do we listen . . . even though he did rise from the dead? Those questions are answered in how we live our lives, what we do with our wealth, and where we are investing ourselves and what we have in the kingdom of God. Are you convinced? You can be, because Christ rose from the dead for all.

PRAY. Jesus, conqueror of the grave and builder of God's kingdom, open our ears to listen and turn our hearts toward you, so that our lives reflect your desire that we keep in proper perspective how we are to live and how we share our wealth. In your name we pray. Amen.

LISTEN. JUNE 12 **1 Timothy 6:6-10**

Trust, Priorities

THINK. One of the greatest challenges to the faith of the modern day disciple is materialism. As part of the wealthiest of the world's societies, we are at risk of being drawn away from God every moment.

Technology, power, class, prestige, security, retirement planning . . . money. Each can easily get in the way of our reliance upon God. Paul essentially told Timothy, "You brought nothing into the world and will take nothing out of it," a reminder that all is transient. If you have food and clothing, be content with that, and don't worry about getting more. "The love of money is the root of all kinds of evil."

Are you content with what you have, or do you worry while your cupboard and fridge are full, closets overflow, and computers and gadgets fill your home? How much money is in the bank? Does that money, or desire for more, get in the way of your relationship with God? Do you rely more on money than God? From the beginning, God's desire has been for us to be content in God and trust God. How are you doing in fulfilling God's desire for your life?

PRAY. Loving God, though you surround us with love, we surround ourselves with things. Assure in us our faith in you, then make sure that our first love is you, so our priorities will be ordered well for your service. In Christ we pray. Amen.

LISTEN. JUNE 13 **1 Timothy 6:11-16**

Priorities

THINK. Our theme for the week is "Godliness and Wealth." At times it seems that these two things can be in conflict. But Paul had a remedy for this:

> Pursue righteousness - right living
> Godliness - God's will and God's way
> Faith - believing in God and trusting in Christ
> Love - giving yourself away
> Endurance - keeping focused on Christ,
> Gentleness - allowing humility and
> compassion to be your guides.

When wealth takes control, we can easily get caught up in ourselves and seek for more and more. When godliness is our aim, we discover true life, which is contentment in Christ.

PRAY. Righteousness, godliness, faith, love, endurance, and gentleness are what I aim for, O God. Make them so in my life, that I may be content in Christ and truly alive in this world. Amen.

LISTEN. JUNE 14 **1 Timothy 6:17-19**

Generosity

THINK. I learn many things from my children; one of the best is to be generous with my love. Often my children run up, give me a hug, and say, "I love you!" Without my request and without reserve on their part, they give their love away as an expression of their care for me, but also as God's instruments of grace to me.

Their love moves me to give more than just a hug, smile, or encouraging word to those around me. It reminds me that all I have is a gift from God, who is the source of all love. It reminds me that I am to give in deed and treasure. Their love reminds me of these words from Paul, to "do good, to be rich in good works, generous, and ready to share."

How well are you doing in goodness, generosity, and sharing?

PRAY. Loving God, you have blessed me beyond measure and call me to bless others with that same wealth. Move me toward goodness, generosity, and sharing, so that others will take hold of the life that is truly life. Amen.

LISTEN. **JUNE 15** **Jeremiah 32:1-3, 6-8**

Sharing Christ

THINK. We live in an extremely transient society. Few people today grow up in the same house from birth through high school, and even fewer from birth to the grave. The roots we put out are shallow, for we know that we'll be moving on. This was not the case in ancient cultures.

Jeremiah the prophet was imprisoned. He was warning Zedekiah that Babylon would soon overtake Judah and the people of God would be enslaved. Despite being in prison and knowing that the land would be taken, Jeremiah heard God's command to buy his uncle's land. As the next closest heir, Jeremiah had the rights to possess that land.

Why would he even think about buying the land? After all, he was in prison and the Babylonians would soon conquer. He contemplated it because God commanded it, and he puts his trust in God and understood that this is sacred land was intended to remain in the family.

In this transient society, what might God require you to "purchase" or hold on to in order for God's legacy of family to be lived out through you? What in your life is a sacred gift from God?

PRAY. God who bestows all gifts, reveal to me those things in my life that reveal your truth in my life. Use them as a means of multiplying your kingdom through me. Amen.

LISTEN. JUNE 16 **Jeremiah 32:9-15**

Faith

THINK. This purchase was more than just an investment. Jeremiah bought this land as an act of faith and a sign of hope. The Babylonians were breathing down their necks. Jeremiah was in trouble for speaking God's Word. Everything seemed to be up in the air. Yet in a deliberately public way, Jeremiah made sure everyone knew that he was buying land, which for all intents and purposes, it looked like he would never see.

Jeremiah listened to God and lived out God's will. This did more than just bless him; it was a proclamation that Israel would overcome what was on the horizon (invasion and captivity) and that one day "houses and fields and vineyards shall again be bought in this land." It was a statement of faith, that with God anything is possible.

PRAY. God of the second chance, help me to hear your voice encouraging me to be more like Jeremiah, witnessing hope to the world, even in dark times. In Christ I pray. Amen.

GO.

Thus says the LORD: Do not let the wise boast in their wisdom, do not let the mighty boast in their might, do not let the wealthy boast in their wealth; but let those who boast boast in this, that they understand and know me, that I am the LORD; I act with steadfast love, justice, and righteousness in the earth, for in these things I delight, says the LORD.

Jeremiah 9:23-24

Using Wealth and Power Wisely

Ka'thy Gore Chappell

PAUSE.

Everybody wants to be rich, right? Even if we accept that as true, we have to ask ourselves what true riches are.

As you take a little time for quietness today, think about what true wealth means—and what it means about how we live.

LISTEN. JUNE 17 **Psalm 113:1-4**

Praise

THINK. Praise God. God's name is to be praised. Praise God all day.

Today's Scripture, as with other psalms of praise, provides us with instructions as to what, when, and how we should praise God. In fact, the Scripture states that we should look for opportunities to praise God even when we do not feel like it. From waking up in the morning to going to sleep at night, we should praise God.

The reason it is important for us to praise God is because God genuinely loves us and cares deeply about us. Yes, we have access to spiritual wealth and power because we are God's children. We have the opportunity to serve God. When we praise God, we celebrate who God is as well as the relationship we share with God. Praise God. God's name is to be praised. Praise God all day.

PRAY. God, you are worthy to be praised. Today I pray for wisdom to know what spiritual wealth and power really look like. Thank you for the love and care you provide in my life. Amen.

LISTEN. JUNE 18 **Luke 16:1-4**
Following Christ

THINK. A parable is a story that is used to teach a lesson. The characters and theme in a parable are symbolic of real people and life lessons. In this Scripture, Jesus told a story about a steward that may have been a real occurrence instead of a parable.

The steward, who was not the owner of the company, managed the business. Based on accurate information, someone complained to the owner that the steward was not managing honestly. The owner initiated a financial audit, which made the steward fearful of losing his position. So the steward began to contact the owner's debtors to negotiate a lower re-payment price. The steward had not been wise in his responsibilities to the owner nor in his relationships with the debtors. In the panic of the moment, the steward redirected his focus on relationships and hopefully realized that wealth and power can be found in relationship with God and others. True wealth and power are found in relationship with Jesus Christ.

PRAY. God, give me the wisdom to choose you and follow the example of Jesus Christ in life and relationships. In the name of Jesus Christ, I pray. Amen.

LISTEN. JUNE 19 **Luke 16:5-9**

Forgiveness, Grace

THINK. Jesus told a story about a steward who managed a company for the owner. The owner discovered that the company was mismanaged; therefore, a financial audit was ordered. Prior to the audit, the steward contacted the debtors, renegotiated the amounts owed, and then collected the debts. It sounds like the steward realized that relationships are more important than wealth and power.

Since the owner actually lost money, it's confusing that the owner complimented the steward for collecting debts. While the steward originally wasted the owner's goods, the steward made a decision to collect funds in order to maintain business relationships in the future. Did the steward grow in wisdom from the experience? Did the owner exhibit grace by affirming the steward for his change of behavior? What can we learn from the story? As followers of Jesus Christ, we can affirm responsible business practices as well as the importance of building genuine relationships. Most importantly, we can affirm the gift of grace that can be offered through the love of God.

PRAY. Dear God, I have made mistakes; forgive me. Grant me grace and help me do the same for others. Amen.

LISTEN. **JUNE 20** **Luke 16:10-12**

Responsibility

THINK. Most of us have heard our parents or teachers communicate the importance of responsibility with whatever task has been assigned. Of course, there are times that we think that the assigned task is insignificant or below our maturity level. Then, the person who assigned the task says "Complete that task, and I will give you a more involved task or greater responsibility." In today's Scripture, this is exactly what Jesus was telling the disciples.

The lesson from the Scripture is to be faithful in your responsibilities, and your responsibilities will grow with your faithfulness. Specifically, if you lie or are dishonest in small things, you will probably lie and be dishonest in big things. The challenge is to be responsible with what belongs to you and with the task that is at hand. Apply the Scripture lesson to areas of your life such as managing homework, resisting the temptation to cheat, recycling, and caring for our environment. Be responsible! Then watch for the greater things God will call you to do.

PRAY. Dear God, you remind me that my ability to be responsible does not appear magically. I must learn, practice, and grow with responsibility. Teach me and help me grow in wisdom! In the name of Jesus Christ. Amen.

LISTEN. JUNE 21 **Luke 16:13**

Putting God First

THINK. Serving two masters? Let's restate that in contemporary language. Masters may mean parents, teachers, or work supervisors. When parents instruct you, it's helpful if they are unified in decision making and discipline. With teachers, it's helpful if there is a principal or homeroom teacher who communicates basic school goals and objectives clearly. With supervisors, it helps if you receive instruction and feedback from one person. The result of service to two masters is miscommunication, confusion, and lower quality of work.

What was Jesus' specific point? Identify your master, build a relationship with your master, determine your goals and objectives, and respond with faithfulness in work to the assigned tasks. Jesus instructs us to establish and commit to God as our master. There is wisdom in identifying God as master; there is freedom in knowing who is master of our lives.

PRAY. God, give me the wisdom to recognize the importance of choosing you as master. Help me develop a right attitude about service with school, work, money, people, and the environment. In the name of Jesus Christ, I pray. Amen.

LISTEN. JUNE 22 **1 Timothy 2:1-7**

Following Christ

THINK. When Paul wrote a letter, he was eager to provide instruction on how to live and proclaim Jesus Christ. Paul was committed to the God he served and the message he proclaimed.

Today's Scripture is part of a letter Paul wrote to Timothy. Most likely, Timothy would have read the letter at church. First, Paul instructed that we pray for ourselves, others, and world leaders. Paul's idea was that prayer for leaders was a prayer for peace. Second, Paul reminded us that God desires salvation for all people and that the way to salvation is through our mediator, Jesus Christ. Third, Paul confirmed who he was, a preacher and teacher to the Gentiles.

We can follow Paul's instruction by praying for wisdom for ourselves, others, and world leaders. Remember that we serve God, the one true God. Celebrate those who have come before us to instruct us in the way to follow in faithfulness.

PRAY. Dear God, I pray for wisdom and strength to follow you and serve you in all of my life. Thank you for salvation through your son, Jesus Christ. Amen.

LISTEN. JUNE 23 **Psalm 113:5-9**

Love, Generosity

THINK. Praise God! God's name is to be praised. Praise God all day.

Today's Scripture is a song of praise to God that describes God as powerful. The psalm states that God "looks far down on the heavens and the earth" and is capable of raising "the poor from the dust . . . to make them sit with princes." The fact that God sits the poor with royalty shows us that God loves all people. In God's eyes, we are all equal.

The psalm also states that God makes the barren woman a joyous mother. A woman who could not have children became a mother. We do not know if the woman actually gave birth or adopted children. What we do know is that she became a joyous mother. God cares about our concerns and responds with generosity.

PRAY. Dear God, help me to grow in wisdom. I am realizing that you are a powerful God, and through you I also have spiritual power. I am also beginning to realize that in a world where material possessions and money are so important, you provide wealth in forms of equality and joy. Thank you. Amen.

Go now, grateful for all God has given you, offering all you have, all you own and all you are, to be used by God today.

The Dangers of Wealth

Elizabeth Mangham Lott

PAUSE.

Riches bring great opportunity, but also great temptation. What we do with what we have goes deep into the heart of our relationship with God.

Consider today what you have materially, what it means to you, and how it impacts your spiritual self.

LISTEN. JUNE 24 **Psalm 91:1-6, 14-16**

Trust, Priorities

THINK. Pop culture can be a lot of fun. In fact, it can be so fun that it is downright addictive. How many reality shows bombard us with images and information about the lush, exciting lives we could be living if we weren't sitting on our couches watching reality television? There are the competition shows for the newest, thinnest top model or the most exciting, most dramatic new fashion designer. Then there are the shows about people who aren't really famous, but they somehow live out their days shopping and fighting and looking attractive in front of TV cameras.

Even if we do not watch them, these steady flashes of "reality" permeate our culture in ways that sometimes make us think our own lives aren't real enough. Or decadent enough. Or rich enough. Figuring out who we really are is a tough task. Even centuries ago, the psalmist knew the human struggle to look for the keys to real life. But it is God and not the world who is faithful. It is God and not the world in whom we trust. It is God who promises to satisfy us and show us what real life is all about.

PRAY. O God who loves me and knows my name, you promise to satisfy me. Help me to trust you. Amen.

LISTEN. JUNE 25 **Psalm 146**

Priorities

THINK. It is pretty common and really tempting to look at folks who have significant material possessions and say, "Wow, they are really blessed." Our culture so prioritizes having the newest and latest everything that even in the church we start to think that "stuff" is a sign of God's blessing.

Does God bless us? Absolutely! The sky, the seas, and the land "and all that is in them" are evidence of God's provision and protection. The psalmist tells us, however, that God has a different set of priorities than the culture around us does. Not only does our creative God speak to us through the world God created, God is active in this world giving food to the hungry, opening the eyes of the blind, and upholding the orphan and the widow. If we want to get in God's head or, more importantly, if we want to live in God's way, then our priorities must begin to line up with God's.

PRAY. O God who made the heaven and earth, the sea, and all that is in them, I want to know your ways. Help me to move like you. Amen.

LISTEN. JUNE 26 **1 Timothy 6:6-9**

Contentment

THINK. What makes you really happy? We're talking deep down to your toes happy. If you could plan the perfect day from morning to night, what kind of happy would be in that day? Think of a moment when you realize for just a second that everything is just as it should be. In Paul's letters, he wrote a fair amount about contentment. Sometimes we think of being content as kind of a neutral state between really great and really lousy. Or worse, we think of contentment as settling for something less than the best, but that's not what Paul meant.

Paul knew that deep down to your toes happiness comes from living the life God has created you to live. This is that abundant life that Jesus talked about. At times, we get distracted by wanting someone else's life, and sometimes that distraction includes wanting the things that someone else has. Whether it's the other life or the other stuff, the wanting is distraction from a rich, joyful life that God desires for each of us. Don't waste another moment. What might contentment look like right now, today?

PRAY. O God, you give me everything I need and you want such a full, good life for me. Teach me the deep down to my toes contentment that comes only from you. Amen.

LISTEN. JUNE 27 **1 Timothy 6:10**

Trust

THINK. In writing about choosing between ways of living, Robert Frost's poem famously reflected, "Two paths diverged in a yellow wood." Paul's words to Timothy contain a similar sentiment as he laid out two paths: the way of money and the way of faith. Things get a little prickly when we talk about wealth being separate from faith. If we listen to Paul's words, we hear a lesson about trusting God to provide for our needs and to gift us with all we need as we seek to live our lives in faith.

Paul was describing a trust that feels something like relaxing in an overstuffed armchair; the way is not anxious because one is at rest in knowing God provides enough. The other way, "the love of money" way, is a way of anxious hoarding that shows no trust for God at all. Remember the story of the Israelites wandering in the desert when they first encountered manna? Even though they were told to take just enough and that more would come, some still frantically took more than they could eat. The manna went bad, and the lesson was clear: trust God to provide.

PRAY. O God, I want to believe that you care enough about my daily needs to guide the path of my life. Help me to relax in that trust as I discover your path. Amen.

LISTEN. JUNE 28 **1 Timothy 6:11-14**

Trust, Generosity

THINK. At 75 years old, Mr. Biff worked 15-hour days every day of the week cleaning office buildings. Few people knew that Mr. Biff had amassed sizeable savings and provided all of his family's needs, paying cash for everything. Asked why he continued to work so many hours, day after day, he replied, "When you've been as poor as I've been, you're always scared you might go back."

Mr. Biff was a kind man who loved his family deeply, but he also lived in constant fear. Did his fear prevent him from living the life God wanted for him? Does that happen to us at times? Paul knew people who lived this way, too. He urged his friends in the faith to trust God, not just as One who provides, but also as One "who gives life to all things." When we live this life God wants to give us, we are choosing a way of living marked by "faith, love, [and] endurance" rather than steady fear.

PRAY. O God, I want to know life that really is life. Teach me generosity. Teach me to notice you in the moments and movements of my day. Amen.

LISTEN. **JUNE 29** **1 Timothy 6:17-19**

Trust

THINK. After mastering the word mine, one of the first lessons young children must learn is to share. This is almost always an unnatural lesson for toddlers and preschoolers who want to hold onto a favorite toy being spied by a young friend. Are we very different now than we were at two or three or four?

Few people really master that first sharing lesson, but the practice of unending generosity is a key to not only God's nature, but the life God wants us to discover. Paul rightly suspected that when a person's every need and want are met, trusting God to be present in one's daily life becomes much less important. Paul didn't want the false notion of financial security to prevent people from trusting God fully. To miss out on the ways God daily participates in our lives is to miss out on the essence of God's character. Paul wanted all believers to live in the true, real life God has planned for all people. When we open our hands and start to let go of the life we think is true, we begin to discover a life we could never have imagined.

PRAY. O God, I want to know life that really is life. Teach me generosity. Teach me to notice you in the moments and movements of my day. Amen.

LISTEN. JUNE 30 **Amos 6:1a, 4-7**

Service, Kingdom of God

THINK. Few of us think we are wealthy, certainly not the sort of wealthy people Amos talked about.

Our passage today harshly condemns those living lives of leisure with no regard for the anguish of others. Money itself was not the problem, but the way people became consumed by luxury at the expense of those who suffer. According to Amos, "those who are at ease" will soon be the ones cast out from home. That doesn't have to be the case for us, though. How can we be mindful of the world's needs, not just so we are grieved, but so we are moved to act? Visit http://www.globalrichlist.com to find out how you and your family live compared to the rest of the globe. If the United States really does sit at the top of all the world's wealth, how might we use that position to impact the world for God's kingdom?

PRAY. O God, touch my heart that I might grieve for the needs of this world. Inspire me to move and act in simple, daily ways that welcome your kingdom on earth as it is in heaven. Amen.

GO.

Keep your way pure by keeping to God's Word and seeking God with your whole heart. Treasure God's Word in your heart, and seek God's teaching.

Then you will delight in God as if you owned all you can imagine!

Inspired by Psalm 119

JULY

Free to Follow

Tammy Wiens-Sorge

PAUSE.

God made us to be free; we are free to decide for ourselves how we will live. Though God will not insist on it, it is clear that God intends Jesus to be the model for our lives. And so we are free to follow him. How will these next moments impact your decision about following the Lord today?

LISTEN. JULY 1 **Psalm 77:1-2, 11-15**

Hope, Faithfulness

THINK. When a moment of desperation stretches into a day, or a week, or a season, it may seem to us as though the darkness will never end. We stop seeing color, and the world around us fades to shades of gray. This is the plight of the psalmist whose "soul refuses to be comforted." His refusal is symptomatic of a deeply troubled person at prayer. Oddly enough, hope for the future is restored by his memories of the past.

It's a strategy that will work for us, too. When we lose confidence in tomorrow, we should think back on God's faithfulness to us in the past. "Us" is used because we find hope in remembering God's goodness from the first day of creation until this very moment. The psalmist finds hope in remembering how God parted the sea to save the people of Israel. Since God is the same yesterday, today, and forever, every act of God's faithfulness assures us that the future is securely in God's care. This gives any of us reason to hope. The gray in our lives can once again give way to hints of color.

PRAY. Faithful God, give me the courage I need to see beyond my problems and worries. Open my heart to remember the ways you have proved your faithfulness over and over again in the pages of the Bible and in the stories of my life. Thank you for your unchanging love, most obviously shown to us in Christ. Thank you for giving us the Holy Spirit so that, even on the worst day, we can find a reason to hope for a better tomorrow. I pray in Jesus' name. Amen.

LISTEN. JULY 2 **Luke 9:51-56**

Example of Christ, Sharing Christ

THINK. Every summer my nieces come and stay with us for a couple of weeks. It happens only once a year, and so when the visit comes to an end we almost immediately begin looking forward to the next summer. Maybe the young Jews in Jesus' time had a similar enthusiasm about their yearly trip to Jerusalem. Families traveled for three or four days to get to Jerusalem for the Passover celebration. When Jesus made up his mind to go to Jerusalem, it marks the beginning of his journey toward Passover, but also toward the cross.

The next ten chapters of Luke provide a picture of what it means for disciples to follow Jesus. The first glimpse lets us know that there will be some people who misunderstand us or refuse to hear Jesus' message. We may be frustrated or angry with those who respond disapprovingly, but Jesus asks us to calm down and take it all in stride. He is not surprised when we meet resistance. Instead of calling down fire on the ones who don't want to hear our testimony, Jesus asks us to respond with love and grace, and continue on our way.

PRAY. Loving God, thank you for calling me to be a disciple. Thank you that Jesus came and set an example for us to follow. I pray that your Holy Spirit will help me to live out this example. Give me the courage to act out and speak about my faith, but also give me the love and patience I need to deal with those who don't understand or appreciate the message. I pray in Jesus' name. Amen.

LISTEN. **JULY 3** **Luke 9:57-62**

Putting God First, Priorities

THINK. In the previous verses we see that some people simply refuse to accept Jesus' message. In these verses there are some who hear and accept Jesus' message, but other obligations prevent them from becoming disciples. For instance, one guy told Jesus he had to bury his father before he could follow Jesus. It sounds like a lousy excuse. And besides, a funeral shouldn't take too long. What's the big deal?

Actually, it's a much bigger deal than it seems on the surface. It is likely that the young man's father has not yet died. He wants to put off following Jesus so that he can stay home and take care of his father as long as the father is living. It is actually a very virtuous thing he has in mind to do. That's the paradox of believing Jesus' message and yet failing to respond to it. We may have some really good reasons for delaying our commitment to Christ, but Jesus says even things we think are important need to take second place to the call to follow him.

PRAY. Holy God, your plans for me are so much better than anything I could design on my own. Help me trust my future to your care. Let your Holy Spirit search my heart and mind and expose my good intentions for what they really are, an excuse to delay my obedience to you. Take away my excuses and fill me with a willingness to follow you. In Jesus name I pray. Amen.

LISTEN. JULY 4 **Galatians 5:1, 13-15**

Loving Others

THINK. Freedom! It's a popular word on the fourth of July as we lift patriotic voices to sing "My country, 'tis of thee, sweet land of liberty . . . from every mountainside, let freedom ring." All Americans agree that freedom is a good thing, but perhaps not everyone agrees about how best to live out our freedom. Some people may define freedom as the right to do anything they please. Most of us, however, realize that freedom is not the same thing as lawlessness. For example, living in a free country still obligates us to obey the law and respect the rights of other citizens. Christians in this country are fortunate that these laws support our religious freedom. Nevertheless, Christ sets an even higher standard for our lives than obedience to the laws of a nation. Christ calls us to obedience to God's law, which is partly summed up here: You shall love your neighbor as yourself. When Christ speaks of freedom it is synonymous with sacrificial love. As followers of Christ we must choose to live in a way that protects not only our own interests, but the interests of our neighbors as well.

PRAY. God of freedom, I thank you for the privilege of living in a country that does not punish me for worshiping you. I celebrate the blessings of freedom and pray that I would not take for granted what it means for me to be free. Even as I enjoy the privileges of freedom, I pray I will recognize the ways I am not free. Remove from me any attitudes that stand in the way of sharing freedom with those around me. I pray these things in the strong name of Christ my Lord. Amen.

LISTEN. JULY 5 **Galatians 5:16-21**

Actions, Priorities

THINK. When Martin Luther King, Jr. delivered his "I Have a Dream" speech in 1963, he gave new meaning to the words "let freedom ring." It was Dr. King's profound hope that America become a nation where all God's children, regardless of race or religion, could "join hands and sing in the words of the old Negro spiritual, 'Free at last! free at last! Thank God Almighty, we are free at last!'" It was his conviction that when the freedoms of a few people diminish the freedom of even one other person, then none of them is free.

What privileges do you and I enjoy that may be a source of injury to someone else? The question is not only inspired by King's conviction, but it also springs from the heart of the gospel. Paul said that when we reject the Spirit then we live for ourselves. He mentioned a whole list of things that may seem irrelevant to us: sorcery, enmity, carousing. But don't let the big words fool you! Paul's meaning is clear. When we live to gratify our own desires, we end up hurting other people. When our actions are self-centered, we will never know true freedom.

PRAY. God of big dreams, give me a vision of what it means for your Church to live by the Spirit. Help me, as a member of Christ's body to assess my life by the standard of Christ's love. Help me to see the ways in which my actions or attitudes are contrary to Christ's example. I ask these things in the name of the Spirit of Christ who makes me free. Amen.

LISTEN. **JULY 6** **Galatians 5:22-26**

Following, Loving Others

THINK. Freedom is a gift that can only come from God. Without the Holy Spirit, Paul said, we would be slaves of the flesh. The "flesh" was Paul's term for every conceivable human weakness, things such as hate, lust, self-pity, or greed. When God's life-giving Spirit is indwelling us, then we are no longer slaves to every human impulse.

In the same way that we identify a tree by the kind of fruit it produces, Paul identified the Spirit's work by the fruit it produces in a person's attitudes and actions. These fruits of the Spirit are not conjured up by our own willpower. This is good news! It means that loving others is something God does in us and not something we force ourselves to carry out. Every time we are able to think or act with patience, kindness, gentleness, and all the other "fruits" mentioned in these verses, it is living proof of the Holy Spirit living in us and freeing us to follow Christ.

PRAY. Holy God, I thank you for the gift of the Holy Spirit. It is such a relief to know that I am more than just the sum of my feelings and impulses. Sometimes my loneliness gets the better of me, and sometimes I crave what I know it is wrong to crave. I'm so glad your Spirit can live in me and give me freedom to follow Christ. I want to see the fruits of the Spirit in my life. Hear my prayer, O God, and free me so that I can act with love, joy, peace, patience, kindness, generosity, faithfulness, gentleness, and self-control. In Jesus name I ask it. Amen.

LISTEN. JULY 7 **Psalm 16**

Child of God, Unconditional Love

THINK. God's love is such an amazing gift that we're sometimes fooled into thinking that we're the ones doing the giving. We follow Christ in freedom, and so we assume that we should get all the credit for making the right choice. The paradox is that we love because God first loved us, and we follow Christ because Christ initiated a call to do so.

The first verse of one of my favorite hymns expresses it like this: "I sought the Lord, and afterward I knew he moved my soul to seek him, seeking me. It was not I that found, O Savior true; no, I was found of thee."

This psalmist tells God, "You are my Lord." And again: "The LORD is my chosen portion and my cup." But then comes the psalmist's ecstatic realization that God chose him! We can celebrate like this because God chooses us, too. We are also heirs. God is watching us, protecting us, giving us rest, paying our debts, and teaching us to walk the path that leads to life!

PRAY. O God, you are my God, and I love to walk in the way that you lead me. How surprising it is to find that even before I chose you, you had already chosen me! I am so blessed to be your child; so blessed that not one thing happens to me except that fits your purpose for my salvation. Your presence is all around me, and nothing I do can pry me away from your love. Even when I doubt you, Lord, you do not abandon me. You are an awesome God! In Jesus' name I lift my praise and my prayer to you. Amen.

Go now as a free child of God, choosing to serve your Creator.
Go now as a free child of God, choosing to follow your Lord.
Go now as a free child of God, free and alive in the Spirit of Christ.

The Household of God

Dave McNeely

PAUSE.

We all want to belong; we want to be a part of something bigger than ourselves.

We are. We are part of the household of God, the family of all God's creation.

As you pause today to spend time with the Head of our household, do so knowing that you have been accepted, and you are loved.

LISTEN. JULY 8 **Mark 6:30-32**

Rest, Stillness

THINK. When I was younger, I simply couldn't sleep in on Saturday mornings. It wasn't that I was a really industrious child. No, what awoke me with the dawn every Saturday was the fear that I would miss something. What if my family does something really fun while I'm asleep? What if my best friend stops by to see if I want to hang out? What if the Ultimate Warrior wrestles Hulk Hogan this morning on TV? What if the cute girl in math class calls to talk? (OK, so my scenarios were a little too optimistic . . . but what if?)

As I grew older, and my life became busier with school, sports, clubs, friendships, family commitments, and everything else, suddenly Saturday mornings were starting to look a lot better for rest. Believe it or not, it got to the point where I would turn my cell phone off to maximize my rest. We live in a world of constant noise and never ending "busyness." In a world like ours, we do well to reflect on the fact that even Jesus and his earliest followers took a break every once in a while. If even Jesus took the time to rest, why are we in such a hurry?

PRAY. Lord of life, help me to remember that my value is not tied to the amount of activity in my life. Help me to understand that I am a person with limitations and that rest is an important part of giving my life as an offering to you. Amen.

LISTEN. JULY 9 **Mark 6:33-34**

Compassion, Love

THINK. Do you ever get the feeling that the one person who most annoys you is also the one person who just keeps showing up in your life at the most inopportune times? Maybe it's the brother you have to babysit, the girl at school who always wants to tag along, or even the mother who just wants to know every little detail of your day. Whoever it is, we all have that person we seek to avoid.

Jesus seemed to face this problem a lot, too. Everywhere he went, people followed. And it wasn't always the good-looking, esteemed, and powerful people of his day. On the contrary, Jesus seemed to attract a real motley crew of followers, the kind of people everyone else avoided. But there was one big difference between Jesus' situation and ours. These outcasts were exactly the kind of people Jesus wanted to be around. Instead of judgment and exhaustion, these never ending encounters with people who were "different" than him awakened and excited compassion and love. Imagine what the world would look like if we began to act in the same way.

PRAY. Compassionate God, slow to anger and abounding in love, I ask that you give me a heart of compassion toward those whom you have placed in my life. Instead of seeing their presence as a curse, change my heart and mind to see them as a blessing, and to see myself as a blessing to them. Amen.

LISTEN. **JULY 10** **Mark 6:53-56**

Compassion, Healing

THINK. Do you ever wonder what it would be like if Jesus walked among us today? Would he go largely unnoticed, or would he fill football stadiums with people wanting to hear him speak? I'm pained to admit this, but when I'm at the checkout line at our local supermarket, I find it difficult not to glance at all of the tabloid headlines. Whether it's politicians caught in scandalous situations or celebrities misbehaving, the bright pictures and headlines make it hard to look away. But I can't recall one time when I left the checkout line inspired or encouraged by what I (quickly, without anyone noticing) read.

On the flip side of this, we find Jesus, a man whom many people couldn't take their eyes off when he came into their town. They, too, found themselves captivated in their marketplace, but instead of scandal and shock, they were captivated by his healing touch and words. Perhaps the next time I'm in line at the supermarket, I will look away from the tabloids long enough to offer a word of healing to those around me. And perhaps in that moment, I, too, will be healed.

PRAY. God of healing, may I feel your touch. May the stir you cause in our marketplaces be a scandal of compassion and inspire headlines of grace that bring healing to our communities. Amen.

LISTEN. **JULY 11** **Ephesians 2:11-16**

Inclusion, Grace

THINK. Like most people, I hate being labeled. When I was in high school, the labels naturally centered around the sports I played, my body type, and the company I kept. I always hated being pigeonholed. But like most people, I really like to label others. As much as I'd like to justify my stereotyping as fair, efficient, or just normal, I know that when it comes down to it, it's just a form of what one author calls relational laziness.

We're all prone to labels, and one of the things we like about labels is that they separate those who are "in" from those who are "out." (Of course, we ourselves are always in the in group!) It seems that this is precisely what God hates about labels. Every time we draw a circle to fence people out, God grabs our boundary lines and pulls them further out to bring more people in. Every time we find a new label to identify those we want outside of our group, God adds their names to the list of people God cares about most. For every attempt at exclusion we make, God's commitment to inclusion becomes that much stronger.

PRAY. God of grace, the legacy of justice you have given has been abused. Whereas you have always desired to more fully extend compassion, we have sought to corner the market on your love for people "like us." Forgive me my insecure need to draw lines of exclusivity around the privileges of being your child, and grant me the grace to keep pace with your ever-widening circle of inclusion. Amen.

LISTEN. JULY 12 **Ephesians 2:17-22**

Faithfulness

THINK. I often get the opportunity to help on local construction projects that seek to improve the lives of some of our more impoverished community members. Every time, I'm reminded that I know nothing about construction. But I have learned one important lesson. No matter how much work you put into the exterior, it's all for naught if the foundation of the house is not stable.

Our lives are much the same. We, too, often believe that if we just do a little whitewashing on the exterior of our lives, everything will be OK. As long as we wear Christian t-shirts and attend weekly Bible studies, all the necessary work is done, right? As long as our church is respected in our community and we have successful, well-attended programs, our faith is rock solid, right? There's certainly much to be said for the outward expression of our faith. But just as well-painted walls aren't very useful when they're crumbling and falling down, so are well-meaning religious activities often unstable unless they are supported by the strong foundation laid by our religious ancestors.

PRAY. God of our fathers and mothers, I ask that you give me the diligence to build my faith upon a sure foundation. Grant me the patience to be a steady builder and the faith to develop an inward journey that matches my outward one. Amen.

LISTEN. JULY 13 **Jeremiah 23:1-4**

Following Christ

THINK. Many of us have been advised to "be a leader, not a follower," but the fact remains that we're all, in our beliefs and actions, followers. The real question is not, "Will you be a follower?" but rather, "Who will you follow?" Unfortunately, many of us have had poor and disappointing leaders to follow. Whether they were disgraced celebrities, abusive parents, negligent teachers, or just friends who let us down, we have all suffered and found our own lives limited by the weaknesses of those who would direct our paths.

The good news, however, is that God cares about who leads us and won't leave us without good leadership forever. Beyond the stain of steroid allegations, past the fear of hurtful hands, exceeding the vacuum of nurturing attention in our lives, none other than God will send the leaders we need to show us the way to go. And as we follow, we will find our true pasture, where we have always been meant to live.

PRAY. God, I am never so weak as in my willingness to follow weak leaders who would lead me astray. Help me learn to be led more fully by your ever-faithful Spirit and to seek out those leaders who would lead me in paths of righteousness. Lead on, O King Eternal! Amen.

LISTEN. JULY 14 **Jeremiah 23:5-6**

Kingdom of God, Justice

THINK. I have to admit that it's very difficult to read the news today and not grow deeply cynical toward the people who guide the affairs of our fragile world. Whether it's corrupt regimes in Africa, arms-amassing dictators in North Korea, or duplicitous, partisan politicians in the US, our hearts cry out for leaders who would "deal wisely" and "execute justice and righteousness in the land." But where are they to be found?

This question is not a new one, and as the message of Jeremiah testifies, it is a question that troubled the Israelites just as much as it troubles us today. But Jeremiah's message was not one of apathy or cynicism. Rather, the Israelites were instructed to place their hope in God's commitment to justice and righteousness. As one hopeful follower of Christ has put it, we are to "believe in spite of the evidence, and then watch the evidence change!" In faith and in hope, we await the day when God's King will rule in justice, and we will celebrate and trample upon the trail of injustices that are left behind us.

PRAY. Faithful God, I await the time when your justice and righteousness will be the ever-present air I breathe. May you hasten the day when your righteous King establishes the peace of the world. Amen.

GO.

How good to be a family!
God has made a church of you and me.
We're not alone; we've found a home . . .
The family of God.

Paul Duke and D.E. Adams[8]

The Lord Forgives

Joann Lee

PAUSE.

It doesn't take much to convince us of our own shortcomings. Most of us, much of the time, are fully aware that we fall short of God's ideal. But the Lord forgives us. Set aside your failures for a time, and hear the offer of God's grace.

LISTEN. JULY 15 **Psalm 51:1-8**

Unconditional Love

THINK. Sometimes, our hearts are heavy. And like the psalmist, we sigh and ask for God to hear our prayers. In these times, we often look to God as our Comforter.

We find comfort in the familiar names of God, such as "Lord" and "King." We find comfort in remembering that God is good and detests evil. We find comfort in hearing that evil cannot abide with God. We find comfort in knowing that God lifts up the humble. We find comfort in believing God hears our voices.

But perhaps where we find the most comfort is in understanding that the steadfast love of God is abundant. God's love for us never ends; it is steadfast, constant, and unchanging. God's love for us is more than we need; it is abundant, overflowing, and plentiful. No matter what we do, we cannot be separated from this great love. Thanks be to God!

PRAY. Holy God, sometimes I forget how much I am loved. Thank you for loving me unconditionally. Help me to fully experience the abundance and power of your love in my life today, and help me to share your love with others. Amen.

LISTEN. JULY 16 **Luke 7:36-39**

Inclusion, Forgiveness

THINK. Jesus the Messiah had a wide circle of friends and acquaintances. Many people were drawn to him, from the strictest religious leader to the prostitute. In today's story, a Pharisee invited Jesus to his home for a meal, and somehow a woman whom everyone knew to be a sinner began to anoint and worship Jesus. We are not told how she got into the house or how she knew where Jesus would be. We are only told of her bold and grand gesture of devotion and the responses it provoked.

In our lives we act as both the Pharisee and the woman, moving between brokenness and worship before Jesus to rejection and scorn of those whom Jesus calls "friend." We are sometimes surprised at the great diversity of people who are included in the vast family of God, but we are also, at times, surprised that we too are included in this family.

When we come to God honestly and openly, bringing all of who we are, the piety and the sin, we find forgiveness and reconciliation.

PRAY. Loving God, thank you for including me in your great circle of friends. I admit that sometimes I ignore and exclude others whom you also call friend. I ask for your forgiveness with the reassurance that you are a God whose forgiveness never runs dry. Amen.

LISTEN. JULY 17 **Luke 7:40-47**

Forgiveness, Loving Others

THINK. Through this parable, Jesus revealed to us the proper response to forgiveness. Assurance of forgiveness should not encourage us to act any way we please, knowing whatever we do will be forgiven. We are not to abuse this wonderful gift and continue to behave in ways that are displeasing to God.

Rather, Jesus said the appropriate response to the forgiveness we find in Christ is to "show great love." Our love is first shown to the one who forgives us. The woman in the story lavished Jesus with her tears, kisses, and oil, unafraid and unashamed to show her love and devotion to Christ.

But we are also to show our love to one another. The Gospel of Matthew tells us that whatever we do to the "least of these" who are members of Jesus' family we have done to him (Matt. 25:40). Therefore, when we love and care for one another, it is simply another way of expressing our love to God. Let us thank God for forgiving us, and let us respond in love.

PRAY. Forgiving God, please give me the courage to forgive others as an expression of my love for you today. May I lavish your love and forgiveness on those least expecting and least deserving of my forgiveness. Amen.

LISTEN. JULY 18 **Luke 7:48-8:3**

Assurance of God

THINK. There is no record of who the woman in this story is. Earlier this week, we saw that she approached Jesus, and weeping, bathed his feet with her tears and her precious oil, but she never said anything to him or the others in the room with them. Yet Jesus said to her, "Your sins are forgiven." The woman did not ask Jesus for forgiveness, and yet somehow the Messiah knew exactly what she needed in order to go in peace. In the same way, God knows us intimately well. Even before we say or ask anything, God knows what we need and the desire deep within our hearts. God grants us peace and understands what we need to attain that peace. Sometimes, like the woman in the story, what we need is forgiveness. Sometimes what we need, however, takes different forms. Whatever we need to go in peace today, God can provide.

PRAY. Loving God, you knew me even as I was being formed in my mother's womb. You know my needs and my desires just as you knew what the woman in the story needed. Grant me peace today. Amen.

LISTEN. JULY 19 **Galatians 2:15-16**

Faith, Actions

THINK. The end of this passage says, "No one will be justified by the works of the law." The truth of the matter is no one can be justified by simply obeying the law alone because it is impossible to fully obey all of the law, all the time. No matter how much we may try, we will always fall short.

For example, the law commands that we should not covet or be jealous of what our friends and neighbors have, but we have all envied others. Perhaps we covet other people's clothes, or grades, or their talents. Perhaps we see our friends at church who have gifts we wish we could share with others, such as singing or playing an instrument. No matter what sins we struggle with, we should remember—no one is justified by the works of the law because we cannot live up to them.

The good news is we are justified to God by our faith in Christ, not by our works. In fact, our hearts, rather than our perfection, is what God requires of us. Thanks be to God whose forgiveness and mercy are unending.

PRAY. Merciful God, I try and try to live a life that is pleasing to you, a life that honors your creation and your goodness. But no matter how hard I try, I often fail. I thank you that I am not justified by my works of the law or my perfect obedience to it, but by faith in Jesus the Christ. Help me as I walk this journey of faith. Amen.

LISTEN. JULY 20 **Galatians 2:17-21**

Call of God

THINK. Our faith changes our lives. When we live for God, we allow God to transform and use us. That is what "living by faith" means.

And through the Holy Spirit, Christ lives in us and in others. Teresa of Avila said, "Christ has no body on earth but ours, no hands but ours, no feet but ours. Ours are the eyes through which the compassion of Christ looks out upon the world; ours are the feet with which he goes about doing good; ours are the hands with which he blesses his people." In other words, we are vessels for God's activity in this world.

Different people are called to live for God in different ways. Perhaps for you, it's by befriending those whom others ignore and leave out. Perhaps it's by making conscious decisions to be good stewards of God's creation. Perhaps it's by listening to someone who needs a friend's attentive ear. How can you live for God in your life this week?

PRAY. God of grace, thank you for drawing me to you and granting me the faith that transforms my life, the faith that justifies me to you. Help me to be like Christ to others, loving, including, and honoring them. Help me to be used as a vessel for your activity in this world. Amen.

LISTEN. JULY 21 **Psalm 32:1-7, 11**

Prayer, Trust

THINK. Hear the good news: we are the blessed and happy ones, for our sins are forgiven and our faults are covered!

While we are saved once and for all by Jesus' sacrifice, we are also called to confess our sins before God throughout our lives. We do not acknowledge our sins before God to satisfy God's need for confession or to somehow appease God's anger. Rather, we confess to God in order to relieve our own burden of sin and guilt.

Even before the words leave our mouths, God already knows all the things we want to say in prayer—our thanksgivings, our wants, even our confessions. However, like the psalmist, when we remain silent and try to hide our guilt before God, we often find it difficult to receive forgiveness and mercy. Being completely honest with God and acknowledging that every part of us is already known to God helps us to be reconciled to our Creator and to accept God's full and undying love for us.

Let's stop hiding from God and allow God to be our hiding place.

PRAY. God, I admit I have much to confess and I often hide myself from you. Thank you for never hiding from me and for drawing me closer to you every time I reach out for you. Thank you for promising me the everlasting gift of your forgiveness. Amen.

GO.

Have mercy on me, O God, according to your steadfast love; according to your abundant mercy blot out my transgressions.

Create in me a clean heart, O God, and put a new and right spirit within me.

Psalm 51:1, 10

The Healing Eternal Priest

Ruth Perkins Lee

PAUSE.

The same Christ who was present at the beginning, who was present also in Jesus, is with us still today, and will remain through all of eternity.

In Jesus, God was among us, serving us as a priest serves a congregation. This same one is present to you as you take time for devotion today.

LISTEN. JULY 22 **Psalm 34:1-8**

Sharing Christ

THINK. Ever had a good story to tell? I mean a really good story? How excited were you? Whom did you tell? David wrote this psalm when he had a good story to tell. He asked someone to share this really good story, "O magnify the Lord with me, and let us exalt his name together." The rest is this wonderful story about God. In it, we hear David's version of events as he sought God and God answered.

We are still the same as David, calling out to God in times of need. God is still the same today, answering our cries. Our faith is much like David's. Our lives are much like this psalm. God is eternal. Like David, when we encounter God, we can't help but tell others. We seek God; God answers us. Now it's time for us to share this really great story. What is your great story about God? Whom do you need to tell?

PRAY. God, I seek you. I wait for your reply. Give me the courage to tell my story of faith in you. Amen.

LISTEN. JULY 23 **Hebrews 7:15-19**

Relationship with God, Journey with God

THINK. We have to go all the way back to Genesis to find Melchizedek. There we discover that Melchizedek was recognized as a priest even though he was not from the house of Levi. Priests in the Bible, by tradition, came from the house of Levi. Jesus, like Melchizedek, did not come from the house of Levi, but from the house of Judah. Nonetheless, Jesus serves as priest for us, not because he was born into the right family, but because of the life he lived.

Through the life of Christ, we as Christians understand who God is and how to be in relationship with God. The life and teachings of Jesus give us hope and model for us how God loves us. It is no longer about being from the right family, either church family or family of origin. Instead it is about living a life that emulates the life of Christ.

PRAY. O God, Christ taught that you love us no matter what. Help me to know that and do the same for others. Amen.

LISTEN. JULY 24 **Hebrews 7:23-25**

Assurance of God, Thankfulness

THINK. One of my favorite things to do is to hear about people's childhoods and how different they were from my own. The world is changing so fast that each generation's childhood is very different. For example, when I was in first grade, I was in the first computer class in the whole state of Georgia. Now every classroom in my daughter's school has one. I remember when the first smart phone commercials came on TV; it took me over a year to see one and understand how they worked! Now my child can work mine with no trouble.

When I think about all of the changes that happen in the world over time, it's hard for me to comprehend the word eternal. But that is what Jesus is. Jesus does not need to be upgraded or replaced with a newer model every few years. The presence of Christ offers comfort in its consistency and constancy. The text today tells us that Jesus is here "for all time," helping us to know God, wanting to be in relationship with us, pointing us to God, and guiding us through life. In a world that is always changing, what comfort to know that Jesus is the same, now and forever!

PRAY. O God, in the world of change, I rest in your unchanging presence and guidance. Amen.

LISTEN. JULY 25 **Hebrews 7:26-28**
Example of Christ

THINK. Jesus changes things. Before him, the high priests offered sacrifices daily, partly on behalf of others and partly because of their own sins. It was the best way they knew to be in relationship with God. Jesus changed that. Because of him, daily sacrifices are no longer needed. Before Jesus lived among us, the best living examples of how to live for God were people like you and me. Jesus changed that. In him, we see the ultimate example of living in a relationship with God.

I find it hard at times to know how to treat other people or make a good choice when both options seem OK. Sometimes I'm not sure how to go to God. Jesus changes that. Because of the record we have of his life, I find answers in how to treat others and in making good choices. I see examples of how to talk and listen to God. Thanks to the eternal priest and the changes he made and continues to make, I know how to live my life for God.

PRAY. O God, thank you for Jesus. Thank you for the example he set as he lived his life on earth. Thank you for the changes for the better. Thank you for reaching out to me so that I, in turn, reach out to you. Amen.

LISTEN. JULY 26 **Mark 10:46-48**

Courage

THINK. We have a four-month-old baby. She is a great baby. She never fusses—unless she's hungry. Then she cries so hard and loud that it scares everybody. No matter what you do, she will not stop crying until you give her a bottle.

Bartimaeus reminds me of our baby. He wanted Jesus to have mercy on him. No matter what those around him said, he did not stop calling out. The one who healed was walking nearby. Bartimaeus knew what he wanted. He called out, undeterred by the hushing of others. It takes a lot of courage and a lot of want to call out the way Bartimaeus did.

Sometimes we are scared to ask. Sometimes we don't know what to ask or how to ask. Sometimes we are intimidated by those around us. Take courage from the example of blind Bartimaeus, who called out in spite of all those things. The one who heals is always nearby. What is it that you ask for? What holds you back from calling out?

PRAY. God, give me the clarity to know what I want, the boldness to call out to you, and the courage to do it when others try to stop me. Amen.

LISTEN. JULY 27 **Mark 10:49-52**

Healing, Presence of God

THINK. The story after this one is the story of the triumphal entry into Jerusalem. We celebrate it as Palm Sunday. That means this happened about a week before Jesus' death. Jesus walked, surrounded by his disciples and a large crowd. Blind Bartimaeus called out, "Jesus, Son of David, have mercy on me," and Jesus stood still. A week to go, and Jesus stood still.

As a child I often sang and did the motions to "My God is so big, so strong and so mighty, there's nothing my God cannot do . . ." As an adult, I still take comfort in the bigness of God. However, I take greater comfort in the "smallness" of God that allows God to hear my voice among the many and answer me.

With just a week left, time was of the essence. And Christ, surrounded by crowds, heard the prayers of one and responded. Once again, Jesus showed us that the healing of one is as important as the gathering of the many. In the midst of the multitude, the God who heals hears your voice and responds.

PRAY. Healing God who is big enough to handle anything, help me to know that you are also small enough to hear my voice. Amen.

LISTEN. JULY 28 **Psalm 34:19-22**

Doubts, Questions

THINK. Why do bad things happen to good people? There are many answers to this question; none of them satisfy me. To know that bad things happen to good people breaks my heart. And yet I feel a small measure of comfort when I hear these words of David's and know that when bad things happen to me, it does not mean I am a bad person.

Even more comforting to know is the healing, eternal presence of God. To be comforted by the one who created me and knows me gives me hope and courage to face the days ahead. God provides refuge for us, not so that we will be protected from life, but so that we will live our lives to the fullest. Live fully as the person God has called you to be, knowing that God walks with you all the way.

PRAY. For strength to live with the knowledge of the refuge you provide, I give you thanks, O God. Help me to remember that you are walking alongside me. Amen.

GO.

Go now as the called of God,
called also to follow Jesus' example,
serving one another as priests.
Caring, loving, walking in the way of companionship,
pointing the way to the eternal God.

Good Instruction

Adrian McMullen

PAUSE.

Every experience, good or bad, brings with it the opportunity to teach us something. The question is whether or not we are paying attention. As you pause to read, pray, and reflect today, consider what you might learn from the living of this day. Listen particularly for God's instruction, meant especially for you.

LISTEN. JULY 29 **Lamentations 3:19-24**

Presence of God, Hurting

THINK. The musical group REM says it very clearly, "Everybody Hurts." In that song they remind us that everybody has struggles, painful moments, and bad memories that are impossible to erase. But the best part of the song is when they sing, "Hold on, hold on, hold on. No, no, no, you're not alone." It's sad and comforting at the same time.

It's true. Everybody hurts, but does everybody learn from it? This might sound weird, but if we don't learn from our hurts, we are wasting opportunities. If we decide not to wallow in self-pity when something goes wrong, and instead look at what we can learn from the situation, we gain knowledge and understanding from our hardships. When we fail a test, when we get cut from the team, or when a friendship goes bad, there is always something to learn.

Even more than that, God can use painful times to open our eyes and minds to the presence of God's Spirit. We may be hurting, but we are not alone.

PRAY. Gracious God, when I have problems, help me to not focus on them; instead help me to focus on you. Remind me that I'm never alone. Amen.

LISTEN. **JULY 30** **Luke 17:5-6**

Faith

THINK. In the movie *The Empire Strikes Back*, Luke Skywalker spends time studying with the Jedi master, Yoda. When Yoda tells Luke to raise his fighter out of the slimy bog he crashed it into, Luke responds with, "I'll try." The wise old master states, "There is no try. Do . . . or do not." That he is telling Luke to do the seemingly impossible task of raising his ship means Yoda knows that Luke already knows how to use the Force.

When the disciples asked Jesus to increase their faith, Jesus basically told them that they didn't need more faith; they needed to use the faith they already had. Jesus said that, even with the most miniscule amount of faith, we can accomplish amazing things.

Taking what we already know along with the faith that we already have and putting it into action can help our faith grow. Don't discount the instruction you have already received. We can't become discouraged. Luke needed Yoda's help to get his fighter out of the bog. In the same way, we have the Spirit who will help us accomplish great things for God!

PRAY. Loving Lord God, I pray that I will use my faith whenever I can, knowing that it is always enough. And when it's not, you will help me. Amen.

LISTEN. JULY 31 **Luke 17:7-10**

Service

THINK. When I was a kid my brother and I had a lawn mowing business. It drove us crazy when my dad would volunteer us to mow someone's lawn—for free! He would say, "Margie's husband is in the hospital, so I told her you boys would cut the grass. She has enough to worry about, so don't go to the door when you're done." This meant, "Don't ask for money."

So often our attitude toward service is one of supply and demand. We supply the service and then demand something in return. That's not service; that's business. If every deed we did had an equal reward, there would be no place for grace. Sometimes we need to do things and not expect anything in return.

If we are focused on a reward, or the lack of one, we can miss the fact that the job is the reward. My brother and I learned that some of the best rewards come in the satisfaction of knowing that you did a good job.

PRAY. Gracious God, even though it's hard, I pray that I will do things without expecting anything in return. I will do your will and know that it is its own reward. Amen.

AUGUST

LISTEN. AUGUST 1 **2 Timothy 1:1-7**

Faith, Relationship with God

THINK. Is there a teacher or friend or relative who shapes you, who helps you discover truths about yourself and about life and about faith? Do you have role models? Do you have faith models?

Growing up in a family of faith and going to a loving church is something I used to take for granted. Now I understand that my faith might not be what it is if it weren't for the grace of God, the faithfulness of my parents, and the wonderful people of my home church.

But my faith is my own now, not my parents' or my church's. Faith is not merely inherited without effort on our part. Faith is learned and experienced. It is a constant process that we need to work at, not just now, but throughout our lives and through the generations. It's great to have role models and even people of faith that you look up to. But, it's also important to make your faith just that—yours.

PRAY. God, thank you for the people you have put in my life to teach me the faith. Help me to be a worthy model of the faith so that others may see you through me. Amen.

LISTEN. AUGUST 2 **2 Timothy 1:8-11**

Following Christ, Child of God

THINK. On my first day of high school, I was walking down the hall when I ran into my sister and some of her friends. She was a senior, so when I said hi to a group of seniors, that was cool. It was not cool, however, when my sister responded, "Hi, Pee Wee!" This is a nickname that started when I was a toddler and has lasted to this day. She meant well.

Our families love us, but they can also cause us pain. Our friends can be wonderful support, but they aren't always on our side. We can be good people, but we don't always make the best decisions for ourselves. We have to take the good with the bad.

Following Christ is an amazing journey, but we will encounter struggles along the way. Paul was in prison because of the faith, and he still managed to celebrate it! The blessing is that the joy of faith far, far outweighs the sorrow of the world. Any obstacles to faith that the world puts in our way can be overcome by the grace of God through Jesus Christ.

PRAY. Almighty God, help me to put behind me the pain and hurt others have caused in my life. I will look for the joy and celebrate that fact that I am yours! Amen.

LISTEN. AUGUST 3 **2 Timothy 1:12-14**

Journey with God

THINK. One of the problems with secrets is that if you tell someone to keep a secret, they think it won't hurt anyone to just tell one person, as long as that person keeps it a secret. The other problem with secrets is that they are usually told with little alterations. So it ends up like that game of telephone. One by one, people get the message wrong.

In the Scripture for today, Paul said to Timothy that what he had received he should repeat over and over (hold to the standard). Seems like the opposite of a secret to me. Paul also said to take care of what he had received (guard the good treasure). This is also the opposite of what happens to secrets. So, what's the opposite of a secret? An announcement? Common knowledge? News? Good news?

The good news that we have been taught is not a secret and is not to be kept to ourselves. And we are to get it right. We have a responsibility to the message and the messenger, and we need to be faithful to both.

PRAY. Gracious God, thank you for letting me in on the good news. Help me be faithful to you, the message, and to those who have given it to me to share. Amen.

LISTEN. AUGUST 4 **Lamentations 3:25-26**

Waiting, Trust

THINK. I am the youngest in my family, and my older siblings always got to do things before I did. I didn't like it. I wanted to learn the same things they did at the same time they did. When they learned to tie their shoes, I wanted to tie my shoes. When they learned how to tell time, I wanted to tell time. The problem was that my brain and my body just couldn't handle all the things that my older siblings were doing. This usually led to a great deal of frustration and tears on my part.

Sometimes we just have to wait. Just because we want to do something doesn't mean we can or should. There's a reason why things happen in a certain way, even if we can't understand why we have to wait. In waiting we learn things. Then maybe we are ready to hear, accept, learn, use, whatever. We will then receive after waiting—or not receive in spite of waiting. Even during the waiting, we receive things such as patience and hope. Things happen in God's time, not ours.

PRAY. Loving Lord God, waiting is so hard. Please grant me patience and understanding to know that things don't happen when I want them to. I will trust you to do things when the time is right. Amen.

GO.

Go now to learn the lessons of the day.
Go with your eyes and your ears open
to see and hear what God has to teach you.
Go knowing that the Teacher is with you
to guide and instruct you in every moment.
Go, willing to learn.

The Future: 101

Phillip Fackler

PAUSE.

God has given us a sense of time, a sense of the past, present, and future. Despite living only in the present, it is the future that captures most of our attention. God calls us to meet the future with hope and faith by living fully in the present.

Take a moment to turn your eyes from the future toward seeing God in the here and now.

LISTEN. AUGUST 5 **Matthew 28:16-20**

Courage, Assurance of God

THINK. Sometimes we get anxious about the future because the tasks seem beyond our ability. How will we ever have the time to finish papers and projects, study for exams, or finish chores around the house? When confronted with a difficult task or deadline, we're afraid to fail or look silly in front of friends and family.

Jesus told the disciples to do something beyond their ability. As they stood there shocked, some doubting it was really him, Jesus told them to leave home and proclaim his message to all people everywhere. They didn't have language training or particular skills for public speaking, just Jesus' promise to be with them always. Jesus makes us the same promise when difficult tasks confront us. He promises to be with us, giving us strength to face fears and anxieties with confidence, putting other people in our paths to help when we struggle.

PRAY. O God, I know that you are with me always, even though it is easy to forget when I feel fear and anxiety. Give me courage to face my fears with confidence. Give me the faith to fail boldly or succeed gracefully in the knowledge that your presence will sustain me. Amen.

LISTEN. **AUGUST 6** **Ecclesiastes 3:1-8**

Waiting, Trust

THINK. I'm nearly 30 now, but people still ask me one way or another what I want to be when I grow up. I think it has to do with still being in school. When we're in school, we get asked to think about our futures a lot. Will you go to college or find a job after high school? If you choose college, where do you want to go? What will you study? What job do you want to do? These questions can create uncertainty or leave us feeling inadequate when we don't have answers but our friends seem to have it all figured out.

Today's text encourages us to look at the bigger picture and see that there is more to life than what we want to be when we grow up. There is a season for everything, including uncertainty and waiting. It is often in the times of attentive waiting that we find ourselves and the answers we seek. God asks us to trust that there will be a time for all these things; perhaps now, perhaps in the future.

PRAY. God, all times and seasons are in your hands. Give me trust to wait attentively while in seasons of uncertainty. Help me to discern the best course when I must make a decision. Amen.

LISTEN. AUGUST 7 **Romans 8:35-39**

Presence of God, Questions

THINK. We face separation every day, one of the many things that creates anxiety. As we start a new school year, many of us are separated from friends and family, whether we now go to different schools or have left home to start college or a job. We part from our loved ones for hours, or even days and months at a time. We wonder when we will see them again, and how things will be different then. The new things the future holds can be hard to face because it seems like we face them alone, separated from those who support and care for us.

Today's Scripture reminds us that absolutely nothing can separate us from the love of God in Christ; nothing in the present moment and certainly nothing the future might bring. Separation will never be final because the love of God binds all people and things together, bridging the distance even when we are apart.

PRAY. Ever-present God, thank you for loving me through everything, through my mistakes and missteps as well as my successes. Help me to face change and separation in the security of your love. Amen.

LISTEN. AUGUST 8 **Romans 8:18-25**

Hope

THINK. Have you ever worked hard to achieve a goal? One summer as a kid I collected aluminum cans in order to buy a bicycle. I already had a bike but wanted one that wasn't a hand-me-down. I hated most of it: the smell of warm soda from cans that weren't empty, the time spent crushing them so I could fit more in my parents' car. The hope of a bicycle at the end of all that work kept me going.

Sometimes we struggle through tough times and worry without knowing what our goal or prize is. God's promises of life and community with God are the hope that keeps us going. We experience the fruits of this community with God here and now in the love shared with family and friends and in the joy we find at different times in life. With little nudges, the Spirit reminds us that with God there is always hope, always a future that will be better than anything we could hope for, even a new bicycle.

PRAY. Loving God, I sometimes have trouble finding hope for the future. Continually remind me of your love and care, and send your Spirit to comfort me when all seems dark, for my true hope is always and only in you. Amen.

LISTEN. AUGUST 9 **1 Timothy 6:17-19**

Generosity, Thankful

THINK. Have you ever said to yourself, "If I could just have that car (or that stereo or those new clothes), I would be happy"? It's surprisingly easy to be unhappy when we see all the things we don't have and imagine that everyone else is much happier having them. TV commercials and magazine ads always show how much happier some product makes people. The strange thing is that the more we give way to these ideas, the less happy we become. Happiness is always delayed until we have enough stuff.

In today's Scripture, the author suggests that present and future joy have less to do with getting stuff and keeping wealth than with finding joy in generosity, a willingness to share what we have. When we look at what we don't have, we are always unhappy with what we do have. But when we look to share and rightly use what we have, we enjoy the present and build the foundation for a joyful future.

PRAY. Merciful God, teach me to be grateful for the things I have rather than always being concerned with what I lack, so that I may fully enjoy the gifts you have given me this day. Amen.

LISTEN. **AUGUST 10** **Matthew 6:25-33**

Doubts, Comfort

THINK. We spend a lot of time worrying about the future. Most of us probably don't worry too much about where our next meal will come from or how we will find clothes to wear, though these are real concerns for millions of people. Nevertheless, we worry about school, what's coming next in our lives, the big math test, or the countless other things that distract and worry us through the course of a day.

Jesus tells us to stop. Stop worrying. It's not doing you any good. Jesus reminds us that God provides for the needs of everything, even the birds and the flowers, so we too will have what we need. That doesn't mean we will have everything we want or that the math test will go exactly as we hope, but that we can face the future confidently because we will have what we need. As Jesus tells us, strive for the kingdom of God and the rest will take care of itself.

PRAY. Gracious God, you give me what I need before I even ask. Teach me to spend less time worrying about the future and more time working for your kingdom so that all people may have what they need. Amen.

LISTEN. AUGUST 11 **Revelation 21:1-5a**

Kingdom of God, New Beginnings

THINK. There are a lot of voices in our society telling us to worry about the end of the world. Movies and street preachers warn us that the end is near; many people tell us the problems we face are signs of something worse to come. They tell us that war, famine, and disease will grow to such proportions that nothing else will remain. Many of these people point to Revelation as their guidebook, but even Revelation tells us that such things are not the end. War and famine do not have the final word. God does. God promises to put an end to all the things that cause suffering and pain; God promises to make all things new.

Rather than worry about the end of the world, perhaps we should concern ourselves with working for the new world, working with God to build God's home here on earth where death and pain and crying will be no more.

PRAY. Eternal God, my beginning and my end are in your hands as are the beginnings and endings of all your creation. Help me to work for justice and peace now rather than fretting over those things that are beyond my control. Amen.

GO.

Give your entire attention to what God is doing right now, and don't get worked up about what may or may not happen tomorrow. God will help you deal with whatever hard things come up when the time comes.

Matthew 6:34 (The Message)

Pep Rally

Andrew Kellner

PAUSE.

Celebrating can be a big part of going back to school. With back to school celebrations and pep rallies for football, soccer, and other sports, there can be a lot of excitement around achievements and what a team or individual can do or has done.

Every individual is meant to be celebrated just because they were created by God. Celebrating who you are can be hard, especially when others don't see you for who you truly are.

Think about your life and what things you would celebrate. Try not to focus on things you have done. Celebrate your life just because it is a gift from God.

LISTEN. AUGUST 12 **John 8:48-56**

Image of God

THINK. Have you had someone assume something about you and be wrong? Or have you ever had someone misunderstand you and in turn think badly of you? This can happen to anyone and happens to most of us. It is one of the ways we can begin to tell ourselves that we are not as good as we really are.

Even Jesus had people who made incorrect assumptions about him and took what he said the wrong way. They judged him harshly because they only saw what they preferred to see.

God wants us not to see ourselves through the eyes of others, though. God wants us to see ourselves through God's eyes, to see the good things God has placed within each one of us. God also desires us to see other people like this as well, and celebrate the good within them, too.

PRAY. God, help me to see myself and others through your eyes. Help me to see the good you have created in all of humanity. Amen.

LISTEN. AUGUST 13 **Mark 14:61b-65**

Confidence in God, Courage

THINK. Trying to celebrate your life can be hard when there are people who are trying to bring you down. You might not have people trying to put you to death like Jesus did, but we all encounter people who do not seem to want to see us succeed. In today's passage, Jesus gave us an example, which is not that far out there for us to do. He told the truth. He did not change the story of his life to try to please the people who were trying to bring him down. Jesus spoke the truth about who he was and about his life.

If we are going to do the same thing when we are faced with adversity, we will need to make sure that we know the stories of our lives. Where is your life going? What is your story? Be prepared to share it.

PRAY. God, help me to know my story. Give me the courage to share it, even when it is hard. Amen.

LISTEN. AUGUST 14 **Mark 14:66-71**

Friendship

THINK. Friendship is a great thing, blessed by God. But we do not often think about that fact. We think about what we want to share with our friends or do with them. We focus on what we can give and get from the relationship. And sometimes when a better deal comes along, we take it.

Peter did this. He needed a better deal because his friend was going to be killed, and I guess he did not want to be brought down with him. So he pretended that he did not know him, and by doing so he joined the crowd.

If we forget to celebrate the gift that our friendships are, we can trade them off with little thought. Celebrating our friendships and God's blessings in them reminds us of their importance in our lives, and that it is not just about what we give or get.

PRAY. Thank you for my friends and for making me to be in relationships. Amen.

LISTEN. **AUGUST 15** **Mark 15:1-5**

Actions, Sharing Christ

THINK. Have you ever had to explain your actions? To explain why you did something? It can be very hard to be completely honest, first of all with yourself and second with the person you are trying to explain to. I find that I always want to paint myself in the best light, and therefore take minor liberties with the details.

Jesus, though, let his life speak for itself. He did not argue or try to defend against the attacks of others. Jesus let his actions speak for themselves.

Our lives are like this; people see our actions and words and judge us based on their observations. It can be helpful for us, then, to think about our actions each day, trying to be as honest as possible about them. This way we, too, will have an idea about what our life is speaking to the world.

PRAY. Help me to see my life honestly and let it speak goodness to the world. Amen.

LISTEN. AUGUST 16 **Mark 15:16-21**

Image of God, Putting God First

THINK. Have you ever had someone treat you really nicely, but in doing so they actually made fun of you? It is the scene of many a high school movie. Usually the popular kids begin to befriend someone, only to hurt or make fun of them.

But it is also as close as your school's hallway. It can seem fun, to have a laugh at someone else's expense. It is a strange way to celebrate your life, and yet we all sometimes celebrate ourselves at the expense of others.

The reality, though, is that no one is truly being celebrated. When we try to show how much better we are than they are, or by making fun of them, we only celebrate how hurtful we can be. It is a celebration based on externals, and we are not seeing ourselves or others through God's eyes.

PRAY. Give me your eyes to see myself and others. Help me not to celebrate myself over others. Amen.

LISTEN. AUGUST 17 **Mark 15:25-32**

New Life, Hope

THINK. Death is not an occasion where we look for celebration. We think about it as a time of sadness, and it is. But death is also a place of beginnings. While the individual might be gone, we think about how they lived their life and what they taught us. These seeds, which have been dormant in our lives, begin to grow. Life is happening.

Death is not just something that ends life. We each experience a little bit of death when we hurt or are in pain either physically or emotionally. We experience something that is the opposite of life; we experience death.

What matters at these death-like moments is the life that comes out of them. We might not feel life during them, but we are people of faith, people of hope. So we celebrate these moments for the life that they might bring in our lives.

PRAY. Help me to celebrate even the deaths in my own life. Show me the way to new life. Amen.

LISTEN. AUGUST 18 **Mark 15:33-39**

Following Christ, Example of Christ

THINK. We often want people to see us and to think about us in a particular way. We may even spend a lot of time working on this appearance. We will buy a certain type of clothes, and participate in activities that make us look good.

But what if our lives spoke loudly enough? What if the ordinary things we did every day and the way we treated others were all people needed to know what we are all about? Jesus' life was very much like that. He did not need to wear a t-shirt that said, "I'm the Messiah." The way he lived and even how he died let people know who he was. He was authentic.

We are invited to live authentic lives as well, celebrating who we are and not what we do or do not do.

PRAY. Help me to be authentic and see others for who they are. Let my life speak. Amen.

GO.

Celebrate the life that God has given to you.
Celebrate the potential God has placed within you.
Celebrate what God is doing through you.
Celebrate all people for the gift their lives are.

Accepting God's Call

Grier Booker Richards

PAUSE.

Accepting God's call requires courage to follow. It's normal to feel fear and self-doubt, but ultimately God knows we can handle the calling that God places on our hearts.

Are you listening for God's call? Prepare yourself today to hear and respond!

LISTEN. AUGUST 19 **Exodus 3:4–5**
Putting God First

THINK. "What made him Moses," writer and theologian Barbara Brown Taylor once wrote, "was his willingness to turn aside." When I think about this familiar story, I sometimes wonder, what if Moses had received a text message right before he came upon that lit-up bush? Would he have looked up? Or what if Moses had been running late for an appointment? Would he have kept going and missed the message that would change his life?

Our world tells us that if we want to be successful then stay the course, put your blinders on, and don't look back. Update your status along the way, but don't stop until you reach your destination. Yet God's call often presents itself most clearly when we make the choice to go off the beaten path, to try something new, to let our minds and hearts wander, to observe stillness in the midst of everyday chaos. Extraordinary things happen when people stop to pay attention to God's creative and mysterious presence.

PRAY. Help me, Lord, to turn aside in the midst of my everyday chaos and turn instead toward you. Amen.

LISTEN. **AUGUST 20** **Exodus 3:6**

Presence of God, Actions, Service

THINK. I remember exactly how I felt the moment I stepped foot in Port au Prince, Haiti, for the first time. I just about had a panic attack. The sight of swollen bellies and fly-ridden hair, tattered clothes, and lifeless eyes was enough to send me running straight for the comforts of home—until, of course, I realized that our living Lord himself was standing right there, summoning my faith to be put into action. "Feed me. Clothe me. Get to know me. Love me."

Sometimes meeting God face-to-face can feel downright terrifying. It certainly did for Moses! But the God we worship is a patient and wildly creative God who knows us far better than we know ourselves. So when you are anxious or afraid, when God's call has taken you so far out of your comfort zone that you think you might have a panic attack, remember Moses. And then remember the words of the one who knows you best: "Fear not, for I am with you."

PRAY. Merciful God, stir my heart and hands to action, and when I am afraid, be patient with me and call to my mind your comfort and promise: Fear not, for I am with you. Amen.

LISTEN. AUGUST 21 **Exodus 3:9–10**
Call of God

THINK. We tend to think that when God calls women and men like Mary and Moses, Saul and Peter, and you and me, our response to God somehow operates inside a vacuum where the rest of life simply stands still, waiting for us to make up our minds. But think about the Israelites, who had been suffering at the hands of the Egyptians for generations. Wasn't the call of Moses just as much about the Israelites' future as God's chosen people as it was about Moses' call to leadership?

As you discern your call, thinking and praying about where you'll go next or what you want to do later in life, remember that you are not in this alone; God is using you and working through you to accomplish great and miraculous things! Remember that your yes to God may just be the yes that many have been dreaming about and waiting for, for generations.

PRAY. Just as you used Moses to deliver your oppressed people, use me, O God, that I might be a blessing to others. Amen.

LISTEN. AUGUST 22 **Exodus 3:11–12**

Promise, Hope

THINK. How many times have you heard the phrase, "God will never give you any more than you can handle"? Every time I hear these words, I wince a little. Anyone who has ever tasted suffering, anyone who has lost a parent, sibling, or close friend; has received a horrifying medical diagnosis; has been bullied or abused, any of these people will tell you they have experienced moments, days, weeks, or years when they felt they were carrying far more than they could possibly handle. And don't you imagine that Moses must have felt that way when God called him to deliver an entire people out of Egypt?

What our good and merciful God promises is not a life free from pain or hardship, but a way to make it through. "I will be with you," God says. "No matter where you go, no matter how bad it is, I will be with you. This is who I Am, and this is the promise I have made to you."

PRAY. Thank you, God, for sharing my load—my sadness, my grief, my struggles, and my pain—when it's far too heavy for me to carry by myself. Thank you for always providing me with a way to make it through the hard times. Amen.

LISTEN. **AUGUST 23** **Isaiah 6:6–8**

Image of God, Call of God

THINK. When I was a young girl, I thought that being a Christian meant I needed to be perfect. Seeking God's forgiveness looked something like, "I'm sorry, God, for not being perfect enough today." It's taken years to re-wire my understanding of God's mercy, goodness, and grace, because there are still many times when I feel so . . . unholy, so imperfect, and like such a disappointment to others.

Perhaps you are experiencing a call to a particular ministry, mission, or outreach project, and you're feeling a bit unprepared, unacceptable, and unclean yourself. "Why me, Lord?" you might be thinking. Remember that God does not choose perfect people, because there simply are none to be found . . . anywhere. Rather, God calls us, as wondrously imperfect as we are, because God knows who we are and who we are becoming. Our job is simply to answer, "Here I am. Send me."

PRAY. Spirit of the living God, fall fresh on me. Convert and consecrate my heart, that I might see myself through your eyes and my future as a part of your greater plan. Amen.

LISTEN. AUGUST 24 **Jonah 1:2–3**

Unconditional Love

THINK. When God said go, what did Jonah do? He took off in the exact opposite direction in a foolish attempt to beat God at God's own game. My prayer is that you have heard clearly that there is simply nowhere you can run where God cannot and will not find you. My prayer is also that you've read and heard the many stories of our faith that witness to this truth over and over again, because this is the centerpiece of what we believe as Christians: We belong to God who loves us.

We have plenty of good news to share, beginning with the fact that the power of God's call, God's love, and God's mercy are relentless! God has and God will continue to move heaven and earth for you, even as you're running for Tarshish, because even when we run, we can never hide from God.

PRAY. Every time I turn and run from you, O God, meet me where I am and guide me to where I belong. Amen.

LISTEN. AUGUST 25 **Luke 5:10–11**

Child of God, Following Christ

THINK. "They left everything and followed . . ." insert any current popular celebrity or trend.

Our media-saturated culture tells you thousands of times every day exactly who and what is worth your time, your attention, your money . . . your everything. But your faith tells you something different.

Following Jesus is no easy task, because all of who you are is called to action: your heart, your mind, your talents, your values, your shortcomings, your reputation, your everything. And everything is all you've got. So give thanks to God for all that you have, for all that you are, and for all that you are becoming! Get ready, because God fully intends to put your everything to work.

PRAY. Loving God, use my everything to glorify you, and mold me into the disciple you need me to be. Amen.

GO.

God's presence and call often show up in unexpected places and at surprising times. We should all be changed by God's presence each time we encounter God. Have you sensed God asking you to do something differently in your life? Have the courage to say, "Yes!"

Be the presence of Christ today as you give back and share your life with others.

Inspiring Others

Dale Tadlock

PAUSE.

Everyone needs to be reminded that God creates us with a calling for each of our lives. God has given everyone gifts that need to be shared with the world.

You can be an agent of change in our world. You can empower anyone, no matter what age, to make a change in their life and to follow God's call.

LISTEN. AUGUST 26 **1 Timothy 4:12**

Boldness, Image of God

THINK. Ever have to sit at the "kids' table" at family get-togethers? I remember sitting at a small table with my cousins and being separated from the adult conversation.

Sadly, many of us feel removed when it comes to the area of faith. We are led to believe only our church leaders and adults are the people who really possess knowledge and gifts. However, what about those who are not pastors or deacons or elders or teachers? Writing to Timothy, a teenager, Paul reminded him that in Christ there is no kids' table. Timothy was told to demand respect, pull up a chair, and join the conversation. Surely Timothy was shocked when Paul told him to be the leader in the congregation!

Don't sit at the kids' table because you do not feel worthy or able to contribute to the cause of Christ! You have something to say. You have a gift to use. You have something to contribute. Welcome to the table!

PRAY. God, thank you for your invitation to the table! Help me to step up and offer all that I have in service to you, even when I feel inadequate or that my opinion does not matter. I offer myself to you. Amen.

LISTEN. AUGUST 27 **1 Timothy 4:13–14**

Talents, Call of God

THINK. I heard of a woman who, when someone gave her a card with money in it, whether for a birthday or other special occasion, always saved it—not in a savings account, either. She tucked the card away with the money in it. She so valued the gift from the other person that she couldn't bear the idea of ever getting rid of the money or the card. As an adult, she had boxes of these cards tucked away with countless dollars hidden in the cards. Even when she was in desperate need for money, these gifts from loved ones went unused.

We often do the same. Many of us have talents and gifts that no one knows about or that we use or share hesitantly. You have been gifted with many talents and abilities. They may be small or large. They may be public gifts or gifts that you use privately. Whatever your gift may be, God can use it. Have you tucked them away? Have you developed your gifts for God to use?

PRAY. Gift-giving God, please accept my smallest and most hidden gifts today. Allow me the chance to share my gifts in a way that shows others your love and acceptance. May others be inspired as I use my gifts to serve you. Amen.

LISTEN. AUGUST 28 **1 Timothy 4:15–16**
Faith to Action

THINK. One of the most well-known advertising slogans belongs to Nike. You know it—JUST DO IT!™ In fact, some have identified this slogan as one of the most successful and recognized slogans ever created. Millions may know and recognize it, but do we really heed the advice?

In today's passage, Timothy was given that same advice. He was reminded that he knew what to do. The instructions from Paul were simple. He told Timothy to "put these things into practice." The advice is simple—just do it! Many of us have listened to more than our share of sermons and Bible studies. Our problem is seldom that we do not know what God wants us to do. We have already heard it. We just need to begin doing what we have learned.

You have probably attended summer camps, retreats, and other church events this summer. What have you learned? How have you heard God? What must you do now? It's simple—just do it!

PRAY. God, you have taught me, challenged me, and helped me to better understand you. Give me the courage to do what I know you want me to do today. Help me to finally live and serve the way you have taught me. Amen.

LISTEN. AUGUST 29 **1 Timothy 5:1–2**

Actions, Sharing Christ

THINK. "Mind your words!" My grandmother's advice reminds me of the importance of taking seriously the words I speak. In a world full of social media status updates, tweets, and text messages, we should take my grandmother's advice each day. It is easy to type an update or send a tweet or text message without thinking about the harm that may be done to someone else or to ourselves!

Today's passage comes right after Paul instructed Timothy to stand and make a difference in his church and in the world. Here, he cautioned him about the words he spoke. Our words do make a difference!

Think about the words you say. Do your words encourage others to seek God? To seek "purity"? To be their best? Do our words demonstrate respect? Kindness? Humility? Our words alone have the ability to inspire others or to greatly discourage them. What will your words accomplish today?

PRAY. Life-giving God, you spoke words and the world came into being. Help me to speak words today that will inspire and bring life to others. May I not speak words that discourage and damage. Speak through me today so that my words may reflect you. Amen.

LISTEN. AUGUST 30 **Psalm 24:3–6**

Priorities, Putting God First

THINK. What kind of life inspires others? What kind of life makes God look good? In essence, that is the question in today's passage. We are told that we should do things for the right reasons, honor truth, and not be deceitful. Those instructions seem simple, yet it is becoming more difficult to live that way. In a world where people only look out for themselves, it is not easy to live an inspirational life. In a world where gossip and unnamed sources are the norm, it is not easy to live a life that changes others' lives. In a world where cheating and "doing whatever you must" are acceptable, it is not easy to stand above the crowd.

What impact does your life have on others? Does your life draw others toward God? Are you willing to live in a different way so that others may experience the love and acceptance of God? Your life can make a difference!

PRAY. God, as others see my life today, help me to be an example. Help me make decisions today that will cause others to notice your presence in my life. Amen.

LISTEN. AUGUST 31 **Philippians 2:22–23**
Service, Priorities

THINK. "Do you know how much he is worth?" I've always found that an interesting question. When we ask it, we usually are asking how much money someone has in the bank. Whether we intend it or not, we are equating money with how important a person might be.

In today's Scripture, Paul spoke of Timothy's great worth. So how was his value measured? Paul said his worth was measured by his service to the cause of Christ and Paul's ministry.

With what do we measure our worth? The size of our offering? The sports or activities to which we give our time? The neighborhood we live in? The friends we hang out with? As you begin a new school year, why not redefine your worth? Seek to make this a year in which the only thing that matters is how you serve your church and the cause of Christ!

PRAY. God, I do so much each day. Please help me to rid myself of those things that keep me from serving you. Help me to find my worth in things that bring your presence to those who need to be encouraged by you. Amen.

SEPTEMBER

LISTEN. SEPTEMBER 1 **Matthew 5:14–16**

Actions, Light

THINK. Have you ever flown in an airplane at night? I am always amazed that even at very high altitudes, a single street lamp or beams of light from a car are visible. In the middle of the darkness even the tiniest lights make a difference.

Today's passage reminds us of that important truth. We may feel we have little to offer. It may seem to us that our light doesn't shine very brightly. Remember, however, that in the middle of the darkness, even the tiniest of lights make a difference. It isn't how bright your light shines or how large your light may be. What is important is that you shine!

In a world of injustice and hate, shine your light of peace and dignity. In a world of rejection and hurt, shine your light of acceptance and healing. Wherever you may live, there are people who need to see your light of hope shining. Don't hide it . . . shine!

PRAY. God of light, thank you for shining your light into me. Help me to reflect you into the lives of others. Give me the courage to confess those things that might not reflect your presence in my life. Shine through me today! Amen.

GO.

It is easy to feel that we are not inspirational to others. However, each day the Holy Spirit empowers us to be agents of inspiration and change in the lives of others. How has the Holy Spirit empowered you to inspire someone else? How can you make a difference in the world today?

You have the gifts, the ability, and the Spirit of the living God to inspire others.

Go! Be! Inspire!

Praying for the People Around Me

Gina Yeager-Buckley

PAUSE.

Isn't it nice to know sometimes that someone has you on their mind? It's also good to know when someone is praying for you.

Now is a good time to think about others, too, and to offer prayers for them. Who comes to your mind right now?

LISTEN. SEPTEMBER 2 **1 Cor. 14:13-19**

Relationship with God

THINK. Praying . . . it's the thought that counts. It seems that's what Paul was saying to the new believers in Corinth. We need to remember this too, that prayer is simply the movement of thoughts, feelings, and care back and forth with God. It's not meant to be dazzling. Flashy words, fancy prayers, complex and thoughtful illustrations . . . sometimes in church it feels like a contest to form all the SAT words into a church-appropriate prayer.

But Paul was saying ,"Your gift of speaking in a fancy, exclusive language is all well and good—for you. But how does it benefit the world around you?" How does your church praying truly connect your hopes, for yourself or for someone else in your life, to God's ear? That's where the mind comes in. What's in your mind, your heart—this is what God wants to hear. This is what you need to share and what others need.

PRAY. Listening God, hear the words of my heart. They are louder than the words I read or speak. The words of my heart carry with them hope, joy, anxiety, longing, love, and a need for peace. I can be myself with you, O God. Thank you. Amen.

LISTEN. **SEPTEMBER 3** **James 5:13-16**

Prayer

THINK. It's easy to read the Bible and read "you" as . . . you. "Are any of you suffering?" "Why yes, I am." "Are you cheerful?" "Actually, I am pretty cheerful!" Now let's take ourselves into the outsiders' seat. An amazing thing happens when we do this. We can be the church. Not the building, the organ, and the pews. Not the sermons or Ten Commandments memorization. We can be the people of God called to pray, called to notice others.

We get a reminder in the Scripture that prayers and especially prayers offered for others can do amazing things. Who around you in the hallways of school needs a prayer? Who in your circle of friends is suffering? What can you pray for that might bring healing? And don't be put off by the last sentence with the phrase "the prayer of the righteous," thinking that is not you. Being righteous means being of God. You are of God; your prayer is powerful.

PRAY. O God, listen to my prayer today. I watched the news and saw hurting people. I pray for them, that they might feel some peace, some healing, some joy. I saw someone today who looked alone. I pray for them. If they are praying, too, let my prayer join their prayer. If they are not praying, let my prayer carry their longing to you. O God, I am the church. Let me be a place where your love is shared through my prayers, through my actions. Amen.

LISTEN. SEPTEMBER 4 **Matthew 5:44-45**

Inclusion, Prayer

THINK. Draw a circle. Place yourself in that circle. Now place in that circle those who love you, who care for you, that you call friend. Don't forget that God is in your circle. Now, who is outside this circle? Who in your world would you say is not your friend and is even out to get you? You might feel like putting all of those people in another circle. That's OK to feel. But here's the amazing thing: "Those people" are also in the first circle, the one that includes God.

That's what Jesus told his followers; his very intentional, rule-following followers. Enemies (what those people are to us) feel like they are a world away from us. But God is the God of everyone. And God asks us to pray for those people. So take a moment and pray for your enemies. Pray that they will feel God's love. Pray that they and you might, through God, come to see the good in each other.

PRAY. There they go, God. My enemies. (Silently name those you might see as enemies.) God, thank you for loving them. Help me to see them as you do. Help me figure out how to love them, even the slightest bit. I pray that the circle of love surrounding me might also be a place where I can begin to love others . . . even when I don't. I can do it with your help, God. Amen.

LISTEN. **SEPTEMBER 5** **Matthew 6:6**

Prayer, Relationship with God

THINK. Prayer is basic to being a follower of Christ. We state our longings for . . . whatever; we name them, saying them out loud or silently. Something about the simple act of saying these things puts something in motion. Jesus understood this deeply. As the person God put in the midst of humankind to help us understand God and what it means to follow God, Jesus must have had lots of needs in the prayer department.

When he told the people around him to go into a room and shut the door, it kind of messed with the status quo. "But Jesus, we thought we were supposed to memorize long lists of laws, genealogies, and stories and then pray to remember!" Jesus suggested something different, more like a one-on-one conversation with a trusted, loving parent or friend. So try it again. In your room. In your car. Say those things to God that you need to say.

PRAY. God, here is what I need to say to you today, tonight, right now: I pray to you because I hope that . . .

I thank you for . . .
I pray for the following people . . .
I pray for the following things . . .
I confess that I . . .
You are here with me. Amen.

LISTEN. **SEPTEMBER 6** **Romans 8:26**

Priorities

THINK. Going back to school brings the great overload, that somehow allowable, even celebrated thing where it's OK to be completely busy. "Should I study? Should I be at practice? Should I follow my dreams of being a musician, an artist, a good person, a mentor, a person who makes good grades, a punk, a prep, a skater, a Christian, a friend? There's what my parents want for me, what the school wants for me, what college expects of me, what the church says I should be, and what I want for myself. I need to identify what's truly important."

"What justifies the time, the energy, and the dedication? What helps me be me and glorify God? I might need help figuring that out! Oh, I have help. God, in the form of an invisible but powerful presence, is already helping me pray, already understands what I feel and what I really need. I don't need the words. I have them."

PRAY. They might be mumbles or whispers, but the prayers are here, God. And this Spirit, this force that is you, is moving these words around in my head, in my heart, closer to you. God, help me find the ways to sort through the longings of my life. To figure out what you want for me and from me. To figure out how to take this great, deep mixture of me, and make it into something that it should be. I don't even know how to ask for this. I can't figure out the words. But you can. Please do. Amen.

LISTEN. SEPTEMBER 7 **Philippians 1:3-4**

Prayer, Loving Others

THINK. Who do you need to see every day? You want to catch up, walk with them, hang out. Friends, most of the time, are simply part of the air we breathe. Their presence is so normal that we forget to acknowledge the important place they have in each day. Occasionally there's a birthday card or yearbook signing at the end of year, a time when the words come out—saying what we feel for our friends.

But what would happen if, from the beginning of the school year, we took on a silent mission—the mission to pray for our friends? To simply thank God for their presence in our lives and for the way they support us, make us laugh, accept us, challenge us, and stand up for us? Paul wrote his letter to his friends in Philippi. How amazing that we read Paul's letter, his prayer of thankfulness to God for his friends! Look where that prayer took us, as a church, as followers of Christ! Pray for your friends today.

PRAY. God, I thank you for ___________________ (name of a friend). Every time I think of _________________ today I pray that you will know how much they mean to me. I pray that I might be as good a friend to them as they are to me. Help me to be a good friend, God.

*Repeat this prayer throughout the day as you see your friends in class, in the hallway, after school, at lunch, and when you are out having fun.

LISTEN. **SEPTEMBER 8** **Proverbs 1:1-6**

Thankfulness

THINK. Why do teachers teach? You might ask one or two of your teachers, "Why did you feel called to teach?" or "What got you into teaching?" There are lots of reasons: love of a particular subject such as science or music, love of young people, passion for the actual act of teaching, even their own experience as a student (whether that was good or bad).

God granted Solomon gifts of wisdom and teaching. Wisdom is something you don't just pick up from a cereal box or a casual conversation. It's something you learn, something you are taught, something you observe in a person with a passion. Today, think of your teachers. Consider how they came to teaching. Give thanks for the time they spend preparing and for their patience. And if they seem to be out of patience, you might pray about that, too! Give thanks for the wisdom God has given your teachers. Pray for the wisdom to do your share of teaching in your life.

PRAY. O, God, your own son was called "Teacher." I pray that today I will begin to see the skills and passions of my teachers. I pray that they might feel confidence and fulfillment as they face their next class full of students. I pray that the wisdom they carry might transfer to my mind and heart. And I give thanks today for the women and men in my life who teach me all the mysteries of your world. Amen.

Therefore . . . pray for one another, so that you may be healed. The prayer of the righteous is powerful and effective.

James 5:16

Time of Your Life

Lars Rood

PAUSE.

What would you do if you knew that there was no way you could possibly fail? What is something you would try? How might you live your life differently for your faith if you knew God was always with you?

Today and every day, right now and in every moment, God is with you. So think about your answers to these questions—with that in mind!

LISTEN. **SEPTEMBER 9** **Joshua 1:1-5**

Relationship with God

THINK. Can you picture this moment? After wandering in the desert for 40 years, the Israelites are about to enter into the land that the Lord has given them, and they are going in with the promise that it is all theirs; no one can stand before them. I think that night must have been quite a party. I'd be dancing and singing knowing that God had just given us the greatest present, and nothing could stop us. If there were ever a time of your life moment, that would be it. "We are about to go. Are you ready?"

Do you ever feel this way in your relationship with God? Like you have been given a great gift and nothing can stop you? The reality is, it's true. That's exactly what's happened; you just have to follow God and your life will never be the same.

PRAY. God, there are days that I feel like I am on one side of the Jordan waiting to cross into the Promised Land. Please use those times in my life to mold me into a person that trusts and follows God in all ways.

LISTEN. SEPTEMBER 10 Joshua 1:9

Presence of God

THINK. If I were going to get another tattoo, I would get this one; it's my favorite Bible verse. God was commanding Joshua, just before he was to enter into the Promised Land, that there was a specific way God wanted him to live his life.

I love this! I think that life is so much more exciting and incredible when we live in this way. I like to say that when God is this big, our problem seems so much smaller. We can literally do anything God wants us to do when we go boldly following God. As a student, this verse should give you great comfort in knowing that God will always be with you. There is literally no place you can go and not be with God.

PRAY. Many of us don't do things for our faith we know we are supposed to because we worry and are scared about the results. Pray today that this verse will become real to you.

LISTEN. SEPTEMBER 11 **Joshua 6:12-16**

Journey with God

THINK. What a great picture that started out pretty funny. Can you imagine if you were in the city and saw these people marching around for six days? You'd probably be laughing at them by the seventh day. But that's the day that everything happened. What a fun life the Israelites were having! They may not have known what God was going to do, but they'd been following God for a long time and they must have known it was going to be something.

Do you live in a way that shows you believe God may actually be up to something? If you do, you are on an amazing journey. Don't get off that path. You will have the time of your life watching God.

PRAY. Pray today that God will give you faith big enough to believe that God has power to defeat even the biggest problems with simple means.

LISTEN. SEPTEMBER 12 **Joshua 7:19-22**

Putting God First

THINK. One summer I had the opportunity to stand next to the place they call Gideon's Spring in Israel and read this text. I love this story because it reminds us of the amazing power God that has and how it is so important that we give God the credit for doing great things when God uses us.

This school year will likely have some tough parts for you. It might be that you are trying to do too much on your own. Maybe you will need to stop trying to be in charge and allow God to both lead and get the glory when things are resolved. You will likely find that you can do so much more and feel so much better about the results when you let God be in charge.

PRAY. Today pray for two things. First, pray that God might make it clear how you need to follow God. Second, pray that when God makes your path clear, you will give God the glory.

LISTEN. SEPTEMBER 13 **Judges 15:16**

Power of God

THINK. Sometimes the Bible teaches us by using a really good example of a bad example. This is the case here. Samson seems like he was a pretty OK guy, but his story shows us his one major flaw. He thought it was all by himself and his own power that he defeated all these men. He didn't give credit to God at all, and in fact took the credit away from God and put it on the jawbone of a donkey. It was a pretty arrogant statement, and the main reason he ended up in a pretty bad place right before he died.

What can we learn from Samson? How about this: Live a great life but constantly remind yourself that God is the reason it is all happening. Put the power where it is supposed to be and stop thinking it's all up to you.

PRAY. Today pray that you don't take any of the glory God should get and put it on yourself. When things go great, praise God, and when things don't, keep praising God.

LISTEN. **SEPTEMBER 14** **Ruth 4:14-15**

September 14

THINK. Everyone likes a happy ending. This story didn't start out well. A girl got married, her husband died, and she was left with just her mother-in-law. But she stayed faithful and followed her back to her town. Eventually, after a journey, she ended up getting married. Out of that marriage came the direct line of King David and, ultimately, Jesus.

This last week we've thought a lot about God's faithfulness in several Old Testament stories. We've also talked about how we need to give God credit. Ruth experienced God's faithfulness and gave God credit. This is a great reminder for us that God can and will work out of tough circumstances.

PRAY. Today pray that God might use you to be hope for those who can't see it.

LISTEN. SEPTEMBER 15 **1 Samuel 3:19**

Presence of God

THINK. Every time I read Bible stories about the faith and commitment of different people, I can't help but question my own faith a little bit. If I'm honest, I say I don't think I'm ever satisfied with my knowledge of God's Word. I wish I took more time reading and thinking about what God has revealed in the Bible. Then I read verses like this and realize that there is a path toward that knowledge; I just always forget about it.

This verse says that the Lord "let none of his words fall to the ground." I'm encouraged by this because I realize that what I need to do is to pray a lot more that the Lord will be with me in all of this. It's not solely based on my own knowledge, memory, and skills. God was with Samuel, and God will be with you.

PRAY. A simple prayer for today: "God please be with me and help me as I try to understand you and your word more. Amen."

GO.

Go now with thanks that God has given you time—
This day, this hour, this moment.
Make the most of the time of your life,
And offer it all to the God who provides it!

Getting Along

Brian Abel

PAUSE.

Reconciliation. That's a pretty big word and a very big idea. The Bible's entire story is that of a God who seeks to be in a new relationship with all of creation. God seeks that same reconciliation within creation, so that we all would find a way to be in a right relationship with one another. Consider today how God is calling you to this way of newness.

LISTEN. SEPTEMBER 16 **Psalm 149:1-5**

Inclusion, Child of God

THINK. New songs endlessly filter into our lives. We're instantly aware of the latest music through TV, radio, laptops, and even phones. While music saturates youth culture, it also creates strong preferences and differences of opinion. The chosen anthem of one crowd at school may stand in contrast with the choice of another group. The psalmist flips this dynamic around. Instead of receiving new music, we're invited, even called, to give new songs! God eagerly welcomes our offerings of praise. Unlike the latest TV singing contest, we stand before an audience of One without being compared or judged. The new songs we offer to God emerge from our hearts and take many expressions.

Learning to sing or play an instrument, especially in public, can feel awkward at times; it can also take time to feel completely comfortable in God's presence. Look around at the global family of believers with a shared commitment to offer praise. We're a diverse people with a common anthem. Your contribution to our collective sound matters!

PRAY. God, encourage me as I offer my new songs to you. Help me to lift my voice with a fresh word for you rather than raise my voice with a harsh word for others. Amen.

LISTEN. SEPTEMBER 17 **Matthew 18:15-17**

Loving Others

THINK. People at church can let us down. How we respond when this happens makes all the difference. Too many people choose to get in someone's face and launch accusations. God asks us to consider and pursue reconciliation. Despite feeling wronged or hurt, we need to value restoration. A caring minister once told me, "You might be right, but you're not correct." Sometimes, we settle for being right, and we resist forgiveness. The correct and best outcome is a healed relationship.

We're encouraged to address the problem one-on-one. Sometimes it becomes necessary to include others who truly care about both parties involved. Our efforts to resolve differences might benefit from the presence and limited input of others. We don't gang up on someone just because we know we're in the right. But we all remain capable of digging in our heels and refusing to apologize. God doesn't let us off the hook. The call and example of Christ remains to love others. Is getting along easy? No. Is it possible? Always.

PRAY. God, I don't always want to give people second chances. Help me be more like you. I want to be more merciful and loving, even when I'm disappointed by others. Amen.

LISTEN. SEPTEMBER 18 **Matthew 18:18-20**

Priorities, Putting God First

THINK. Have you ever been traveling with some friends while deciding where to eat? Agreeing on a restaurant can take forever! The strong opinions come out first. "I love that place!" quickly followed by someone else saying, "Oh, I can't stand eating there." Neutral people claim, "It doesn't matter to me," only they chime in later, "Well, anywhere except there."

Sometimes people view things so differently that they conclude, "Let's agree to disagree." An impasse keeps them from reaching an agreement. God believes we can find common ground. Whenever we gather together and intentionally include God in our conversation, the outcomes of our dialogue know no limits. Let's set aside preferences and want what God wants.

Consider becoming passionate about something more important than a menu item. Huddle up with others who welcome God into the circle. Agreed?

PRAY. God, help me to want what you want. Free me up from making demands. Reveal yourself to me more fully when I gather with others to pray. Amen.

LISTEN. **SEPTEMBER 19** **Matthew 18:21-22**

Forgiveness

THINK. How often do we need to forgive the same person? Few of us would ask simply because we want God to provide clarification. We don't really want to hear a specific number. We get tired of shabby treatment and want to know how long God expects us to put up with it.

Imagine God asking, "How often do I need to forgive?" I don't know about you, but I don't want a limit placed on God when it comes to forgiving me. Keep those second chances coming! How curious that we reach our saturation point and want to bail on other people. As the recipients of abundant grace and mercy, we know what it feels like to be forgiven. Forgiveness heals us and makes us free to fly again.

Holding onto grudges bogs us down. Hands clutching old resentments are not open to receive new gifts from God. Relationships sometimes must change. Certain actions deserve consequences. Pain caused by someone else cannot always be forgotten. But, forgiveness remains an option—every time.

PRAY. Lord, you are so patient with me. Where would I be without your forgiveness? Comfort and quiet my wounded places and help me forgive. Amen.

LISTEN. SEPTEMBER 20 **Romans 13:8-10**

Loving Others, Faith to Action

THINK. "Keep your hands to yourself." We start hearing this at a young age. Early on, we figure out that things don't go well for us when we pull hair and kick shins. "Share your toys." We get a little cranky at any age when someone messes with our stuff. Sharing is all good and fine if someone asks first, although Mom or Dad might need to nudge us a few times now and then.

The commandments make it clear that taking things that don't belong to us is not cool. "Hold hands." We felt someone grab our hands to cross the street or form a circle. This instruction from childhood presents a big challenge as we get older. It's hard to hold hands with someone if we've made a fist or pointed fingers. Loving our neighbors requires us to reach out. Long before social media encouraged us to like or unlike, God asked us to love.

The choice to unlove doesn't show up anywhere. Pretty cool.

PRAY. Lord, I owe you everything for loving me. Help me treat others with kindness and respect. Forgive me for failing to love those you love. Amen.

LISTEN. **SEPTEMBER 21** **Romans 13:11-14**

Life in Christ, Priorities

THINK. Parents get frustrated with their kids when reminders need to be given over and over. "Put your coat on!" The barometer parents use to gauge the temperature or rainfall can differ vastly from their children's. "Put your things away!"

The tolerance parents have for kid clutter reaches a breaking point if the house or a bedroom becomes out of control. We feel like rolling our eyes in protest. What's the big deal? Parents often remind us to do stuff because we don't, plain and simple. So grab a jacket and straighten up a bit. Honoring a parent teaches us to value something beyond ourselves.

"Put on the Lord Jesus Christ." Paul spoke to believers; folks who already had a relationship with Jesus. Like a caring parent, he encouraged them to make wise choices. He wanted them to live their faith in Christ with intentionality and discipline rather than being indifferent and casual. Our urgent response is a big deal.

PRAY. God, I need to remember it's not all about me. Help me become more deliberate and less spontaneous. Amen.

LISTEN. SEPTEMBER 22 **Psalm 119:33-40**

Trust, Faith

THINK. Teach me what I want to know. Give me what I think I need. Lead me where I want to go. Imagine praying like that! It sounds a little bossy, even outrageous.

We know better than to dictate what God should be doing. So we don't actually say things like this. But do we ever wish we could?

The psalmist makes a habit of acknowledging God's leadership.

We could make the mistake of assuming someone like that is so super-spiritual that we can't even relate. On the contrary, here we've encountered someone who frequently admits to weakness and desperation. What a gift to recognize the only way to make it through is by leaning on God!

We will get along much better in life and with others as we follow the model given by the psalmist.

PRAY. God, help me recognize when I find myself slipping into the driver's seat. Teach, give, and lead as you see fit. Amen.

GO.

So if anyone is in Christ, there is a new creation: everything old has passed away; see, everything has become new! All this is from God, who reconciled us to himself through Christ, and has given us the ministry of reconciliation.

2 Corinthians 5:17-18

Whom Do You Follow?

David Burroughs

PAUSE.

Stop. Take a slow, deep breath. Open your heart.

Take time today; give attention to the One you follow, the One to whom you have given your life. Offer your life again.

LISTEN. SEPTEMBER 23 **1 Thessalonians 2:12**

Grace, Security

THINK. "Lead a life worthy of God." No small task there! There is a famous *Saturday Night Live* skit of Wayne and Garth on their knees at the feet of 80s rocker Steven Tyler, yelling, "We're not worthy!" We can laugh at this mock "worship" of mad guitar or vocal skills, but the reality is that when we think of being worthy of God, most of us know we fall way short—like miles.

And yet it was a common theme of Paul's, used in several of his letters: You should lead a life worthy of God. I wonder if it means that we follow a loving, caring God who, while being worthy of our praise and adoration, is more interested in a relationship with us. So doing the basic stuff that Christ has called us to do can mean that we lead a life God would consider "worthy" to save, worthy to heal, and worthy to forgive. Indeed, I am not worthy. But through God's grace I am whole and complete and can feel God at work in me. No small task there either.

PRAY. God, I'm not worthy of your love and grace. Thank you for giving it to me anyway. Amen.

LISTEN. **SEPTEMBER 24** **Matthew 23:1-3**

Grace, Following

THINK. You may have heard, "Do as I say, not as I do." I recently heard that fourth through sixth graders begin to match words with lifestyle. So the D.A.R.E. program reminds parents that if they tell their kids not to smoke while constantly lighting up in front of them, they are sending a mixed message. Imagine!

Whom do you follow? This is a tough one because no one we follow on earth lives up to our expectation, not even ministers. Does this mean I don't have to follow anyone? Does this mean that because each of us is a sinner, no one can be a spiritual leader? No. It means that we have to exhibit a God quality, grace, in dealing with our leaders. We must hear the best they have to teach us from God's Word and from their understanding, while not necessarily modeling our lives after theirs.

After all, the church is not a place for the healthy but for the sick. That is why we must always offer up our best. We are hoping others will hear our words and be inspired to change and reach and grow, all in spite of our own shortcomings. Aren't we glad God is a God of grace?

PRAY.

God of grace and God of glory, On Thy people pour Thy power. Crown Thine ancient church's story, Bring her bud to glorious flower. Grant us wisdom, grant us courage, For the facing of this hour, For the facing of this hour.

Harry Emerson Fosdick[9]

LISTEN. **SEPTEMBER 25** **Matthew 23:4-7**

Following, Kingdom of God

THINK. It is so fun to read in this passage about "those people," those shallow and small people who work and connive for a place at the table. I love to laugh at these people, and I often do so behind their backs. Ha!

OK, wait. What am I missing here? Could you step to your left, because I seem to have something in my eye, blocking my vision a bit. It's a twig of some sort, a big one.

Instead of asking how our leadership is involved in small and pitiful acts of self-congratulation, let's turn the focus toward ourselves. Whom do we follow? We follow a God who in humility became a human to show us the way. I must admit I love a place of honor, having the best seat. But the One I follow said that the last shall be first; I follow an upside-down kingdom model. I am to carry the heavy burden myself so that others can be free. In my best moments I have a place of honor—in the cheap seats, helping others find their way. It's great work if you can get it.

PRAY.

Joy is a song that welcomes the dawn,
Telling the world that the Savior is born.

When God is a child there's joy in our song.
The last shall be first and the weak shall be strong,
And none shall be afraid.

Brian Wren [10]

LISTEN. SEPTEMBER 26 **Matthew 23:8-12**

Putting God First

THINK. Not bad really. We have but one master, one teacher, one Father, one instructor. While it sounds like a Bruce Lee movie where the English translation finishes way before the Chinese, it is really a clear call to follow—a call to follow the Messiah.

There is a scene in one of my favorite TV shows, *The West Wing*, where the president's chief of staff is inviting a young lawyer from the other party to join their team. He says rather bluntly that a call like this, a call to work in the White House, doesn't come along that often. After the call has come, he says, "nothing else matters."

It is this same emphasis, but a hundred times more powerful, that Jesus uses in this passage. The terms of respect we toss around all pale when put beside "Messiah." The best we can hope for in this regard is to truly humble ourselves as we serve the risen Lord. And really, after that, nothing else matters.

PRAY. God, nothing else matters but you. I know this, and yet so often other stuff seems to matter more. I seem to be all about exalting myself, no matter how good my intentions start out to be. But it isn't about me. As a leader in my faith tradition, I pray for courage to be last, for the gumption to keep silent when I have something to say, and for the wisdom to sit and listen when I have advice to give. Lord, I humble myself today, and I am ready to learn what you would have me learn. Amen.

LISTEN. SEPTEMBER 27 **Joshua 3:7-8**

Following, Putting God First

THINK. In this passage, Moses has died and a new leader has been chosen to lead the people into the Promised Land—Joshua. This is a big moment. The Israelites have been waiting for over 40 years to cross this river. God's presence rests in an elaborate box, the Ark of the Covenant, real Indiana Jones stuff. You could die for just touching this box. And the Lord said to Joshua, "I will begin to exalt you." Wow! Now that is a leader I want to follow.

More dangerous, let's assume the Lord wants to exalt us. Exalt means "to raise high." Is it absurd to think that the Lord wants to raise us high? I don't think so. I think God truly wants the best for us. I think God wants to love us and wants us to be happy and fulfilled. All we have to do is learn to bear the ark, the very presence of God. But the ark is now set free, and God's presence lives with us as close as our next breath, and the burden is light.

God is on our side, not against us, no matter what some preachers say. God wants to help us move across the river to what is next, bigger, deeper, with more meaning. Now that is a leader I want to follow.

PRAY. God, here I am. I am standing in the river. My shoes are wet, and my heart is full. I want to follow you. I want to go where you lead me, and I am ready. Hear the prayers of the deepest part of my heart this day. Amen.

LISTEN. **SEPTEMBER 28** **Joshua 3:9-13**

Following, Journey with God

THINK. We know that God separated the Red Sea for Moses, but we may not remember that God did the same thing for Joshua, who brought the ark into the Jordan. So the escape from Egypt came full circle. It started with a salvation moment in water, and it ended with a salvation moment in water.

Now, crossing the river doesn't bring heaven. It doesn't bring peace. It doesn't bring eternal happiness. But it does move the people of God one step closer. When done in faith it is a sign, held out for a long time since, that God is with us. There are a bunch of "-ites" (like Canaanites and Jebusites) in our way, but the Lord is going to pass before us. That is a pretty good bet. I will pick God's team any day.

Remember this: We follow a God who has gone before us and is ready to stand with us. All we have to do is stick our foot in the water.

PRAY. God, give me the courage to take that step into the water, the step I have known for a while, the step that I have been avoiding. God, help me to lay down the things I am clinging to and to trust and follow you, because you have already walked this path, and I am ready to follow. Amen.

LISTEN. SEPTEMBER 29 **Joshua 3:14-17**

Journey with God, Courage

THINK. This is the end of a very long journey. The Israelites had spent 40 years in the wilderness, wandering and waiting. A new generation had come into leadership. They had seen the Promised Land and were staking their claim, with the blessing of the Lord. I wonder if the elders had told stories of crossing the Red Sea so many years before and if they made the connection to what was happening. God is faithful. God always finds a way.

And I find it interesting that as the ark of the covenant was in the middle of the river, every person had to pass right by it, young and old, male and female, everyone.

The lesson for us today seems simple enough: Things work better when we walk with God. God is faithful. God finds a way. We work better in community, all of us together being faithful and walking the path. What river is God calling you to cross? Who can make the journey with you? Following God's call doesn't have to be done in isolation. Step in.

PRAY. God, you always find a way. You are always reminding me in subtle and obvious ways the path that I should be on. As I follow, I am thankful for a community of believers and family who walk with me. I have some things to pray about today, and I thank you in advance for hearing me. Amen.

The LORD your God you shall follow, him alone you shall fear, his commandments you shall keep, his voice you shall obey, him you shall serve, and to him you shall hold fast.

Deuteronomy 13:4

A Discerning Faith

Arianne Lehn

PAUSE.

We face decisions every day, some big, some small. God is committed to growing a discerning, wise faith in you as you make these decisions. A discerning faith takes both courage to risk and patience to wait.

To hear God's voice and direction, we turn all that we are—body, soul, and mind—toward God. Center yourself on how you hear God speak to you right now.

LISTEN. **SEPTEMBER 30** **Isaiah 51:1-3**

Listening, Call of God

THINK. Discernment can seem like a desert. When we face decisions, we sometimes feel short on supplies. We lack clear direction, knowledge, understanding, or support. We may feel lost, afraid, or alone, scorching under the sun and not sure what to do.

Today's Scripture has a promise for us desert-dwellers. God is bringing us to the garden of "joy and gladness!" God will transform our time of waiting and confusion. God will transform our desert. As we travel through our desert of discernment, God calls us to listen—to pay attention.

What is clouding our eyes, plugging our hearts, or closing the doors of our minds? Where is God speaking to us today? God may surprise us. In fact, God probably will. A foundation for our discernment is remembering our true identity. We take comfort in recalling the "rock," or place from which we came. We came from God. God formed us (Psalm 139), walks with us (Josh. 1:9), has good plans for us (Jer. 29:11) and will complete the good works God began in us (Phil. 1:6).

PRAY. Creator God, thanks for the desert and thanks for the garden. Open my eyes to see what you want me to do, and give me the courage to do what I see. Amen.

OCTOBER

LISTEN. OCTOBER 1 Matthew 16:13-17

Relationship with God, Following

THINK. Who do you say that I am? Our most important discernment comes in how we answer Jesus' question. Most of the disciples parroted what they'd heard others say. Peter responded differently. He boldly staked his security on an understanding of Jesus that stood apart from others. When others said so many things, Peter discerned God's voice.

Franciscan friar Richard Rohr describes this deeper voice of God: "It will sound an awful lot like the voices of risk, of trust, of surrender, of soul . . ." When we claim Jesus as Lord, we risk raising eyebrows. We trust God's staunch commitment to see us through. We surrender ourselves to a selfless way of life. What is the guiding source in our discernment? Whose voice is most important?

At times we know what is true and real, but we are afraid to speak up. We hesitate to share what we've discerned. We will answer Jesus' question through how we live today: in the humble and loving way we talk with others, the devoted way we work, and the gentleness we show ourselves.

PRAY. Jesus, you are the one who makes me bold. Please give me courage to declare your love and leading in my life through all I do today. I give my mind, my heart, my mouth, and my body to you. Amen.

LISTEN. OCTOBER 2 **Matthew 16:18-20**
Listening, Sharing Christ

THINK. When you think of keys, what comes to mind? Some immediately think of unlocking or opening doors. Others picture securely locking or shutting doors. Keys can open a hidden place; they can also protect the place of safety, security, and comfort inside.

Jesus points to discernment as an important key in opening the path to life with God. Jesus' answer to Peter shows that his identity as God's Son was not obvious; such a full understanding of Jesus' love and identity required discernment. This discernment was a powerful key in opening the disciples' hearts and lives to the abundance, hope found in Christ.

Jesus also commanded the disciples to use these keys carefully and to keep his identity a secret. Sometimes our discernment involves timing. How are we using the keys of discernment God gave us? Are we jealous or afraid, shutting others out from God's grace and life for all? Or are we using them to open the kingdom of heaven more and more in others' lives as well as our own?

PRAY. God of openness, please help me unlock doors for others and lead them into your grace, love, and compassion. Give me a discerning heart and a courageous spirit that follows your leading. Amen.

LISTEN. **OCTOBER 3** **Romans 12:1-2**

Call of God, Confidence in God

THINK. "What is God's will for my life?" I've asked it many times, often with a heavy heart. I thought God's will for my life was a very specific path. A step too far right or left would take me off course. Paul brings us back to the true qualities of God's will—it is good, acceptable, and perfect.

We tightly wind ourselves into a cocoon of narrow thinking about God's will. God can transform us in that cocoon if we're willing to be changed. We discern what is good and pleasing to God through a transformed mind, a holy cleansing of all that we are. God washes, brightens, and shapes our thoughts so that we can see the world and our lives through God's eyes.

What is God's will for your life? To love God, to love God's world, and to love yourself. Live into the freedom and bigness of God's will. Take joy in open doors, the light you have, and grace in each step. God's promises will nourish your heart for the journey. Wherever you step, God goes with you.

PRAY. Thank you, God, for the freedom and goodness of your will. Please transform my body, spirit, and mind to joyfully live out my love for you, your world, and myself. Thank you for taking each step with me as I journey. Amen.

LISTEN. OCTOBER 4 **Romans 12:3-5**

Listening, Transformation

THINK. Authentic discernment involves other people. Their voices speak truth and bring holy clarity. Their hands carry our problems, their smiles share in our joy, and their prayers lift us. We need other people on our journey of discipleship.

Just as important, other people need us. Desmond Tutu points to an African saying that "a person is a person through other persons. I need you in order to be me as you need me in order to be you."

Being a Christian is being in relationship with each other. Faithful discernment reveals this in our lives. A discerning mind is humble, careful, and attentive. We recognize our place in the family of creation. May we not be consumed with ourselves and forget our need of others. May we never get so bummed out about ourselves that we think no one needs us. We understand ourselves by looking to who God is, our faithful and loving Creator who commits to transformation. Who is God using to transform you? Who is God using you to transform?

PRAY. God, thank you for relationships in my life that encourage and transform me. Please breathe your transforming Spirit through me into the lives of all those I see and connect with today. Amen.

LISTEN. **OCTOBER 5** **Romans 12:6-8**

Image of God

THINK. You are gifted. God delighted in placing gifts within you. Watching you develop these gifts brings God joy.

What gifts do you discern in your life? Maybe you are a natural listener in whom people find a safe shelter to share their stories. Perhaps you have a gift for encouragement; you speak just the right words to help someone along and bring hope. Maybe you are gifted with compassion. You reach out to those who feel alone.

Ask those closest to you what gifts they see in you. Tell your family and friends the gifts you see shining through them. Sometimes, our most innate gifts are the hardest to recognize. We use these gifts so naturally that we don't even notice them as being special. We can easily feel jealous of others' gifts, compare ourselves to them, or try to be people we are not. God loves when we live out our own gifts authentically and joyfully. Using your gifts is an expression of your love for God.

PRAY. Creator, thank you for the gifts you have placed in me. Please open my eyes to discover, cherish, and use these gifts today. Help me to encourage to others gifts too. Amen.

LISTEN. OCTOBER 6 **Isaiah 51:4-6**
Waiting, Listening

THINK. Are you waiting for God's instruction? Maybe you are trying to decide on a college or career. Perhaps you seek God's direction in a difficult relationship. Maybe you need God to show you how to live faithfully in your work. Is God calling you to change course? Or to remain steady in where you are? You do not wait alone. Today's Scripture lifts up the whole world's waiting. But God promises the waiting will end in good. God will bring teaching, justice, deliverance, and hope.

Lift up the things for which you wait. Hope and wait expectantly. Pray for God to instruct your heart, then open yourself to all kinds of possibilities—those that scare you, those that comfort you, those that convict or challenge you. Though much of what surrounds us will vanish, God's presence is forever solid. Turn your eyes toward God. Look at the decisions for which you need God's wisdom. Reflect upon the long-lasting qualities of these decisions. Trust that God will lead you into lasting good.

PRAY. God of wisdom, I lift up to you the decisions on my heart and the things for which I wait. Please wrap me in your hope and lead me on the path of good that will last. Amen.

GO.

Your teacher will be right there, local and on the job, urging you on whenever you wander left or right: "This is the right road. Walk down this road."

Isaiah 30:21 (The Message)

Recognizing the Good

Bentley Manning

PAUSE.

We go through much of life focused on the bad news that seems to so often surround us. The negative is our focus; in our frustration, we might not even try to look for the positive. But ours is a good God, the Creator of every good thing, the giver of every good gift. As you take these moments for devotion, think about the good that surrounds your life today.

LISTEN. **OCTOBER 7** **Psalm 106:1-6**

Forgiveness, God with Us

THINK. The cry of the psalmist is our cry. It is my cry, and it is your cry. "Remember me, O Lord!" It is easy to feel small and insignificant. The world we live in is vast, and it is filled with a lot of people—billions. What can I do so God will remember me?

Surely you have experienced this fear of being forgotten in the immensity of it all. God is bigger than this world. Please don't forget this truth. Like the psalmist, we know that we have sinned, but being a sinner in a big world does not make us insignificant to God.

God has not forgotten you. The Lord is good, his mercy is everlasting, and his faithfulness endures forever.

PRAY. Almighty God, source of comfort and strength: Come near and take root in my life, that my sins may be forgiven and my fears transformed through Jesus Christ our Lord, to whom, with you and the Holy Spirit, be honor and glory, now and forever. Amen.

LISTEN. **OCTOBER 8** **Matthew 22:1-6**

Priorities

THINK. In this parable from Matthew, Jesus tried to tell us what the kingdom of heaven is like. He painted a picture of abundance and a wedding banquet fit for royalty. Both you and I have been invited to this banquet! Though the parable is speaking of our future in heaven, surely Jesus is also referring to the here and now. God's invitation to the banquet is that still small voice that continues to call us into deeper relationship with Christ.

Just like the people in the parable, we sometimes make light of this call and find other priorities to structure our life. It is worth thinking about the things that demand our time.

What distracts you from the banquet God has prepared?

PRAY. O God, source of life and light, open my ears to hear your voice and give me the courage to answer when you call that I may have a taste of your heavenly banquet, where with Jesus Christ and the Holy Spirit you live and reign for ever and ever. Amen.

LISTEN. OCTOBER 9 **Matthew 22:7-14**

Following Christ

THINK. There is no doubt that this is a difficult and somewhat troubling passage. What should we make of this banquet, and do we really want to go? It is not clear whom we are called to identify with in this parable. Maybe, in some way, we are asked to think about ourselves as each of them.

There is a saying I once heard that might be helpful here. The saying goes, "I can put on your jacket, but I can't wear it for you." Imagine for a moment replacing the word jacket with the word robe.

This parable does not ask for simple solutions, but as Christians we affirm that Jesus understands and has compassion on our lives, both yours and mine. Jesus has worn our robe and through his life, death, and resurrection, the shackles of death have been destroyed while the doors of heaven have been flung open.

Thanks be to God!

PRAY. Almighty God, redeemer of the world and forgiver of sins, guide my heart and mind, that with clarity and strength I may follow your ways through the worthiness of your Son Jesus Christ our Lord, who lives and reigns with you and the Holy Spirit, one God, now and forever. Amen.

LISTEN. **OCTOBER 10** **Philippians 4:1-3**

Gifts, Sharing Christ

THINK. Our journey of faith is not a road we have to walk alone. Why should it be? Christ did not live alone, nor did his disciples. We have too much to share and too much to offer each other to remain in solitude. We are all children of God in one family; we are members of the body of Christ.

You have been given heavenly gifts, more than you probably know. Offer these gifts to the world—to your friends, neighbors, family, and strangers. It is in this deep sharing and trust that we will see the face of Christ in amazing and unexpected ways.

PRAY. Let your continual light, O God, shine through me, that my friends, family, and neighbors may see your face in all that I do. I trust that in caring for others I, too, will be given the grace to see the face of Jesus, who lives and reigns with you and the Holy Spirit now and forever, in them. Amen.

LISTEN. **OCTOBER 11** **Philippians 4:4-7**

Prayer

THINK. The Lord is near! Surely this is cause for rejoicing! Have you ever stood so close to something you didn't know what you were looking at? I'm sure you have been in an art class where the teacher told you to take a step back from a painting. Your perspective shifts, and suddenly you see the painting in a new way. The Lord is near. Sometimes I think God is so close that we miss it.

Step back for a moment and open your eyes. What have you been missing? Where has God been at work in your life?

When God seems out of grasp and far away, pray. In prayer, we are brought back to God and reminded of how close God truly is to our life. When you think your life has strayed far from the Lord, remember this: The Lord is near!

PRAY. Almighty and everlasting God, who became man and dwelt among us, open my eyes to see you, open my ears to hear you, and open my heart to feel you that I may know your life, which through Jesus Christ and the Holy Spirit you have given so freely. Amen.

LISTEN. **OCTOBER 12** **Philippians 4:8**
Transformation

THINK. Our lives can get cluttered and filled with stuff, lots of stuff. Fears, doubts, frustrations, hurt, jealousy, pride, envy, greed, and shame just to name a few. The list could go on and on, and if you are like me, I bet your list can get pretty long. These things often get so big and heavy that they take control of our lives. I don't believe we should carry all of this stuff around. Neither did Jesus.

Ask Christ for help with this; it is too much to do on your own. Make room for things that are true, honorable, just, pure, pleasing, and commendable—anything worthy of praise. Think on these things. Pray about these things. Recognize these things in others. Find peace in these things, and find rest in these things.

PRAY. Blessed Lord, source of all goodness, you have promised that whatever I ask in your name will be done. Clear the clutter from my life, and remove the weight of fears and shame that I may have room for those things worthy of praise through Jesus Christ who with you and the Holy Spirit lives and reigns for ever and ever. Amen.

LISTEN. **OCTOBER 13** **Isaiah 25:1, 4-9**

Grace, Forgiveness

THINK. In Isaiah we have been promised that the Lord will "destroy . . . the shroud that is cast over all peoples" and "the sheet that is over all nations." God has been faithful to God's Word and people. As Christians, we have experienced this removal in the life, death, and resurrection of Christ. This is the good news. Nothing can separate you from the love of God. There is nothing you have done to earn this; it is a gift given freely from God. Take rest then, and give thanks.

It can be easy to think that we have done something or said something that has separated us from the love of God. Please let this go in prayer. Surely you will stumble again; you are human. But God has removed the sheet from the nations and has brought us into God's presence. For this we give thanks and praise!

PRAY. Almighty God, redeemer of the world, remove those things in our lives that separate us from you, so that being reconciled in love we may find life abundant through Jesus Christ our Lord, who with you and the Holy Spirit lives and reigns now and forever. Amen.

GO.

May grace and peace be yours in abundance in the knowledge of God and of Jesus our Lord. His divine power has given us everything needed for life and godliness, through the knowledge of him who called us by his own glory and goodness.

Straight Talk

Rob Fox

PAUSE.

One of the great things about our relationship with God is that it is a direct connection. We can talk straight to God, and God speaks directly to us. Not only that, but our conversations can be very honest as well.

Take this time as an opportunity for direct conversation with your Lord. And be prepared also to listen as God speaks directly to you.

LISTEN. OCTOBER 14 **Leviticus 19:1-2**

Call of God

THINK. Holy? Now, let me get this straight: God was calling the people of Israel, and really all who call themselves believers, to be "holy"? What exactly does that mean?

Being holy is not something that comes easily to us. When I was a child, people in my neighborhood used to refer to me as a holy terror. I was always getting into trouble or cooking up trouble for others. However, that is not the kind of "holy" that God is asking of us here. Or is it?

To be holy is to be set apart for a purpose. That means you were created different than others, and God has equipped you with special gifts. What others interpret as misbehavior could be one of your greatest attributes if you choose to use your talents for holy, God-intended purposes. Take the apostle Paul, for example. He was one holy terror toward the early Christian church, but God changed him and used his gifts for holy purposes. How is God calling you to use your gifts to be holy?

PRAY. Holy God, like a paper marked and scribbled upon with unholy thoughts and deeds, I ask you to renew and recycle me. Take my life and my gifts, and make my page fresh and new. May I use my gifts for God-given purposes, and in doing so may I become more holy as you are holy. Amen.

LISTEN. **OCTOBER 15** **Leviticus 19:15-16**

Loving Others, Friendship

THINK. Social media websites have become one of my new favorite web pastimes. These clever websites allow me to connect with new friends and reconnect with friends I haven't seen in a number of years. Recently, however, one of my friends invited me to join "Top Friends" on one of these sites. This application allows you to choose who are your top friends, and whomever you don't choose, by default, remains merely a friend.

How rude! I politely rejected my Top Friends invitation by asking, "How could I choose who is 'top' and who is 'not'?" The writer of Leviticus echoes the importance of this kind of impartiality and asks us to keep balance in our relationships. Don't be partial to the poor or defer to the great: with justice you shall judge your neighbor. Justice is not just something handed down in a courtroom. Justice happens in the way we treat our friends, our neighbors, and even our enemies. Resist the temptation to choose who is top and who is not, and love all your neighbors as you love yourself.

PRAY. Loving God, thank you for the gift of friends and neighbors. Whenever I talk with my friends, may justice be the words on my lips. Whenever I walk through my neighborhood, may justice be the path I trod. Today make me a friend to the friendless and a neighbor to the one in need. Amen.

LISTEN. **OCTOBER 16** **Leviticus 19:17-18**

Forgiveness

THINK. Ouch! This straight talk from Leviticus hurts because it hits so close to home. Home can be a place of great comfort but also a place of great pain. When you think about it, how many of us haven't experienced significant hurt from a close family member or friend? I know I have, and the truth is we all have. A sad fact about humans is that we hurt one another. It may not be intentional, but it happens all the time in families and in friendships.

God asks us, not to take vengeance or bear a grudge. Turn the other cheek, because forgiveness is the key that unlocks the chains that hold you captive to the pain of another. When you forgive that family member, friend, or enemy, you are set free! No longer do they have any control over you; you are free to live the life God has called you to live.

PRAY. God of great strength, when I want to lash out against family or friends because of the pain I have endured, teach me forgiveness. Help me to remember the cross and how I am called to forgive others because you first have forgiven me. Amen.

LISTEN. OCTOBER 17 **Matthew 22:34-40**

Loving Others

THINK. My desk is such a mess. There are stacks of paper, books, and files covering every inch of the workable space. I crafted a solution to my desktop problem: a "to-do list." On a clean sheet of notebook paper I made a checklist. Each time I finish a task, I check it off my list and remove one or more of the supporting materials from my desk. Read a book. Check, and I remove the book from my desk. Finish a project. Check, and I remove the file from my desk. Before long, I can see my desk again! Transformation occurs because of a simple list.

Jesus calls us to transformation, and there are only two items on our to-do list: 1) love the Lord your God, and 2) love your neighbor as yourself. That is so simple. Or is it? When Jesus taught this to the Sadducees, it silenced them. Even a lawyer sent by the Pharisees found himself stumped. What seems so simple really is complex. They are, indeed, so complex that each of us will spend the rest of our lives learning and doing the two things on Jesus' to-do list.

PRAY. Creator God, thank you for your infinite love. Love seems so simple, yet it is complex. Like stars shining brightly in the heavens, may your love shine through everything I do and say this day. Allow my friends and neighbors to see this light in me and be reminded of your love for all the world. Amen.

LISTEN. **OCTOBER 18** **Matthew 22:41-46**

Journey with God

THINK. When I was a child, I watched *Batman* on television every afternoon. Batman and his sidekick, Robin, were heroes of mine because of their uncanny ability to recognize and solve great mysteries around Gotham City. My favorite episodes involved the Riddler. The Riddler was obsessed with riddles, puzzles, and word games, and he always delighted in forewarning Batman of his capers by sending him clues.

In today's text, Jesus is the Riddler. He invited the Pharisees to answer the riddle, "What do you think of the Messiah?" No one could answer the riddle, so they didn't dare ask him any more questions. But that is not how this is supposed to end! You don't simply give up and leave a good riddle unsolved. So, you and I are left to answer Jesus' riddle, picking up where the Pharisees failed. We are called to offer an answer to this great mystery, not for the sake of Gotham City, but for the entire world.

PRAY. Awesome God, great is the mystery of faith! Guide my steps as I uncover more clues and questions. As I seek your truth, may my journey lead to discoveries that will enrich my faith, helping bring in your kingdom. Amen.

LISTEN. OCTOBER 19 **1 Thessalonians 2:1-4**

Courage, Following

THINK. "Why did you bring us here?" my three-year-old daughter asked me as we unloaded from the church bus in the inner city. "We came to visit with these people, do some cleaning, show them the love of Jesus, and we might even find the love of Jesus already here," I suggested to her. "I'm not so sure, Daddy," she responded with a puzzled look on her face. "This looks like a very scary place, and I don't know if even Jesus would come here."

Although this is an understandable worldview for a three-year-old, this should not be the mentality of a maturing believer. Have some courage! That is what Paul was screaming in his letter to the Thessalonians. Paul reminded them of how he had suffered for the gospel and how he did it all to please God. Are we willing to suffer like Paul did? Are we willing to put ourselves in harm's way? If so, we may find the love of Jesus already at work there.

PRAY. God of refuge and strength, give me courage. No matter how high the mountain, with you I can climb it. No matter the challenge, you can see me through. Give me the strength to follow you wherever you may lead. Amen.

LISTEN. **OCTOBER 20** **1 Thessalonians 2:5-8**

Sharing Christ

THINK. There is a famous West African proverb that reads, "Speak softly and carry a big stick, and you will go far." President Theodore Roosevelt used this proverb to describe how the United States should conduct its business around the world. Since then, many government and business leaders have adopted this mantra. It is a mantra of power that is based upon silent force.

Paul suggested that the kingdom of heaven, however, is much different. Ours is a kingdom that does not prevail by force but by the living word of God. Therefore, Paul insisted that God's people should substitute the above proverb for a new one: "Speak loudly and carry a shepherd's staff, and you will go even farther." Often Christian people are mistakenly soft-spoken. Speak up! Be heard! How? By loving God and neighbor so earnestly that the world cannot help but stand up and listen. Your straight talk has the power to transform a bruised world.

PRAY. Alpha and Omega, you have called me to be hope for the hopeless, friend to the friendless, and a voice for those who cannot speak. Give me courage to find my voice today. Help me to speak words of peace and justice that have the power to change this world for the good. Amen.

GO.

The mighty one, God the LORD, speaks and summons the earth from the rising of the sun to its setting. Out of Zion, the perfection of beauty, God shines forth. (Psalm 50:1-2)

Today, let your life shine with the perfect beauty of God's love.

The Word of God

Valerie Burton

PAUSE.

God has something to say to us, and the Word of God comes in many ways. In these next moments of reflection, be open to how God's Word may come to you as you pause, read, and reflect.

LISTEN. OCTOBER 21 **Nehemiah 8:1-3**
Word of God, Listening

THINK. Some of my most enjoyable memories of elementary school were the times that a teacher read aloud to the class. Pippi Longstocking, Ramona and Beezus, and the poems of Shel Silverstein were among my favorites. When I read aloud, I stumbled over the words, but my teacher read the story with the appropriate amount of enthusiasm or sadness, bringing the characters and situations to life. I listened attentively so as not to miss anything!

When I hear a Scripture passage read aloud, the words linger on my ears. I appreciate a reader who speaks the Word of God with appropriate emotion. The words come to life, and the Word comes to live in me when I hear them as they may have been spoken originally. Ezra must have read with a passion that rang in the ears of his listeners, for they, too, listened attentively. This week, read the Scripture passages aloud with expression, and see if the Word doesn't come to dwell in you more richly. And as Jesus often said, "Whoever has ears, let them hear!"

PRAY. Gracious God, thank you for the gift of Scripture that helps me understand who you are, Creator, and who I am, your beloved. Open my ears, Lord, that I may hear your voice intermingled with mine in your divine Word. Help me to listen attentively when your Word is spoken. Amen.

LISTEN. OCTOBER 22 **Nehemiah 8:5-6**

Word of God

THINK. The word that comes to mind upon reading this passage is posture. Ezra's hearers were literally moved by the Spirit. Is that so unusual, where one's posture follows the movement in one's heart? There are plenty of other times when we are literally moved to respond—applause, for example, for those who deserve celebration, honor, or praise. When applause is not enough, however, we rise to our feet for a standing ovation, showing our respect and utmost admiration as well. And then there are those times when we jump up and down, whoop and holler, or stand silent and still. Moses took off his shoes. Elisha tore his clothes. Mary Magdalene knelt and washed Jesus' feet. Paul fell on his face. Each of these was moved by a God-encounter.

In this passage, the Holy Scripture received a standing ovation. The people expected to receive a word from God within it. They expected to encounter the God of Abraham and Sarah. At its opening, they stood. At Ezra's greeting, they lifted their hands, praised the Lord, and then bowed low with their faces to the ground. My heart desires to greet God and God's Word with the same expectation we witness in this passage.

PRAY. Merciful God, meet me in the text of your word. Draw me back to it again and again for a fresh encounter. Let me be moved as I find inspiration in the history, the poetry, the instruction, and the stories of those holy pages. Amen.

LISTEN. OCTOBER 23 **Nehemiah 8:8-10**

Word of God, Listening

THINK. It is my personal conviction that God can speak directly to me through God's Word without a preacher or priest telling me what God really said. However, many times I approach Scripture with apathy, even fear. Why should I spend time reading the Bible? Isn't it more important to serve others? Why do these ancient texts matter for my life today? What if my interpretation is nothing like what the writer really intended? What if God speaks to me about something I'm not ready to hear? It is at these times I am grateful for wise preachers and teachers who give insight into the Word of God.

In today's text, the crowd wept during the reading of the Law, but when Ezra, Nehemiah, and the Levites offered their explanation, they encouraged their listeners to receive the words with joy and celebration. So when the Scripture text is one that pricks my heart, jabs my pride, or convicts my attitudes, my pastor gently reminds me that God's message is always one of love, mercy, forgiveness, and justice. I need not fear the meaning I find in God's Word. It is the Word of God for the people of God. Thanks be to God.

PRAY. Eternal God, your Word is timeless, for I know it offers healing alongside instruction and hope alongside wisdom. Help me to approach it honestly and willingly, allowing it to shape me into the potential only you can imagine. Grow in me a love for the holy Scripture. Amen.

LISTEN. OCTOBER 24 **Psalm 19:7-14**

Word of God, Actions

THINK. The psalmist has written a beautiful piece of poetry in the 19th psalm. The Law of the Lord is said to be sure, wise, joyful, and enlightening. It is described as being more valuable than pure gold and sweeter than honey from the honeycomb. In other words, there is nothing that can compare to the Scripture's worth to your life.

Hmm. I tend to think that if we really believed this, we would read our Bibles more. If we thought Scripture could make a difference in our lives, we would study it with passion. If we thought that it could bring comfort to the hurting, peace to the distraught, and rest to the weary, then wouldn't it be written on our hearts and spoken to those in need? If we believed it to be so valuable, would we forget where we put it or ever risk misplacing it? If you resonate with any of these statements or questions, then join me in asking God to renew within us a desire for God's Word.

PRAY. For a timeless Word that has inspired generations before us and will influence generations to come, we are thankful. Lord, awaken our appetite for your law, your truth, for the gospel story. Give us a hunger for communion with you that can only be satisfied by the inspired conversation given to us by Moses, the prophets, the psalmists, the Gospel writers, and all those contributors to your inspired Word. Amen.

LISTEN. **OCTOBER 25** **1 Cor. 12:12-20**

Kingdom of God, Community

THINK. Paul orchestrated one of the best metaphors in all of Scripture in today's passage comparing the human body to the body of Christ, the church. Do you imagine yourself as an ear? An eye? A hand? A pinky-toe perhaps?

My one-year-old son is learning to find his ears, his eyes, his mouth, and his toes. He loves to clap his hands together to play patty-cake. He likes it when I tell him about the little pig who went to the market, giving each toe a squeeze. With his fingers, he wants to explore my eyes, ears, and even my tongue if I'll let him. He is genuinely intrigued with the human body because he doesn't take it for granted. It's all new to him.

We would do well not to take Scripture for granted either. It offers instruction and wisdom for individual followers of Christ and for the greater community of faith. This passage offers a beautiful word of encouragement to the body; work together and celebrate our diversity and our giftedness, which will benefit the whole kingdom of God.

PRAY. Great Creator, I praise you for the wonderful way you designed humanity to live together in community. Thank you for the Bible's beautiful image of the body of Christ where there is room enough for all of us to express our gifts and be who you created each of us to be. Help us to treat one another with respect as we would our own bodies. And finally, guide us with your Word as a lamp to our feet and a light to our path. Amen.

LISTEN. OCTOBER 26 Luke 4:14-15

Following Christ

THINK. Luke shows us the beginning of Jesus' ministry. Where better to begin than Jesus' hometown? It seems that his fellow townspeople were proud of their native son! Did they realize that he was actually the promised Messiah? Or did they merely believe this was Joseph and Mary's oldest boy? It has always puzzled me how quickly Jesus' public turned on him. One minute he was Israel's golden boy, and the next he was being sold out to the Roman guard in hopes of a quick trial and execution.

Then, I remember one of my favorite baptism stories. There was an older man who became disoriented after his immersion in the baptismal pool of a Baptist church. Before a whole congregation, the man started up the stairs out of the pool and suddenly realized he was heading to the women's dressing room. So, without hesitation, he plunged back into the waters and swam to the other side. Before his baptismal robes were dry, he had already lost his way! How frequently this happens to those of us who call ourselves Jesus' followers. Let us be devoted to Christ in such a way that we don't lose our way. We must rely on the power of the Spirit to help us navigate the Scriptures as well as the paths before us.

PRAY. Lord Jesus, forgive me when I lose my way, doing more harm than good for your sake. I want to see your kingdom come on earth, yet I lose sight of that vision when I become self-centered. Instead help me to keep you at the center. You are the way, the truth, and the life. Amen.

LISTEN. **OCTOBER 27** **Luke 4:16-21**

Following Christ

THINK. Does your household have a "family Bible?" This is where important family events are kept on record, such as weddings, births, baptisms, and deaths. That's how I imagine Jesus felt about the scroll being handed to him before his "home church." He was reading from the family Bible.

The ancient scrolls were the people's record of God's laws and the experiences of the Israelites. It was a record of God's ongoing covenant with the people of God. It was also a record of God's numerous attempts to reveal God's self to Israel. God gave them laws to help them make better decisions and to help them see what was important to God. Then God sent the kings, the judges, and the prophets to make the message of sacrificial love and redemption even more clear. But ultimately it would take a person, someone who would walk this earth alongside the people, to expose God's true heart. Jesus is the ultimate revelation of who God is. That means you will never find a better representation of God than Jesus. When you enter into a relationship with Jesus, your name gets written in the family Bible.

PRAY. Eternal God, thank you for persistently pursuing relationships with your people. Thank you for loving us enough to send Jesus, your only Son, who revealed to us the lengths you are willing to go to know us and for us to know you. Thank you for your ultimate sacrifice that cost you everything and ultimately set us free. Amen.

GO.

In the beginning was the Word, and the Word was with God, and the Word was God. He was in the beginning with God. All things came into being through him, and without him not one thing came into being. What has come into being in him was life, and the life was the light of all people.

John 1:1-4

Responsible Stewardship

Aimee Wallis Buchanan

PAUSE.

Responsible stewardship means keeping our eyes open to the gifts of God all around us and in us. God asks us to work so that these gifts grow, are shared, and become blessings to others.

It's a matter of seeking, seeing, and serving what God has so abundantly already given.

LISTEN. OCTOBER 28 **Psalm 90:1-4**

Gifts, Sharing Christ

THINK. When I think about stewardship and being who God wants me to be in the world, it's nice to know that I don't have to be everything. Neither do you. You don't have to be all things to all people. We don't have to save the world all on our own. The good news is that God, through Jesus Christ, has already done that.

We are free to simply look around and in ourselves for the gifts God has already given. Our job is to claim the gifts so graciously already given and put them to work for God's glory in the world. We don't have to muster up something we don't have or that doesn't exist. There's no need, because what God wants you to share with the world already exists in you and around you. You just have to look. Be bold enough to open your eyes and look. Take a moment to look now. What do you see?

PRAY. God of all time, of all gifts, and of all of us, open my eyes to the gifts you have given me already. Help me to claim the gifts and faithfully use them in the world. Amen.

LISTEN. OCTOBER 29 **Matthew 25:14-18**

Sharing Christ

THINK. So what's a talent, anyway? A talent was a lot of money! One talent equaled what a day laborer made in 20 years. So five talents was more than a lifetime's worth of money.

Jesus described a person who dealt in abundance! This guy was playing his own version of "Who Wants to Be A Millionaire?" but you didn't have to do anything to win except stand there while he gave out the cash. The man trusted all three people to take the money and do something with it.

God also deals in abundance. God has given everything—even the Son, Jesus Christ. So since this is true, wouldn't God give you much to share? If you know God trusts you enough to give you gifts, then what do you do? If you were given a million dollars, would you hide it under your bed and not text anyone to tell them what just happened? No. You would spread the word via social media and text messages as fast as you could!

PRAY. I praise you, God, for trusting me. You give me everything. You make me a millionaire in heart and soul. Help me to be in the business of actively sharing your abundant gifts in the world every day. Amen.

LISTEN. OCTOBER 30 **Matthew 25:19-23**

Service

THINK. My work is to put youth to work in the city helping others. Youth learn to make friends with those on the margins and to open their eyes to issues they may have ignored for a long time. Youth discover the significance of their own gifts in God's world. They work hard, sweat, and have sore muscles. They eat with folks who are homeless. They listen, and they have sore hearts from hearing hard stories.

When the end of their mission immersion comes, we always discover the amazing joy of what it means to see gifts used. Whether the gift is the ability to build a shelter, to listen to a stranger, or to give a financial offering, God multiplies all of it! Sometimes we run out of wall space as we write all the blessings of the week. We laugh and smile and praise God for these good things.

Just as the master and the servant in the parable entered into joy together, there truly is joy in giving. Giving makes you smile.

PRAY. Oh God, help me to see where you need me to be. Help me to go there. Help me to experience the joy of being your servant and following you. Help me to be courageous enough to give gifts away in your name. Amen.

LISTEN. **OCTOBER 31** **Matthew 25:24-28**

Gifts, Image of God

THINK. Fear is a powerful motivator. It can make us fight. It can make us freeze. It can make us run away. This servant was afraid, and he let the fear control him. He got stuck in his list of all the bad things that could happen. So he dug a hole and hid the master's gift deep down in it.

I'm always amazed when I ask young people to list their gifts. So often, they don't want to write a thing. They are afraid. They don't want to be boastful. They don't want to write something down because others might judge them. Even kids who appear confident seem to have refined the skill of judging themselves and deeming many things about themselves as "not good enough."

I believe God not only is sad when we do this, but God is angry, just like the master in the story! God did not create you to bury yourself and hide yourself away. God did not entrust us with gifts so that we might waste them. God demands that we do something with them.

PRAY. God, I don't want you to be angry, so help me to live in your light. Help me to walk with you and through my fear, so that I can share my gifts. Help me not to hide. Amen.

NOVEMBER

LISTEN. NOVEMBER 1 **Matthew 25:29-30**

Gifts, Generosity

THINK. Making something of the gifts that God has given us means experiencing joy with God. Hiding the gifts that God has given us means experiencing sadness, isolation, and darkness. The servant who hides in our story ends up being even more hidden. Because he brought nothing to the table, he has nothing to experience. For those who give and bring what they have to the table, there is much to experience!

Larry often speaks to our mission immersion groups. Larry doesn't have much in terms of money or status, but he has a very rich story. He uses the gift of his story to share with youth how, with the support and help of many, he has found his way out of homelessness and addiction into a new life. Larry walked a difficult road to discover that the gift of life God had always given, the gift Larry ignored for years, was right there for him. Now Larry lives in joy, and even though he has few material possessions, he lives in the great abundance of God's gifts. He says it is his calling to share them.

PRAY. Good and generous God, I promise to share what I have. I promise to open myself up to generosity. Amen.

LISTEN. NOVEMBER 2 **1 Thessalonians 5:1-5**

Child of God

THINK. In this letter, Paul was saying to the church that just because they were assured of the saving grace of Jesus Christ doesn't mean they can disregard their behavior. Why would you act like you are a child of the dark when you are a child of the light?

My friend who is a marathon runner says she must run some amount most every day to maintain her ability to run marathons. However, she's also learned that her body is so used to running that she feels irritable and out of sorts if she doesn't run. She is a runner, so she must run to feel like herself.

You are a child of the light, so you must live like it in order to feel like yourself. You are not a shade plant. You are a bright flower that needs the sun. Stewardship means remembering you are a child of light every day, so that you can bloom as a gift to yourself, to others, and to God.

PRAY. Creator of us all, remind me every day that I am a child of light. Turn my face toward you so that I will bloom. Amen.

LISTEN. NOVEMBER 3 1 Thessalonians 5:6-11

Confidence in God

THINK. Where I worship, one day a woman who had been homeless rose to sing. Because she was so nervous and inexperienced, she chose to sing along with the recording of the song. When she started, she was terrified. As the song continued, she stumbled on the words and then said, "I have to stop." She looked at us with fear in her eyes and asked, "Can I start again?" The congregation voiced "amens" and "yeses." "Go for it!"

She started the song again, and this time her voice united with the professional on the recording. Her eyes lit up as she sang right along with the voice she heard. When the song was over, there was clapping and more amens and tears.

When we live a life in Christ, Jesus' voice is right there backing us up. Jesus provides the support that encourages us. Jesus asks us to be the ones shouting amens to others and building them up. Through it all, Christ's voice keeps singing, urging, and supporting us along. So sing on, friends. Even if you stumble and have to start over, sing on.

PRAY. Praise to you, God! You are the one who saves me again and again and again. So as you sing with me, I sing with you in love and hope. Amen.

GO.

Go now with a thankful heart for all that God has given you.

Go also with a determination to share all you have. And . . .

Like good stewards of the manifold grace of God, serve one another with whatever gift each of you has received.

1 Peter 4:10

Just Living

Bronwyn Clark Skov

PAUSE.

Sometimes it's a struggle just to live through a day. And sometimes it is harder to live in a way that is just. God is here to help you live well today and to guide you in living in the way God desires. Listen now, and watch for God.

LISTEN. **NOVEMBER 4** **Psalm 46:1-7**

Storms of Life, Trust

THINK. I recall a canoe camping trip with college classmates in the Everglades of Florida. We were Midwesterners on a spring break adventure in an unfamiliar land. We watched a spectacular sunset from East Cape, the southernmost point of the continental US. The moonrise occurred at the same moment as sunset, and for one disorienting instant it was impossible to tell which glowing orb was which.

In the depth of the night, our slumber was interrupted by the deafening noise of terrific wind and waves. Did we landlubbers pitch our tents too close to the high-tide mark? The wind hurled one of the canoes against our flimsy tent, knocking my friend in the head. We sprawled on our stomachs, heads down, holding the broken tent stakes in the wind, certain that we would die that night. My friend began to pray words from this psalm, "God is our refuge and strength."

We climbed from the tent, emboldened by prayer to meet our Maker, eyes wide open, no longer afraid of the tempest outside. The storm wasn't nearly so frightening in the pre-dawn light. God was with us. We would certainly live another day.

PRAY. God of power and might, help me to overcome my fear of living in the moment, my fear of facing the storms that blow through my daily life. Give me grace to know your strength and love in the uproar of change. Bless me with peaceful refuge bound in Christ's love. Amen.

LISTEN. NOVEMBER 5 **Matthew 7:21-23**

Word of God, Faith in Action

THINK. It sometimes seems that church is a competition to demonstrate who is more Christian. I remember a youth group Bible study when kids were asking tough questions and adults were paging through their Bibles, trying to find answers. It felt uneasy to me, like we were playing God, claiming to know the mind of God, showing off our faithfulness by our ability to quickly locate and cite Scripture and verse.

Aren't we taught that God is the judge? Didn't Jesus tell us that it's about what we take to heart and how we act on it?

At one point I responded to a question with a re-telling of the story of the prodigal son from Luke's Gospel. One of the boys in our youth group was impressed that I didn't have to look up the chapter and verse and could just tell the story. I explained to him that I wasn't trying to be impressive, but that I had taken that story to heart.

Christians are not called to quote Scripture for personal status. Jesus calls us to be faithful in our hearts and compassionate in our actions, loving our neighbors as ourselves.

PRAY. God of compassion, help me to claim you with integrity, to take your Word to heart. Give me courage and grace to proclaim your way by my actions, acting faithfully on your commandments. Bless me with humility through Jesus, my advocate. Amen.

LISTEN. NOVEMBER 6 **Matthew 7:24-29**

Faith, Confidence in God

THINK. Is my faith built on a rock or in sand? It sometimes feels like sand shifting under my feet when someone questions my belief. When life gets tough, will my faith be strong enough to withstand the winds of anger, floods of emotion, and rain of questions?

Driving home from a youth retreat, a young man asked me from the back seat, "Do you really believe in God?" I was stunned by the question. I was silent at first, trying to think how to respond. I finally replied, "Have I ever said or done anything that makes you think I don't believe in God?" "No," he said.

He then asked another question. "Why should I believe in God?" Now that question I was prepared to discuss. I found my footing in my solid foundation of belief, and entered into a conversation about the everyday miracles that are presented to us day in and day out. I began with my acceptance of the authority of Jesus, and invited him to ponder his many experiences of Christ at work in his life. We started shoring up the foundations of his faith with some solid teaching and by reflecting on his own experience of God.

PRAY. God of creation, help me to be grounded in you with deep roots of faith. Give me grace and confidence to hold forth in the storms of questions and doubt. Bless me with confidence in the teachings of Jesus my Savior. Amen.

LISTEN. NOVEMBER 7 **Deut. 11:18-21**

Sharing Christ

THINK. My sister and I grew up in a home where the adults didn't believe in God. They didn't go to church, and they didn't talk about God or Jesus. The kids next door talked about God all the time. They were Jewish; we were nothing. They talked about God at our house, at their house, and at the beach. They talked to God at bedtime, and mealtime, and when we woke up in the morning. Their parents thanked God for stuff all the time, too. I wanted to know God so badly. I wanted what they had.

On my own journey, I found God through Jesus in a church when I was 12 years old. I vowed that when I had my own children they would grow up knowing God because I would follow this commandment and follow these instructions. I do my best not only to love God with all my heart, mind, and soul, but also to hold these words in my heart and soul and share them every chance I get, sometimes by actions, and sometimes with words.

PRAY. God in heaven, help me to hold fast to your commandment, remembering to love you as you love me. Give me grace, wisdom, and strength to share your love in as many ways as I can. Bless me with your promise of eternal life through Christ. Amen.

LISTEN. NOVEMBER 8 **Deut. 11:26-28**

Prayer, Faith, Trust

THINK. This passage represents a crossroads for me. God has been revealed to me through Scripture and the actions of faithful people around me. God has created me with free will to make choices for myself. Do I follow the road that I know, attempting to live in the commandments given to me? Or do I choose the unknown path, rejecting that which has been revealed?

I know that my life is full of blessing. I know that even when I seem to be wandering down a dark and cursed path, if I look for the light in Christ, blessings will be revealed to me.

In the darkest moment that I can remember, when I thought my son might be close to death, when I was tempted to reject God in anger and fear, I still found myself able to pray. That still, small voice burst forth from my heart and soul, reminding me that nothing can separate me from God. Warmth. Light. Blessing.

PRAY. God of all, help me to remember your abundant love. Give me the grace to choose you and not reject you when the path before me seems unclear. Bless me with the courage to remain faithful and obedient to your commandments, assured in the knowledge of your love through Jesus. Amen.

LISTEN. NOVEMBER 9 **Romans 1:16-17**

Faith to Action, Sharing Christ

THINK. My 16-year-old son recently designed a zippered, hoodie sweatshirt for himself. I was a little taken aback when he showed up at home wearing a bright white sweatshirt with a big red crusader's cross silk screened on the front left side. I asked him what had inspired him.

He looked at me like I was nuts. It was one of those "Mom, you are so clueless" sort of looks. He then explained to me why this particular design was so important. He helped me understand that the culture at his school doesn't tolerate the "Jesus freaks" very well. He said that a lot of the relatively quiet and confident Christian kids have a hard time identifying with their more evangelistic brothers and sisters in Christ. He said that the non-believers assumed that all Christians were pushy and judgmental.

"This sweatshirt," he explained, "is my way of wearing my faith on my sleeve. I can make my statement without arguing. People can judge me by my actions. I'm not afraid to say I'm a Christian."

This young Christian is unashamed of the gospel, faithful in God's power for salvation. His mother is humbled and proud.

PRAY. God of salvation, help me to live out my faith in thought, word, and deed. Give me grace and courage to proclaim your good news in my own way, rejoicing in your righteousness. Bless me with faithfulness through your Son, Jesus. Amen.

LISTEN. NOVEMBER 10 **Psalm 46:4-11**

Stillness

THINK. Does life ever feel as though it's spinning out of control? Do you ever feel you are at war because everyone is coming at you from all directions and you can't defend yourself? I sure have times like that.

I find that when I am overwhelmed and stressed and have a zillion things to get done, I can't figure out where to begin. I can't even find my way to being playful because my life has become so serious. I don't know where to start.

Usually I can find my way to pray. When my life is spinning this quickly, the words of this psalm melt over me, "Be still, and know that I am God!"

Be still.

I am not very good at stillness or quietness. But this psalm reminds me that it's not my job to fight back. It's my job to remain faithful. It's my job to take a deep breath, be still, seek God, and let God help me see my way through the chaos. Life is to be lived, not simply endured as a never ending battle.

I take comfort in the sure knowledge that God is with me. God is my refuge.

PRAY. God most high, help me to be still and know you. Give me grace to make space for you in my life. Bless me with peace through my savior, Jesus Christ. Amen.

GO.

Now may the God of peace, who brought back from the dead our Lord Jesus, the great shepherd of the sheep, by the blood of the eternal covenant, make you complete in everything good so that you may do his will, working among us that which is pleasing in his sight, through Jesus Christ, to whom be the glory for ever and ever. Amen.

Hebrews 13:20-21

True Hospitality

Jim Somerville

PAUSE.

The image of God's kingdom as like a banquet table, and God being the host is one of the most compelling images in Scripture. God has set the table for you again today and invites you to the feast. Will you accept that invitation?

LISTEN. NOVEMBER 11 **Psalm 81:1, 10-16**

Trust, Food that Satisfies

THINK. When my daughter, Ellie, was just a baby I used to try to feed her those strained peas and carrots out of a baby food jar. She didn't like them. She would clamp her mouth shut. She would jerk her head from side to side until her cheeks were painted green and orange. So, I had to get creative. "Here comes the airplane!" I would say, flying the spoon all around and then zooming in toward her mouth, hoping to get her to open wide.

Sometimes it worked.

In this psalm, God says to the people of Israel, "Open your mouth wide and I will fill it." These people had been stubborn, rejecting God's help, refusing his love. And so, like a father feeding his baby girl, God tried to give the children of Israel just what they needed, even if it wasn't just what they wanted. What about you? Has God ever had to get creative just to give you what you need?

PRAY. Dear God, teach me to be a trusting child, to open my mouth, my heart, my mind, and my hands so you can give me exactly what I need. Amen.

LISTEN. NOVEMBER 12 **Luke 14:1, 7-11**

Trust, Security

THINK. When I was in college I used to spend a lot of time at the salad bar in the cafeteria. It wasn't because I liked salad so much; it was because I could pretend to be interested in garbanzo beans while I looked around for a place to sit. What I always hoped for was a place at the "cool" table, so I could sit with the cool people so everyone would think I was cool, too.

In today's Scripture, Jesus said, "When you go to a banquet don't sit in the place of honor. Instead, take your seat in the lowest place." He says it because, as embarrassing as it is to stand at the salad bar looking for a place to sit, it's even more embarrassing to sit with the cool people and then be told that you don't really belong. "Those who exalt themselves will be humbled," Jesus warned, "but those who humble themselves will be exalted." How cool is that?

PRAY. God, help me trust your love so much that I don't have to look for affirmation anywhere else—not even at the cool table. Amen.

LISTEN. NOVEMBER 13 **Luke 14:12-14**

Inclusion, Relationship with God

THINK. Yesterday we talked about wanting to sit with the cool people. Today Jesus talked about sitting with the most uncool people in the room. "When you give a luncheon or a dinner," he said, "invite the poor, the crippled, the lame, and the blind."

What?

Jesus seemed to understand that people sometimes do things just for what they can get in return. In his day, people would sometimes give big parties just so they could be invited to even bigger ones. "Don't do that," Jesus told them. "Don't invite people who can pay you back. Invite the people who could never pay you back. Then your party becomes a real gift, and you will be blessed by God because that's just the kind of thing God would do. In fact, that's the kind of thing God has done."

PRAY. Dear God, thank you for inviting me to your party. And even though there is no way I can ever repay you, I'd like to spend the rest of my life trying. Amen.

LISTEN. NOVEMBER 14 **Hebrews 13:1-6**

Image of God, Loving Others

THINK. This is one of those passages that haunts me.

The writer of Hebrews says that "some have entertained angels without knowing it." Can you imagine? What if that homeless man you bought a hamburger for turned out to be a messenger of God? Then again, what if the homeless man you didn't buy a hamburger for turned out to be a messenger of God?

That's the part that haunts me.

So I try to imagine that everyone might be someone God has put in my path, that anyone might have a message from God for me—the old man sitting in his wheelchair at the nursing home, that girl with the bright orange hair and nose ring, the child with the sunken cheeks and hollow eyes. I try to think of all of them as angels without wings, but sometimes I get so busy I don't even see them.

And that's what haunts me.

PRAY. Lord, when you came to us, we didn't know it was you. Help me to look more closely for your image in every person, and to treat each stranger as if they were you. Amen.

LISTEN. NOVEMBER 15 **Heb. 13:7-8, 15-16**

Example of Christ, Following

THINK. We learn math from our math teachers, and English from our English teachers, but there are some people who teach us much more than how to balance an equation or conjugate a verb—some people teach us how to live.

The writer of Hebrews asked us to remember our leaders, those who "spoke the word of God" to us. I remember some of the good Sunday School teachers and youth ministers of my youth and childhood, and some of the good pastors who have taught me since. But it wasn't only those people who taught me to be a Christian. My mom and dad did; the members of our church did; sometimes even my ornery brothers did.

People who know about such things say the best way to develop Christian character is not by reading books on the subject but by imitating the lives of faithful Christians. Surely there is someone you know whose life is worth imitating. Watch that person carefully. Learn to live like that.

PRAY. Thank you, God, for those people who have shown me how to live. Let the life that is in me be more and more like the life that is in them. Amen.

LISTEN. NOVEMBER 16 Jeremiah 2:4-8

Faithfulness

THINK. Has anyone ever blamed you for something your ancestors did? Have they ever asked you why your parents let our country get into the shape it's in? That's what was happening in this passage from Jeremiah: the prophet asked the people why their ancestors abandoned the Lord and why their parents didn't do a better job of keeping the faith.

I don't know what you would want to say to the prophet, but I would want to say, "It's not my fault! Don't blame me for something my parents did." But the prophet seems to understand—we learn far more from our parents than we care to admit, and if they have abandoned the Lord and neglected the faith, they have probably taught us to do the same.

So, this is the prophet's appeal to break the cycle, to stand up for yourself, to take your stand. People may blame you for something your parents failed to do, but for God's sake don't let them blame you for something you failed to do.

PRAY. Dear God: My ancestors may have abandoned you, but not I. My parents may have neglected the faith, but not I. I promise you that I will remember your goodness to all generations . . . even to mine. Amen.

LISTEN. **NOVEMBER 17** **Jeremiah 2:9-13**

Priorities, Putting God First

THINK. Have you ever heard someone say, "That idea just doesn't hold water"? Maybe they got the expression from Jeremiah, who, in this passage talks about "cracked cisterns."

A cistern is an underground storage tank made for holding rainwater. We had one on the farm where I grew up. The rain would run off the roof into the gutters, down the downspout, and into the cistern, so that we would have plenty of water for our livestock and garden. At least, that was the idea. But our cistern was made of concrete, and it had a big crack running across the bottom. When the rainwater flowed into the cistern, it flowed right out again into the ground. The whole thing was useless.

Jeremiah said that's how it was with the people of Israel. They had traded the one true God—a fountain of living water—for dumb idols, false gods who were like cracked cisterns. Jeremiah might add, "That idea just doesn't hold water."

PRAY. God, we don't have idols like the people of Israel did, but we do spend a lot of time chasing after the false gods of money, sex, power, and popularity. Help us see that those things just don't hold water, and that they can never quench our deepest thirst. Amen.

GO.

As He gathered at His table
Those who longed to know the way,
Christ proclaimed a holy mystery,
Still His words call us today.
Tho' this feast be one of symbols,
What we celebrate is real:
Still Christ welcomes to His table;
Still Christ serves us at His meal.

Paul A. Richardson [11]

Food That Sustains

Amy Butler

PAUSE.

There is no way to get every little thing we might want. Our desires always extend beyond our capacity for obtaining them.

But God, the great provider, is always there to make available what we actually need.

Listen and watch now for what God offers you today through the Word and by the Spirit.

LISTEN. NOVEMBER 18 **Ps. 145:8-9, 14-21**

Trust, Confidence of God

THINK. Sometimes it's hard to remember that we have everything we need.

When change comes and stress builds and we feel there are so many expectations being placed on us, it's easy to start to panic and think that we can't make it through with the resources we have. Once we survive the rough times, though, we can easily see that God is there, satisfying every need we have.

I wonder if this was how the writer of Psalm 145 felt. Here, he remembered times when God's provision met every need he had, plus some.

God's compassion and provision came through in the hardest times with sustenance, justice, presence, purpose, and protection—just what we need and more than we ever expected! How does God provide for you?

PRAY. God, I want to remember today that you always provide just what I need, even when I don't even know what that is. Help me to trust in your care and provision. Amen.

LISTEN. NOVEMBER 19 **Matthew 14:13-14**

Food that Satisfies

THINK. After starting his prophet's career as a nobody from the backwater town of Nazareth, Jesus suddenly started getting popular. In today's reading, Jesus was processing the death of his cousin, John the Baptist, so he left the crowd to try to get some perspective. But everybody followed him, crowds of people the text says, drawn to the message they'd heard him preaching.

Why were they all trying to get close to Jesus? They were hungry, of course. Maybe they weren't hungry in the physical sense of the word, but they were definitely hungry for the things Jesus was always talking about: justice, peace, healing, and relationship with God. And they were willing to trek out to where Jesus was, hoping to have their hunger satisfied.

We're not so different. There are things we deeply long for, hungers we can't seem to satisfy on our own. And we're drawn to this unlikely prophet because we suspect that Jesus just might be able to help us. Do you know what you are hungry for?

PRAY. I know that I am hungry. My heart longs to be filled and satisfied. Help me remember today that it's you who can satisfy the deep longing of my heart. Amen.

LISTEN. NOVEMBER 20 **Matthew 14:15-18**

Courage, Faith, Trust

THINK. It's a common human response to crisis to spend our time wondering where solutions will come from. After all, we're taught to logically solve our problems, to figure out a way to fix things.

In Matthew's Gospel today, Jesus' disciples were doing just that, taking a logical approach to problem-solving, after Jesus gave them the impossible task of feeding a huge crowd. They looked around, scratching their heads, counting up supplies, and coming up short. Terribly short.

"Bring them here to me," Jesus said.

As much as they'd seen, as much as they believed, it must have taken some courage to gather up just the five loaves and two fish to bring them to Jesus. I wonder what it would take for you and me to look around at what we have, gather it up, and take it to Jesus. And if we could manage the courage and audacity to do that, I wonder just what miracles might result.

PRAY. Open my eyes, God, to see possibilities all around me. There are so many gifts you've given me, ways that you have provided everything I need. Make me mindful of those today. Amen.

LISTEN. NOVEMBER 21 **Matthew 14:19-21**

Promise, Assurance of God

THINK. We should know by now that God provides what we need—and many times even more than we'd ever dreamed. A homeless wanderer, Jesus talked eloquently about God's lavish provision for us. Sometimes, though, we're too set in our ways to even imagine that God will provide.

The disciples in Matthew's Gospel today certainly had the shock of their lives when, after bringing to Jesus the five loaves and two fish they'd been able to scrape together, Jesus blessed the food and began to pass it out . . . until everybody in that huge crowd had had more than enough to eat.

Who would have thought it was possible? Certainly not the disciples, and they'd been hanging out with Jesus for a while. It's not surprising, then, that you and I would wonder about God's ability to provide what we need. But take a moment to think back: when in your life have you brought trying situations to God only to see God work in lavish and unexpected ways to provide just what you need, and often more than you could ever imagine?

PRAY. I know, God, that you are not bound by the limits of this world. When I cannot imagine how my need could be satisfied, remind me that the solutions I can see are vastly limited compared to the possibilities you dream for me. Amen.

LISTEN. NOVEMBER 22 **Isaiah 55:1-2**

Comfort

THINK. My mother always says that life is not fair, and sometimes it seems that people who don't deserve it get all the breaks. The writer of Isaiah's prophecy today reminds us that God offers provision and satisfaction to everybody, even those of us who sometimes feel that it's other people who get all the breaks.

God's good gifts are right here, offered to anyone who would ask. "Why do you spend your money for that which is not bread?" the writer asked. Why do you waste your time thinking that life is unfair, that God would never have time for the likes of you, anyway?

The writer of Isaiah had no patience for that sort of attitude. "Everyone who thirsts, come to the waters." That means all of us. To receive God's provision, to have what we need, our only task is to open our hearts and come to God, who offers the things that really satisfy.

PRAY. When I'm feeling smug about my relationship with you and when I am feeling that life is unfair, remind me that your good gifts are offered to everyone who would ask. Amen.

LISTEN. NOVEMBER 23 **Isaiah 55:3-5**

Courage, Trust

THINK. Do you ever find it hard to ask for help? It seems like a no-brainer to the writer of Isaiah's passage for today. The truth of the matter is that we need the everlasting covenant of God, Scripture says, "so you may live."

In other words, dependence on God to provide what satisfies our hearts is not really a matter of preference or taste, but is rather a matter of life or death. How could we have missed that?

When we finally recognize the fact that God provides lavishly for our every need, other people around us will start to notice the changes in our lives. They will see that we live in relationship with a God who provides for our needs over and over again, and they will wonder how they might learn to live in relationship with God. Our courageous dependence on God will be a life-giving witness to everyone around us.

How does your life reflect dependence upon God?

PRAY. Teach me, O God, to reach toward you for what I need. Remind me that you are the source of my life, and I need you. Amen.

LISTEN. NOVEMBER 24 **Psalm 17:1-7, 15**

Relationship with God, Contentment

THINK. Relationship with God is what makes our lives complete. At some point in his life, the writer of today's psalm decided to look to God to meet his needs. What he found as a result of his dependence on God was a heart that sought God and a life that walked in the way of righteousness.

It's easy to think that a satisfied life comes from the pursuit of material things or following the crowd. But give relationship with God a try! The psalmist found the end result was that when he was in need, he called on God. God heard his concerns, answered him, and wondrously showed steadfast love. What results? The psalmist said it was a life of recognizing God all around him and living a life that was satisfied. Content.

What wouldn't we give to have lives that are satisfied and content? Seek the face of God; look to God for food that satisfies. When you do, you'll quickly find that God answers and provides.

PRAY. God, make my life content and satisfied. Remind me to always look to you for what I need to be fulfilled. Amen.

GO.

Then you shall call, and the LORD will answer; you shall cry for help, and he will say, Here I am. If you remove the yoke from among you, the pointing of the finger, the speaking of evil, if you offer your food to the hungry and satisfy the needs of the afflicted, then your light shall rise in the darkness and your gloom be like the noonday.

The LORD will guide you continually, and satisfy your needs in parched places, and make your bones strong; and you shall be like a watered garden, like a spring of water, whose waters never fail.

Isaiah 58:9-11

Thanks to the King

Dixie Ford

PAUSE.

Think for a moment about thanksgiving, the expression of gratitude. For what are you thankful? Could it be someone you know, an experience you have had, or something you possess?

Now to whom do you give your thanks?

In these next moments, offer your thanks to the ruler of your heart, to the giver of every good gift.

LISTEN. NOVEMBER 25 **Psalm 100**
Presence of God

THINK. Have you ever felt afraid of God? Sometimes, when we imagine God as a king sitting on his throne, we feel a little nervous. God can seem so big, holy, and good. We can feel so small and sinful. What right do we have to be in God's presence? What will God expect of us? Who are we to be talking to God, anyway?

But here is good news. According to today's psalm, we don't have to be afraid. We can come into God's presence joyful and noisy, even singing! What we find is a God who loves us, a God who takes care of us like a shepherd takes care of sheep. What we find is a good God who will never leave us. Yes, this is good news. We do not have to be afraid to be in God's presence or to talk to God. Instead of fear, our hearts can feel gladness. Instead of worry, our hearts can feel thanks.

PRAY. God, thank you for inviting me to know you. Thank you for loving me like a shepherd loves sheep. Please help me to know that I can come to you just as I am; I don't have to be afraid. Thank you, God. Amen.

LISTEN. NOVEMBER 26 **Matthew 25:31-36**

Generosity, Priorities

THINK. Many of us spend lots of time and energy trying to make a good impression on people. Some of us use our choice of clothes and music to impress our friends. Some try to make a good impression on our parents with our grades or willingness to help out around the house. Making a good impression might be hard work, but it often seems worth it.

Have you ever wondered how to make a good impression on Jesus? In today's text, Jesus is a king sitting on a throne, judging the people of the world. But Jesus is not your typical king. Clothes, money, music and good grades do not impress Jesus. Jesus is most impressed by those who spend their time and energy offering care and love.

Jesus himself is our model for this. Jesus did not worry about trying to impress people. He did, however, spend his days caring and loving others. When we act like Jesus, God blesses us and we are part of God's kingdom. That's a good impression worth making.

PRAY. God, thank you that you are not impressed or disappointed by my ability to dress well or by my taste in music. You are impressed when I am generous with my time and resources, just as you are. Help me to act like you today. Amen.

LISTEN. NOVEMBER 27 Matthew 25:37-40

Caring for Others

THINK. What do I do that matters? Sometimes I ask myself questions like this. Did I end world hunger today? Did I bring an end to war? Did I find a cure for cancer? On and on the questions go, and the answer to each one is, "No." I want to make a difference. I want to do something that matters, but it's easy to feel overwhelmed by the world's need.

I suspect that most people probably want to do something important. In today's Scripture, Jesus was recognizing a group of people who had made a difference. Jesus wasn't interested in their popularity or money. He didn't even mention their church attendance or how many times a week they read their Bibles. According to Jesus, these people had made a difference because they offered their food, drink, friendship, clothing, and care to people who didn't seem matter to the rest of the world.

We may not save the world today, but maybe we can give what we have to help someone who seems not to matter much. In God's eyes, when we care for someone who seems unimportant, we are caring for Jesus. I'm pretty sure that matters a lot.

PRAY. God, thank you that I am important. Thank you that I can make a difference in my world. Help me today to remember that I am successful when I help other people. Amen.

LISTEN. NOVEMBER 28 **Ephesians 1:15-19**

Following Christ

THINK. Parents often stress the importance of wisdom and knowledge. I remember my mother asking, “Is that a wise decision?” Most parents want their children to have wisdom and knowledge so that they can make good decisions and be successful in life.

In today’s text Paul wants his listeners to have wisdom and knowledge (or revelation), too. However, Paul doesn’t want them to be wise so that they make good financial decisions or get a good education or choose the perfect job, though these things are important. Paul wants his listeners to have the kind of wisdom and knowledge that will help them know who they are as followers of Christ.

God wants this wisdom and knowledge for us as well. We’ve got it good, really. Following Christ isn’t easy. Sometimes it’s overwhelming; sometimes it’s lonely. However, as we continue to get to know God more and more, our hearts wise up to the fact that we have hope, relationships, and power that make life worth living, whether or not we pick the best school or find the perfect job.

PRAY. God, thank you for the daily invitation to know you more and more. Please give me the wisdom and knowledge I need to know who I am as a follower of Christ. Amen.

LISTEN. NOVEMBER 29 **2 Cor. 9:6-9**

Caring for Others, Generosity

THINK. Followers of Christ have been given a lot. We have a God who loves us just as we are. We have hope and joy. We have friendship with God. We have the power we need to follow Christ. Many of us also have a lot of material blessings. We have plenty of food to eat, clean water to drink, and more clothes than we ever need. Yes, we have been given quite a lot. So what do we do with it?

We share it! Paul said that God is able to provide us with abundance so that we can share with others. Of course that means sharing our physical blessings—food, water, and clothes. It also means sharing our hope, joy, friendship, and love.

God doesn't force us to share with others. God isn't going to make us give food to the hungry or friendship to the lonely. However, if we are truly following Christ, we will imitate what we see God doing. Because God cheerfully gives to us, we will cheerfully give to each other.

PRAY. God, thank you for the abundant blessings that you have given me. Please help me to be like you and share them—cheerfully! Amen.

LISTEN. NOVEMBER 30 **2 Cor. 9:10-15**

Generosity, Loving Others

THINK. As Christians, we try to cheerfully give to others. We give what money we can. We go on mission trips with our churches. We visit nursing homes. Sometimes we give and give and give, yet we don't see a lot of change. We're tempted to wonder if there really is a point to giving.

According to today's Scripture, at least two things happen when we give to others. First, when we share what we have such as money, food, clothing, time, and prayers, we help meet other people's needs. What a privilege to be able to take the blessings God has given us and use them to bless someone else!

Second, when we give to others, God gets thanked. Again, what a privilege! We have the opportunity to use what God has given us to bless someone else and to cause people to thank God. I'd say that's making a pretty big difference.

PRAY. God, thank you for blessing me so that I can bless others. Thank you that I can make a difference in my world because of you. Please help me to share all that you have given me with other people today. Amen.

DECEMBER

LISTEN. **DECEMBER 1** **Deut. 8:7-10**

Following Christ, Kingdom of God

THINK. Following Christ is a journey; a long one. We face challenges. We try to be like Jesus. We try to take care of each other, and those no one cares about. We try to give cheerfully. We try and try. Sometimes we do well, sometimes we mess up, but we keep going. Why? Because it's worth it. Because throughout the journey, God is with us, and God is bringing us to a good place. God is bringing us into God's kingdom, where we have everything we need. A place where we have love, hope, peace, and good relationships with each other and with God. In God's kingdom, we help meet each other's needs, we all have enough, and we are thankful. It's a difficult journey, but a great adventure. God is bringing us to a good place.

PRAY. God, thank you for calling me to follow Christ. Thank you that on this journey you are with me, and will never leave me. Help me to follow you even when it's tough. Help me to remember that it's worth it. Amen.

GO.

O give thanks to the LORD, call on his name, make known his deeds among the peoples. Sing to him, sing praises to him; tell of all his wonderful works.

Psalm 105:1-2

Following in Peace

Michael Harper

PAUSE.

Some might think it foolish to speak of peace these days. But for people of faith, the promise remains.

In the midst of war, division, and simple rude behavior, we are still committed to a much different vision.

Set aside this time now for something more . . . the peace that is coming and that has come.

LISTEN. **DECEMBER 2** **Isaiah 54:9-10**

Promise, Peace

THINK. Growing up, the story of Noah's ark ranked high on my list of favorite Bible stories. How can you go wrong with a tale about a huge boat, marching wildlife, and lots of rain? I even remember fighting over who got to play the role of the dove in the church camp skit. It was always more fun to fly around the room instead of being one of the animals crammed into the cardboard box ark. Amidst the drama of Noah's faithful efforts to protect the animals, however, we must remember the end of the story where God makes a covenant with Noah. The prophet Isaiah calls us to remember that this covenant (or promise) of peace holds true even today.

In the middle of busy schedules, holiday stress, and school pressures, God sticks to this promise of perfect peace. Too often, however, we allow ourselves to become so overwhelmed with life that this peace seems unobtainable. What can you do during this season of Advent to connect with God's promise of peace?

PRAY. Compassionate God, help me remember your promise of peace even in the midst of all that is happening in my life right now. Thank you for your covenant and for the perfect peace you offer the world. Amen.

LISTEN. **DECEMBER 3** **Isaiah 11:6-8**

Peace, Image of God

THINK. Bumper stickers can totally affect my mood when I'm driving. I got stuck in a nasty traffic jam the other day, and working hard not to lay on my horn and yell things I might regret, I looked around for anything that could offer a distraction. Fortunately, the back of the van in front of me was covered with bumper stickers. Although most of the stickers were pretty cheesy, one gave me a much needed attitude adjustment. It simply said, "Be nice."

As I reflected on these two short words that completely humbled me, Isaiah's image of God's peace came to mind. Isaiah radically described peace as a time when wild animals with big teeth hang out with the animals that they usually eat for dinner. (Pretty intense, eh?) After reading the bumper sticker, I decided that my image of God's peace includes people being sincerely nice to each other so that there will no longer be a need to fight. What image comes to mind when you think about peace?

PRAY. Holy God, who offers comfort in challenging times, thank you for your perfect peace. Help me to connect with your love as I work for peace in your world. Amen.

LISTEN. **DECEMBER 4** **Psalm 119:160-165**

Peace, Following

THINK. Do you ever get tired of following the rules? Seems like every time you turn around, there's another rule to follow. Schools are built on a foundation of strict guidelines, and controlling policies govern our extracurricular activities and places of work. I don't know about you, but when I'm faced with too many rules, my rebellious side takes over and I end up getting in trouble. Punishment is never fun, and the whole situation certainly isn't peaceful.

The psalmist tells a different story. Instead of rebelling against God's law, the psalmist proclaims love for the law and praises God multiple times a day for God's ordinances. This paints a very different picture than our typical, rule-filled lives. The distinction here is that God doesn't confine us with useless rules that complicate our lives. Instead, God's law offers a way of living that leads to peace. What can you do today to relish the peace that comes from following God's law?

PRAY. God of peace, thank you for your law and thank you for providing me with a way to live. During this season of Advent, help me to follow your law as I search for peace in my life. Amen.

LISTEN. DECEMBER 5 **Zechariah 8:16-17**

Friendship, Loving Others

THINK. Life is all about relationships. Our lives are profoundly affected by those around us. With relationships, however, conflict and speaking the truth in times of conflict aren't easy. It's much easier to go behind someone's back and make yourself feel better by venting to someone else. Especially when feelings get hurt, getting back at the person who hurt you makes sense. Taking control of the situation by saying mean things or finding ways to embarrass your opponent can seem like the right thing to do at the time. Sadly, these relationship battles happen way too often, cause way too much stress, and typically end up creating more problems.

The writer of Zechariah offered a different scenario, one that comes from God. Instead of engaging in the drama of relationship battles, God calls us to speak the truth and make decisions that lead to peace. Not an easy challenge, but one that works toward God's peace in the world. How would your relationships be different if you lived like this?

PRAY. Amazing God, challenge me to speak the truth, make peaceful decisions, and avoid thinking evil thoughts about my friends and family. May I work for peace in my relationships as I continue to live my life for you. Amen.

LISTEN. **DECEMBER 6** **Psalm 28:3**

Following, Faith to Action

THINK. One of my favorite teachers from middle school was Ms. Galvan. At the time, I knew I didn't resent going to her class every day, which was a major accomplishment for any middle school teacher. Once I was out of her class for a few years, I figured out what made her such an amazing teacher. She practiced what she preached, and well, she "preached" a lot. She was constantly telling us about manners and how to be respectful. She even challenged us to do things to change the world. All of her advice fell on eager ears because she lived the life that she was challenging us to lead.

People like Ms. Galvan are the opposite of those described by the psalmist, who talk peace but have mischief in the hearts. Living in God's peace is so much more than talk; it's about answering God's call to give 100 percent of our lives to God. How might today look different for you if you dedicated your entire self to God's peace?

PRAY. Holy God, do not drag me away with the wicked, with those who are workers of evil. Help me live in your peace, working with all of my being to spread your love in the world. Amen.

LISTEN. DECEMBER 7 **Isaiah 34:11-14**

Justice, Faith to Action

THINK. Elie Wiesel once said, "Indifference, to me, is the epitome of evil." I think he meant the worst thing that can happen in the world is for people not to care. As a Holocaust survivor, he had good reason to say this. At age 15, Wiesel and his family were sent to Auschwitz, a Nazi concentration camp. Wiesel's mother, father, and younger sister all died in the camp; Wiesel and his two older sisters survived. When he talks about the evil of not caring, we need to listen.

The prophet Isaiah calls us into action. This call challenges us to move from evil (indifference, doing nothing) to goodness (seeking peace, working for justice). There is brokenness all around us, and God needs each of us to actively pursue peace and justice to heal the brokenness. During this time of Advent, as you prepare for Christ's birth, what can you do today to accept Isaiah's challenge?

PRAY. Healing God, stir me from my indifference. Though the world's brokenness sometimes feels overwhelming, give me strength to accept the challenge of pursuing your perfect peace. Amen.

LISTEN. DECEMBER 8 **Numbers 6:24-26**

Blessings

THINK. Recently I went to church with a friend. Turns out it was a relatively small congregation that loved to sing. In fact, more than half of the worship time found us on our feet singing. The song that seemed to create the most buzz from the worshipers was called "I Am Blessed." I'd never heard of this song, but my friend obviously loved it. Instead of singing the song, he just yelled out specific ways he was blessed while everyone sang around him. When we chatted after the service, he explained that the song was his favorite because it caused him to remember God's blessings in his life and gave him a chance to thank God for each blessing.

As we continue this journey through Advent, spend some time identifying God's blessings in your life. Maybe you are even bold enough to yell them out like my friend did! What does it mean to truly embrace God's blessings as you prepare for Christ's birth?

PRAY. God of all things, thank you for all of the blessings in my life. Walk with me as I strive to live in your love and as I truly embrace the blessings you have given me. Amen.

GO.

Can you feel it?
Deep within you,
There is a quiet confidence . . . growing.

Be patient.
Prepare for it now,
The gentle presence of the Spirit.

Hope

Reggie Blount

PAUSE.

Hope is connected to a vision, an image in the mind of what can be. As we await the coming of the Christ child, what pictures do you have in your mind for the future, your future? Ask God to paint for you a picture of hope, even in these next moments of reflection.

LISTEN. DECEMBER 9 **Jeremiah 33:14-16**

Promises

THINK. It seems as if we live in a world full of broken promises. The news is filled everyday with broken vows, broken covenants, broken commitments, and broken trusts. Politicians find it hard to keep their campaign pledges. Celebrities find it hard to stay together longer than the weekend. People we trust, including our own family and friends, don't always keep their word. People we thought we could always count on are not always there as they vowed.

Advent is a time to remember that there is One who always keeps promises. God did "fulfill the promise [God] made to the house of Israel and the house of Judah." God did "cause a righteous Branch to spring up for David." God did send One who would save and protect not only the house of Judah, but us as well. God kept God's promises, and God still continues to do so. In a world full of broken promises, aren't you glad there is One who always keeps them?

PRAY. Glorious promise-keeper, thank you for keeping your vow, your covenant, your commitment to us. Help me to be a better promise-keeper for you today. Amen.

LISTEN. **DECEMBER 10** **Zechariah 14:4-9**

Storms of Life, Hope

THINK. Have you ever felt down, discouraged, or defeated? I have. I feel this way more times than I like to admit. It happens when life gets crazy and overwhelming. It happens when I feel like I keep fighting one battle after another. A time ultimately comes when all my strength is gone and all the fight is gone, too. What do you do when all of your fight is gone and you start to feel down, discouraged, and defeated? I start to remember the battle is not mine but God's (2 Chron. 20:15).

Sooner or later, I'm reminded that the Lord is king over all the earth (Zech. 14:9). Sooner or later, I'm reminded that the Lord promises to fight my battles. Sooner or later, I'm reminded I don't need to allow the battles of life to drain me, discourage me, or defeat me. My hope is in a God who is still fighting for me.

PRAY. Come thou almighty King! Thank you for always coming to my rescue! Amen.

LISTEN. DECEMBER 11 Psalm 25:1-10

December 11

THINK. I'm a news junkie. When I'm in my car I listen to National Public Radio®, and then I change channels to the local news. I read various news magazines during the week and watch network news every day. As much as I like to be informed, sometimes it gets to be too much. War, disease, fighting, suffering, hurting, and crime are all climbing with seemingly no end in sight. It's hard not to experience a sense of helplessness and hopelessness after reading and hearing of so much devastation and destruction.

What are some things you find weakening your hope? Is it discouragement, suffering, disappointment, distress, or discontent? So much is going on in our world that can easily shatter our dreams, but the psalmist reminds us that it is not in the world that we place our trust—it is in God. It is God's steadfast love and faithfulness that have endured and continue to endure. So whether or not the world around us continues to battle against our hope, we can trust that God will always do what is right, what is good, and what is best for us, without fail.

PRAY. Gracious God, when the storms of life are raging, it's good to know I can trust in your steadfast love and faithfulness to see me through. Amen.

LISTEN. **DECEMBER 12** **1 Thess. 3:9-13**

Prayer, Blessings

THINK. Beloved, has anyone ever prayed for you? Has anyone ever offered a prayer to God on your behalf? Has anyone ever offered a prayer of thanksgiving? Has anyone ever petitioned for grace and mercy to come your way? Has anyone ever prayed for safety and protection for your journey? Has anyone ever prayed for healing for your body or for your spirit? Beloved, has anyone ever prayed for you? I'm going to go out on a limb, but I believe everyone has had someone pray for them at one time or another. You may not have been present. You may not have been privy to hear its content. But there someone along the way has stood in the gap, offered intercession, and called your name before God. Beloved, somebody prayed for you. They had you on their mind, and they took the time to pray for you. What a blessing, and what great joy is ours in knowing someone is taking the time to pray for us.

PRAY. Listening God, I thank you for those who pray for me. Hear my prayers as I pray for all who need your strength, your love, and your hope. Amen.

LISTEN. DECEMBER 13 **Luke 21:25-28**

Hope, Waiting

THINK. I don't always get it. Sometimes I miss the punch line of what others think is a good joke. Sometimes I misread the body language and gestures of some people. Sometimes I misunderstand the tone of an email. Sometimes I get the wrong idea about certain situations. There are times when I miss the signs. There are times when I miss the cues.

Advent is a time that reminds us not to miss the signs. Don't miss the signs of distress; we see those every day. Don't miss the signs of hope! Hope is coming! The hope we have for a loved one who is sick. The hope we have for a better future for those on hard times. The hope we have for wars to end. The hope we have for chaos to cease. The hope we have for peace to reign. Don't miss the signs! Hope is coming. His name is Immanuel!

PRAY. O Come, O come Immanuel. Help us not to miss the signs! Amen.

LISTEN. **DECEMBER 14** **Luke 21:29-36**

Waiting, Hope, Patience

THINK. Beloved, have you ever found yourself asking God, "How long, O LORD?" (Psalm 13:1). When the chaos and confusion of my life start escalating, and the times between my prayers for help and the expectation of resolution start to grow wider, I find myself asking "How long, O Lord?" I've come to discover that it's not the asking that bothers me. It's not even the answer that really concerns me. I may not like the answer, but it's still always good to have one.

It's not the asking, or the answer. It's that space between the asking and the answer. Advent reminds me not to give up waiting; hope is coming and coming soon. Advent reminds me that as certainly as Christ came once, he will come again in the midst of my chaos and confusion—and the gift he brings the next time will be greater than any I've ever known.

PRAY. Gracious Lord, give me the patience to wait between the asking and the answer. Amen.

LISTEN. DECEMBER 15 **Romans 15:4-6**

Waiting, Community

THINK. You're never alone. Sometimes I find that hard to believe when I'm going through difficult times. All too often the challenges of life convince me that I'm by myself. In the midst of my troubles, I find myself believing I'm all alone.

But thank God something happens that reminds me I'm not alone. Something happens that reminds me that my situation is not unique; others have been there, too. Scripture reminds me. Family reminds me. Friends remind me. The community of the saints reminds me. God reminds me. They all remind me that trouble doesn't last always, and together we can see each other through. Advent offers us this awesome time to remember we don't wait alone. We wait together offering love and support and hope to one another.

PRAY. May the God of steadfastness and encouragement grant [us] to live in harmony with one other, in accordance with Christ Jesus, so that together [during this Advent season and all the days to come, we] may with one voice glorify the God and Father of our Lord Jesus Christ (Rom. 15:5-6). Amen.

GO.

Come, thou long-expected Jesus, born to set thy people free;
Free from our fears and sins release us, let us find our rest in thee.
Israel's strength and consolation, hope of all the earth thou art;
Dear desire of every nation, joy of every longing heart.

Charles Wesley

Love

Bill Sheill

PAUSE.

Somebody loving you is grace. Loving somebody is grace. Have you ever tried to love somebody?

Frederick Buechner writes these words with the recognition that love comes only by grace; love comes only by the work of God in our lives.

Love is revealed to us with the coming of the Christ child. How will this love be gracefully shown in your life today?

LISTEN. DECEMBER 16 **Psalm 146:5-10**

Faith to Action, Loving Others

THINK. Dora the Explorer was just a cartoon character on Nickelodeon until she became the face of Psalm 146 for me. I met her during our Latino Vacation Bible School. When I introduced myself to this young mother with a baby, she said in simple English, "I'm Dora. You know, like the explorer."

Dora accepted Christ at that Bible School and was baptized. At the time, we did not have a Latino pastor in our town, but we promised to take care of new believers. Weeks later, Dora was admitted to a local hospital. The physician told her she needed a heart valve. She had no immigration papers, no insurance, and little money, so the hospital discharged her. That's when a church member became the hands and feet of God. She contacted friends in Washington and found a federal grant that would pay for the surgery. A few days later, Dora was admitted to the hospital again and received successful surgery.

Every Sunday when she worships, she is living proof that God watches over the strangers and sustains the orphans. And most of the time, God does it through us.

PRAY. God, give me eyes to see and hands to touch the aliens around me. Use me to watch over and sustain your beloved ones. Amen.

LISTEN. **DECEMBER 17** **Isaiah 35:1-4**

Love

THINK. A fully grown tree drinks 200 gallons of water in a region of the country that needs all the water it can get. The simple solution is remove the trees, right? But the saltcedar tree is a common nesting ground for the endangered Willow Flycatcher. Local government is prohibited from removing them. Unfortunately, when the city dredged a local lake for a larger place to catch runoff rain water, the sludge held the seedlings of future saltcedars. Gunk deposited along the side of the lake literally planted seeds of trees that consumed the water.

The water of love can be drained like a lake surrounded by saltcedars. When we withhold love from certain neighbors, friends, or enemies, the water of love is consumed by the trees of mistrust, hate, and vengeance.

God corrects us with purifying love. God uproots hate, vengeance, and mistrust so we can be free to love again. Spiritual renewal requires God's corrective love. Water and love flow when there are no barriers between ourselves and others.

PRAY. Holy God, I confess the deeds that have drained my life of the water of love. Lord, have mercy. Amen.

LISTEN. DECEMBER 18 **Isaiah 35:5-7**
Image of God

THINK. In the ancient world, people believed that physical disabilities signified spiritual problems. If you were lame, people assumed your parents did something to cause it. If you could not speak, you possibly said something wrong to mute your tongue.

We might laugh and assume we'd never do that. The social media world, however, gives in to the same mentality. On the surface you can see what a person looks like, but you cannot know the complete story. We see someone who is obese or gaunt, and we might presume gluttony or anorexia. We look at someone's ethnicity and presume "good athlete" or " smart student."

Isaiah imagines a different world, where water springs up in dry places and pools are built in the desert. This kind of world causes believers to see the lame; mute; and physically, mentally, socially, and culturally disabled and to look past the surface of their lives. Isaiah essentially said, "You can't judge a book—or a person—by their cover." What we see on the outside invites us to leap with the lame, to sing with the mute, and to see with the blind. When we do, our hearts are changed.

PRAY. Lord, help me to see as you see and to reserve judgment. I want to be part of the springs of water that you will cause to spring forth today. Amen.

LISTEN. **DECEMBER 19** **Isaiah 35:8-10**

Journey with God

THINK. The hardest thing about getting a driver's license is waiting for the test. The longest season of life seems to be the months between learner's and driver's permits. Our parents watch every move we make. We can't even back the car out of the driveway without Mom or Dad—or both—getting tense.

In a world without motor vehicles, Isaiah imagined another kind of highway that God creates that we have free access to. It's the way of God. Like getting a learner's permit and waiting for a license, we believers have joined God on the way in this life, and we await the life that is to come.

We drive on this spiritual road through our belief in God, but we do not do so with total freedom. We are not allowed to live with whatever behavior we want. God invites us on the way of holiness, governed not by the rules society imposes but by a relationship with the living God who invited us. This Parent is not tense or worried. God enjoys the ride with us, and invites us to continue the journey. The way lasts a lifetime and ends at an eternal destination.

PRAY. God, thank you for being the calm presence on the stressful highway of life. Help me remember that you are with me all along the way. Amen.

LISTEN. **DECEMBER 20** **James 5:7-10**

Waiting, Patience

THINK. We're always waiting for the next thing—the semester to end, Christmas to come, the school year to break, or for life to begin. We say, "I can't wait until . . ." James said that while waiting for the next thing, we need daily obedience to God.

Today's text uses the example of a farmer who is intentionally patient. He does not throw seed on the ground and hope the sun and rain will do their thing. He is deliberately patient. He takes responsibility for the land—fertilizing, weeding, tilling, and nurturing. He repairs his equipment, works with the tools, and does everything that he thinks is necessary to be prepared for a good crop.

Like a farmer, we have work to do while we patiently await the next thing. We easily get caught up in "when I get to" and forget about the gifts of responsibilities. The gift of showing love rather than gossip to the person who shares a locker. The opportunity to sow secret seeds of kindness to a senior adult. The chance to treat parents with respect and gratitude rather than grumbling and arguing. The next thing you know, we've arrived.

PRAY. As I seek your patience, help me focus on today, God, and the gifts that are in front of me. Make me a patient farmer of your love. Amen.

LISTEN. DECEMBER 21 **Matthew 11:2-6**

Loving Others

THINK. Mind reading. It happens all the time. People love to take a few actions, tie them together, and presto! You know what they're thinking. You hear it in phrases that begin with "everybody thinks." "Everybody thinks that I'm a . . ." "They think that he's a . . ." "She thinks that we're going to . . ."

John the Baptist's followers were playing the "everybody thinks" game about Jesus. They assumed Jesus was trying to be like John. Jesus reminded John the Baptist's followers that no one is a mind reader. You can only read behavior. Here are his actions: healing the blind, curing the lame, treating people with health conditions, and sharing good news.

Love your mind during Advent, and give your mind a gift. Let someone else read minds, and you focus instead on behavior. No matter what "they think," there is a world to discover. Just know by watching others' actions. That will tell you everything you need to know about a person.

PRAY. Lord, I confess that I'm more concerned about what people think rather than what they do. Help me to see the behavior of others and love them as you do. Amen.

LISTEN. DECEMBER 22 **Matthew 11:7-11**

Love, Thankfulness

THINK. Love begins when we realize that we cannot make it through life without looking back. When we turn around, we see significant people who made it possible for us to be who we are today. John the Baptist made Jesus' ministry effective.

John did things that Jesus did not come to do. He opened doors, prepared hearts, and preached sermons that people had not heard in a long time. He wore just camel's hair and used the Jordan River for a sanctuary. If Jesus had done that, few likely would have believed him. Jesus gave credit to the giant on whose shoulders he stood.

Who made things happen in your life? Who shared Christ and life with you and made you who you are today? More than likely they sacrificed a great deal so that you could live, breathe, play, and enjoy. Take time to share love this Advent season with someone who has made it possible for you to live the way you live today. Tell them personally through a note, email, or a personal word of thanks.

PRAY. Thank you, God, that we are not alone and that others have prepared the way for us. Help me be that kind of person also for others. Amen.

O come, Thou Wisdom from on high,
And order all things, far and nigh;
To us the path of knowledge show,
And cause us in her ways to go.

Rejoice! Rejoice!
Emmanuel Shall come to thee, O Israel!

Henry Sloane Coffin

Following in Joy

Amy Whipple Derrick

PAUSE.

Joy might be the most sought-after gift of this season.

Though it can be elusive, people of faith remain ever open to its coming.

Pause now, and open your soul to the joy lurking at the edges of your awareness. Receive the gift with gladness.

LISTEN. DECEMBER 23 **Luke 1:30-35, 37-38**

Trust, Listening

THINK. We've heard this story so often and have obscured it with so much sentimentality and Christmas pageantry that we forget how terrifying it really was. Mary, a young teenager, was visited by a heavenly being and told she would become pregnant, outside of marriage, as a virgin, and that the child would be God's. Surely everyone thought she was delusional or had made up a big whopping lie to cover her shame.

It would be embarrassing enough today for the most godly girl in the youth group to get pregnant, but back in Mary's day, it was enough to get you killed, or ostracized at the very least. Mary surely knew that convincing Joseph of her sanity and purity would be hard enough, if even possible at all—not to mention convincing everyone else! Yet she responded with humility and acceptance of God's role for her. She believed against all odds. She believed with joy, knowing that it would change her life path forever, and that she had no idea what that meant.

PRAY. God, I often don't like the circumstances I find myself in. And I often struggle to see you in them. Help me, like Mary, to trust you when I can't see where the path leads, when I can't make sense of the reasons, when I have way more questions than answers. Help me to have the ears to hear your voice and to have faith in your good plans for me. Help me to believe, and to follow. And may I be surprised with joy in the process. Amen.

LISTEN. **DECEMBER 24** **Luke 1:46-56**

Praise, Thankfulness

THINK. I find myself shamed by Mary's song of joy, her Magnificat. Have I ever, when overwhelmed with God's presence, uttered such beautiful words of praise? Have I ever composed such a work of prophetic perfection? My own words to God seem ordinary, empty in comparison. Comparison, however, is not the point here. Perhaps the point is modeling.

Mary put into words the joy of her spirit. She expressed her awe that God chose her and recounted all of the ways God had worked. She focused on God's heart, God's action in the world, and her resulting faith. It is a model for me. How does my spirit feel? Where do I see God? What have I seen God do before? I can rejoice; I can express my trust in God's goodness and faithfulness, too. Maybe my words won't be so beautifully put together that generations to come will recite them, but pure joy and praise expressed to God are always a precious offering, holy and treasured. My soul magnifying the Lord. My own magnificat.

PRAY. My soul magnifies you, Lord. My spirit rejoices in God my Savior. You have seen me, and you have acted in my life. You know me and claim me as your own. What greater blessing could there be? You are at work in my life in ways I can see and in many, many ways I can't see. You are strong, you are giving, you are holy, and you are just. You are God in my life as in the lives of all who have followed you throughout the ages. Hear my song of joy today, Lord. You are magnificent! Amen.

LISTEN. ## DECEMBER 25 **Luke 2:1-14**

Assurance of God, God With Us

THINK. It seems that nothing of Jesus' entrance into this world was ordinary. After all they had been through, Mary and Joseph had to make a multi-day journey to Bethlehem for the census, which was dangerous under the best of circumstances. But with Mary so late in her pregnancy, this would have been a miserable trip, filled with anxiety for both of them. After the unbelievable path that had led them this far, the birth of this miraculously conceived child would take place many miles away from the familiarity and comfort of home. After all she had been through, Mary gave birth for the first time in a strange place, away from her family. And she placed the newborn Messiah in a feeding trough, because there was no room for them where the other guests stayed.

Ordinary? Far from it.

"Glory to God in the highest!"

PRAY. Extraordinary God, when my journey seems long, anxious, and unfamiliar, remind me that you came to us on such a journey, even when there was no place ready for you. Calm my fears, and remind me that as the angels announced, we shall find you in the most ordinary of places, and in the most extraordinary of circumstances. Amen.

LISTEN. **DECEMBER 26** **Luke 2:15-19**

God With Us, Promises

THINK. Mary had been on quite the journey for nine months. She'd been visited by an angel, experienced conceiving the child of God as a virgin, been validated by her relative Elizabeth who had experienced her own miraculous conception, been accepted and loved by Joseph against all societal norms, and had given birth in a barn. After all that, as they were tired, dirty, and uncomfortable in a smelly stable, Mary, Joseph, and their newborn baby are visited in the middle of the night by a bunch of shepherds who claim they've been visited by an angel choir, and who somehow know that this child is of God.

Maybe by now Mary was getting more used to the surprises. She was clearly paying attention . . . treasuring each word. There was certainly a lot to ponder.

PRAY. God of wonder, help me to pay attention to your unpredictable work in my life. Help me to treasure the miracles you bring across my path, even when, perhaps especially when, they are well disguised, like dirty shepherds. And help me to ponder your surprises, to see more clearly your hand in my life, so that I can follow you in joy. Amen.

LISTEN. DECEMBER 27 **Luke 2:25-35**

Doubts, Comfort

THINK. In spite of all of the strange and miraculous events, Mary was still a brand new mother, a new wife under awkward circumstances, and a young girl. Newlyweds giving birth away from home would be stressed under normal circumstances; imagine it with all of the extenuating factors for Mary and Joseph.

With all of this life change, and all of the divine surprises to ponder, Mary and Joseph were amazed again, this time by the elderly Simeon's prophetic words about their baby and about Mary herself. It was another miracle of God that Mary was able to keep functioning with so much to try to sort through. Other people were responding in joy, believing this child to be the Son of God, exactly as the angel originally said. But with Simeon's blessing came an ominous prophecy. What could it all mean?

PRAY. God of the unknown future, life is full of change, stress, miracles, and blessings. It is also full of fear, mysterious outlooks, strange possibilities, and innumerable questions. You are God of all, including my amazement at the miraculous present and my anxiety over tomorrow's forecast. Guide me, keep me, and remind me that joy is not dependent on happiness or circumstance but is found in you in the midst of change, stress, miracle, blessing, and uncertainty. Help my eyes to see your salvation through it all. Amen.

LISTEN. **DECEMBER 28** **Matthew 2:9-12**
God with Us, Praise

THINK. The visit of the wise men is celebrated in many places on January 6, the Feast of the Epiphany. Epiphany, for Western Christians, celebrates the manifestation of Christ to the Gentiles, the wise men. The Merriam-Webster dictionary defines epiphany as "a sudden manifestation or perception of the essential nature or meaning of something."

For Mary, perhaps the realization that these foreign dignitaries had traveled and searched for months, maybe even years, to come and worship her child as king of the Jews was an epiphany for her, a sudden perception into the reality of her child. Even these foreigners, these Gentiles, recognized him. After the newness of it all had worn off, after the shepherds and angels were only memories, these men from a distant land showed up. They rejoiced that they had found the family, declared her child the Christ, worshiped him, and left very expensive gifts. After the dust settled, Mary was left again to ponder and perhaps to realize anew exactly who it was she was holding in her arms.

PRAY. God of "aha" moments, I often take for granted exactly who you are. In my daily life, I see you as just my own and forget that you are Emmanuel, God with us. God with us. God . . . with . . . us. God, Yahweh, creator, savior of the world, here with us. With me. With all of us. This truth is worthy of searching for and rejoicing over. It is worthy of my worship. It is worthy of any gift I could possibly give. God . . . with . . . us. What an epiphany! Amen.

LISTEN. DECEMBER 29 **Luke 2:43-51**

Trust

THINK. Can you imagine all tthat Mary had to ponder? What must it have been like to be the mother of Jesus? This scene shows that it was not always easy. Mary and Joseph didn't always understand what he was up to or why. I imagine they thought about those early days with the angels, the miraculous birth, the shepherds, Simeon, the wise men, and tried to make sense of it all. Who was this boy? Who would he become?

As Jesus grew into a man and began his ministry, surely Mary was joyful as she remembered those miracles she had pondered long ago. She had questions, and some misunderstandings along the way. And as Simeon foretold, her soul was pierced at the foot of the cross. But Mary, obedient Mary who found favor with God, who followed a difficult path, who was surprised by God over and over, whose heart was stretched and broken, surely no one was more joyful than she on Resurrection day.

PRAY. Incarnate God, it's not always easy to follow you in joy. The path is sometimes difficult. I don't know where I am headed. I have questions and misunderstandings. I am often surprised. And sometimes my soul is pierced with grief. Like Mary, I find myself pondering who you are and what you are up to. Help me, like Mary, to trust you above all. To trust that who you are is Emmanuel, God with us. Help me to remember that "God with us" means God with me, and that this epiphany is enough to cause my soul to sing a magnificent song of praise and to cause me to joyfully follow, today and always. May it be with me according to your Word. Amen.

GO.

Far below the surface,
Your delight finds its source,
Making its way to your heart.

Can you feel it,
Feel its power?
The life-changing rush of salvation.

The Gift

Colleen Walker Burroughs

PAUSE.

In the chaos of the holiday, the reassuring presence of Christ can be lost. Take a moment to slow down and reconnect with God. How has God been present in your life unawares to you?

Acknowledge God's presence and provision in your life. Find your rest in God!

LISTEN. DECEMBER 30 **Colossians 3:12-14**

Gifts, Child of God

THINK. Compassion, kindness, humility, gentleness, and patience—that's quite a Christmas wish list. We all have moments when we feel selfish, unkind, proud, loud, and totally annoyed with the 12-item person in the 10-item checkout line. It is human nature.

But just like any loving parent does, God chooses to love us anyway and wraps up a few other gifts with our name on it. Here they are: a hat of compassion, a t-shirt that reads "kindness," humble sneakers, a warm scarf of gentleness, and the gloves of patience. As Christians, we are supposed to clothe ourselves with these virtues and button them all up inside a red coat of love! It's the love that pulls the whole outfit together and makes it pop. The world will notice and begin to recognize what family you belong to. So, bundle up.

PRAY. Dear God, thank you for choosing me and loving me even when I forget to put on my hat or gloves. Help me not to forget that the world needs love and that you want me to carry it with me wherever I go. I want to be recognized as your child every day. Help me to be more kind, caring, peaceful, respectful, and patient in line so that others can see your presence in me. Amen.

LISTEN. **DECEMBER 31** **Colossians 3:15-17**

Trust, Thankfulness

THINK. Ever ridden out a storm? Like a midnight storm with howling wind, lights out, sirens, rain, thunder, and lightning? I remember surviving a hurricane with my mother as we cared for my ailing grandmother and my father who needed oxygen (and electricity) to breathe. It was like moving through two storms, the loud one outside and the silent one inside. We were scrambling all night. When the lights came back on the next morning, I cheered and headed for the coffeemaker! I was grumpy, tired, and a little bit angry that God would drop a hurricane on top of us in the midst of our sadness. Then my mother passed through the kitchen humming. She looked up and said, "We are so blessed. We have lights, the rain has stopped, and we have survived the storm." Even in our exhaustion and the inevitable grief of losing those we love, the peace of Christ ruled in her heart, and she was thankful.

PRAY. Dear God, help me to remember that the storms of life are simply part of living. I know you don't make them happen to me, but you do promise to walk with me. Help me remember to claim your peace and presence in my life every single day, even when it is sunny. Help me to sing in the dark and to share out loud how thankful I am for you, so that maybe those around me will remember to be thankful too.

GO.

Having experienced the presence of God, live your life today with an assurance of God's continual care and provision. From your abundance, be the presence of Christ in the life of those your encounter today!

CONTRIBUTORS

Rev. Brian Abel	Minister, Beaumont, TX
Julie Ball	Teacher/Writer, Lakeland, TN
Dr. Reggie Blount	Professor, Buffalo Grove, IN
Estelene Boratenski	Writer, Glenwood, MD
Brian Boyd	Professor, Richardson, TX
Rev. Aimee Wallis Buchanan	Minister and Co-founder of AYM, Asheville, NC (deceased)
Colleen W. Burroughs	Passport, Inc., Birmingham, AL
Rev. David Burroughs	Passport, Inc., Birmingham, AL
Rev. Valerie Burton	Minister, Birmingham, AL
Rev. Amy Butler	Pastor, Washington, DC
Ka'thy Gore Chappell	Cooperative Baptist Fellowship of North Carolina, Winston-Salem, NC
Amy Whipple Derrick	Cooperative Baptist Fellowship, Atlanta, GA
Amy Dodson-Watts	Executive Director, Luke 14:12, Nashville, TN
Rev. Phillip Fackler	Ph.D. Student, Philadelphia, PA
Rev. Luke Fodor	Assistant Rector, Oyster Bay, NY
Dixie Ford	Minister, Birmingham, AL
Rev. Brian Foreman	Youth Ministry Consultant, Raleigh, NC
Rev. Nick Foster	Editor, d365.org, Columbia, MO
Rev. Rob Fox	Cooperative Baptist Fellowship of Virginia, Henrico, VA
Cindy Gaskins	Campus Minister, Honolulu, HI
Rev. Cory Goode	Social Media Consultant Springfield, MO
Heidi Hagstrom	Evangelical Lutheran Church of America, Chicago, IL
Rev. Peter Hanson	Pastor, St. Paul, MN
Michael Harper	Youth Ministry Consultant/Editor, Louisville, KY

Dr. Tracy Hartman	Professor, Richmond, VA
Susan Hay	United Methodist Church (retired), Nashville, TN
Rev. Daniel Ingram	Passport, Inc., Birmingham, AL
Andrew Kellner	Diocesan Staff, Philadelphia, PA
Rev. Joann Lee	Minister, St. Paul, MN
Rev. Ruth Perkins Lee	Cooperative Baptist Fellowship, Atlanta, GA
Rev. Arianne Lehn	Minister, Ft. Wayne, IN
Rev. Elizabeth Mangham Lott	Minister, Richmond, VA
Bentley Manning	Graduate Student, Sewanee, TN
Adrian McMullen	Presbyterian Church (USA), Louisville, KY
Rev. Dave McNeely	Minister, Jefferson City, TN
Rev. Kerri Peterson-Davis	Minister, Solon, Ohio
Rev. Bo Prosser	Cooperative Baptist Fellowship, Atlanta, GA
Rev. Bruce Reyes-Chow	Writer/Speaker, San Francisco, CA
Rev. Grier Booker Richards	Minister, Greensboro, NC
Rev. Lars Rood	Minister, Redmond, WA
Rev. Michael Sciretti	Minister, Norfolk, VA
Dr. Bill Shiell	Pastor, Tallahassee, FL
Brownyn Clark Skov	The Episcopal Church, Miesville, MN
Dr. Jim Somerville	Pastor, Richmond, VA
Rev. Dale Tadlock	Passport, Inc., Birmingham, AL
Rev. Tim Tate	Pastor, Roanoke, VA
Rev. Michelle Thomas-Bush	Minister, Charlotte, NC
Dr. Richard Vinson	Professor, Winston-Salem, NC
Dr. Andy Watts	Professor, Nashville, TN
Rev. Tammy Wiens-Sorge	Minister, Pittsburgh, PA
Rev. Courtney Jones Willis	Passport, Inc., Greensboro, NC
Rev. Caela Simmons Wood	Minister, Bloomington, IN
Rev. David Woody	Minister, Charleston, SC
Gina Yeager-Buckley	Presbyterian Church (USA), Louisville, KY

SCRIPTURE INDEX

MARK

LUKE

JOHN

ACTS

ROMANS

1 CORINTHIANS

2 CORINTHIANS

GALATIANS

EPHESIANS

PHILIPPIANS

COLOSSIANS

1 THESSALONIANS

2:9 September 23
2:1-4 October 19
2:5-8 October 20
3:9-13 December 12
5:1-5 November 2
5:6-11 November 3

1 TIMOTHY

1:12-14 May 31
1:15-17 June 1
6:6-10 June 12
6:11-16 June 13
6:17-19 June 14
4:12 August 26
4:13–14 August 27
4:15–16 August 28
5:1–2 August 29
2:1-7 June 22
6:17-19 August 9
6:6-9 June 26
6:10 June 27
6:11-14 June 28
6:17-19 June 29

2 TIMOTHY

1:1-7 August 1
1:8-11 August 2
1:12-14 August 3
4:6-8 May 18
4:16-18 May 19

HEBREWS

5:1-10 April 27
7:15-19 July 23
7:23-28 January 20
7:23-25 July 24
7:26-28 July 25
13:1-6 November 14
13:7-8, 15-16 November 15
11:29-31 May 2
11:32-38 May 3
11:39-12:2 May 4
12:12-13 February 7
12:14-17 February 8
12:18-24 February 9
12:25-29 February 10

JAMES

2:1-4 February 21
2:5-7 February 22
2:8-10 February 23
2:14-17 February 24
5:13-20 June 8
5:13-16 September 3
5:7-10 December 20

1 JOHN

4:7-8 April 15
4:9-12 April 16
4:13-16a April 17
4:16b-18 April 18
4:19-21 April 19

REVELATION

21:1-5a August 11

KEYWORD AND TOPICAL INDEX

FOOTNOTES

1. January 21
Schutz, Johann J.
"Sing Praise to God Who Reigns Above." Trans. Frances E. Cox. Sacred Hymns from the German. 1864.

2. February 25
Perry, Michael.
"In Christ There is No East or West." Carol Stream, IL: Hope Publishing Co., 1982.

3. March 6
Niebuhr, Reinhold.
"The Serenity Prayer."

4. March 8
Miller, Jill Jackson and Sy Miller.
"Let There be Peace on Earth." 1955.

5. March 10
Foster, Richard J. Prayers From the Heart. New York, NY: HarperOne, 1994.

6. April 21
Bayler, Lavon.
"Hear the Voice of God, So Tender." Cleveland, OH: The Pilgrim Press, 1987, rev. 1993.

7. May 12
Rosas, Carlos. "Cantemos al Creador." Trans. Dimas Planas-Belfort. Minneapolis, MN: Augsburg Fortress, 1989.

8. July 14
Duke, Paul & D. E. Adams. "The Family of God." Louisville, KY: Windmill Power, Inc., 1983.

9. September 24
Fosdick, Harry Emerson. "God of Grace and God of Glory." 1930.

10. September 25
Wren, Brian.
"When God is a Child." Carol Stream, IL: Hope Publishing Co., 1989.

11. November 17
Richardson, Paul A. "As He Gathered at His Table." Richmond, VA: The Hymn Society, 1990.